S0-DZN-695

The Modern Totemist.
Copyright © 2019 by Stephanie Brown.
All rights reserved.

FIRST EDITION
First Printing, 2019

Cover art and all illustrations by Stephanie Brown
Image editing, book formatting and design by Scott Brown
Additional image editing by Johnny Mendoza
Edited and copyedited by Ahna Fryhover
Additional proofreading by Ruth Ann Brown and Cassie McDaniel

ISBN: 978-0-578-55242-2

Published by: Painted Caves Publishing
a division of Painted Caves Studio

www.paintedcavesstudio.com

The Modern Totemist

by Stephanie Brown

with Scott Brown

2019

This work is dedicated to pagan folk everywhere: to the canny, the wyrd, and the contraries of the world whose whimsically beautiful meandering paths toward wisdom continue to inspire both humility and humor, and who have generously instructed us along the way;

to Arvel Bird, whose music and teachings introduced us to the nine-fold path of the totem so many years ago;

to Scott, my heart, my love, my other half, who built this tradition with me stitch-by-stitch and who patiently read through every draft and argued it with me until it was perfect;

and to Jaguar, Elephant, Lion, and to Wolf — who worked with me until the very last word.

—Stephanie Brown

Sometimes journeys start in the most unexpected places.

I was living in Knoxville, TN in the early 2000s. I was a novice pagan, still not sure of my path or what it meant to me to be pagan. On a late summer evening, I headed out to the county fair. Performing there was Arvel Bird, a Celtic Indian musician. During his performance, he talked briefly about his own philosophies on totems. Afterward I stuck around and he introduced me to his concept of a 9-totem path. We talked until it was time for him to do another performance. Looking back, it was this chance encounter that started me down the path of the Totemist.

Over the next five to six years, I developed my personal totem philosophy. I learned from the pagan and Native American communities in person and through their writings, and I meditated on what I leaned and applied it to my personal practice.

Then another chance encounter changed things again: I met the amazing woman who authored this book. I introduced her to my personal totem philosophy and by learning and exploring together we began our tradition of the Modern Totemist. In the years since, we have been able to learn more together than we could have on our own, and the resulting tradition is influenced in equal parts by both of us.

Stephanie has a unique way of thinking and expressing those thoughts, and she has pushed me to think of many things in new ways. While we don't always agree, we both find tremendous value in the process. It is my hope that she does the same for you. In my biased opinion she is an amazing author. I struggled to organize my thoughts enough to write this small note to you. This book has been her labor of love. It is an accurate and balanced representation of our tradition and I could not be more proud of her.   —Scott Brown

Table of Contents

Authors' Note

on the subjects of historical context, appropriation, and audience

It is our belief that certain types of magick are the birthright of all of humanity. Regardless of race or culture, heritage or time period, we all have a natural right to know and worship the Earth Mother, Father Sun, and other spirits of the natural earth such as the water, the sky, and the trees. We have a right to learn to benefit from the metaphysical energies, the magick, provided by that natural world through the use of plants, stones, and our own innate cunning. We have a right to honor and revere our ancestors. And we have a right to work with the spirits of animals in our magick.

Ours is a modern totemic tradition. It is not a summary of ancient practices, nor does it provide the customs of totem use specific to any one cultural group, modern or ancient (except perhaps for my husband and myself, a culture of two). Our method of understanding and utilizing personal animal totems is built upon the experiences of our lives, incorporating known elements of totem use from several cultures (including neo-pagan, neo-totemic, and neo-shamanic traditions) and combining them with decades of personal experience and insight to produce a unique and complex working - *modern* - metaphysical totemic path. It is not a reimagining of the cultural traditions of anyone else, either ancient or contemporary.

I understand: a lot of people see the word "totem" and think "Native American." But a common association does not make a case for appropriation, as some may suggest. Many human cultures have honored animal aspects of the self, or tutelary spirits that take an animal form, and simply called them something else. But the word for this concept in contemporary English is *totem*, so for clarity's sake, that is the word we will use here.

Now, despite the fact that from the beginning our ancestors from all over the world likely worked with totems, I will not preface this book with an anthropological summary of animal totem use, as is the status-quo. It's a bizarre reality of pagan literature that pagan publishing has set a hard tradition that the first chapter of every pagan book *must* be a half-assed excuse for an undergraduate-level archaeological research paper. This is usually done in an attempt to legitimize the work, but it's done even if the subject of the book is contemporary practice or theory. It does not benefit the reader, who is often simply fed lazy research and communal **fakelore**; neither is it beneficial to the book itself or the metaphysical work of the author it represents, as the value of the discipline it contains should be self-evident. After all, the neo-pagan treatise "if it works, it works," should apply here, and shaky connections to ancient cultures simply do not affect a metaphysical practice's efficacy one way or another.

It is critically important to remember: *neo-paganism is a modern religion.*

It should not read as rebellious for an author to make that assertion. As a modern religion, commentary on its practice does not require it be concretely linked to any ancient ideas. And importantly, *that's ok!*

But it is equally important to remember that ideas cannot form in vacuums, and all new ideas are inspired by existing thought. Neo-paganism is inspired by the practices of many ancient cultures, with some traditions borrowing more than others. If it is done respectfully, and knowledgeably, then *that's ok, too!*

It is my intent to make the ideas presented in this book accessible to anyone. However, it is written with neo-pagans in mind; most of the information will be presented within the context of neo-pagan thinking. Yet, there is no reason this path of totemism can't be used in tandem with any religious path— or none at all, and instead understood as a tool of deep self-reflection, in a similar vein to how meditation or yoga can be used without holding any greater spiritual belief.

This book provides the reader with our system of animal totemism that simply *works* for the modern person. And whether or not ancient Africans, South Americans, Australians, or Europeans had animal mascots for their kin-groups has nothing to do with it.

Foreword

We live in a world domesticated. The days when humankind walked this earth simply as one animal among many are lost to us, accessible only through dreams of longing or misty imaginings. As a species, we have never lived in an environment so far removed from the one in which we originally evolved, until now. We stare across the conceptional expanse at the wilds of nature like something foreign, abstract, unattainable. *Other.* When we travel to the still-untamed places of the world we do not return to nature, we visit it, tourists in our own environment.

We often hear that modern lives are "unnatural." We are told we sit still too long, or work too hard; we eat too much of a certain food, or not enough of it. We are unhealthy on many levels— physical, psychological, spiritual— when such things never seemed so large or common a problem in the past. But concerns of poor modern health involving gluten and standing desks are only symptomatic of the problem, they are not the solution.

We are an animal that spent more than two hundred thousand years living a relatively undisturbed and unchanged lifestyle of regular and seasonal migration, hunting and gathering our foods, living within closely-knit and relatively autonomous kin groups of twenty to fifty individuals. Five thousand or so years ago, we began to switch to more sedentary agrarian lives, and from there we moved towards stratified societies, hierarchical religions, and abstract concepts of universal law and ethos over situational empathy and common sense. We live in a world of intangible wealth through debt and credit; we have largely removed meaningful labor from work; and we have largely retired from traditional concepts of community and kin and tribe that have sustained us from the beginning. It has taken us until now to name this neolithic shift that changed our species forever: "The Great Forgetting."

And perhaps because of this, we feel spiritually unhealthy, unbalanced, unnatural. And it's not an issue that can be corrected with any specific amount of sleep, or sunlight, or organic kale. Even as others of our species raze the land for profit, those of us with eyes to see and ears to hear the echoes of the ancient wisdom feel our disconnect from nature, from its natural cycles, from its balanced ways. We have extracted ourselves from our original role in the natural world, become observers of it instead of participants in it, lost our instinctual, significant connection to the land and how to live on it. We live in a time when we will gladly pay money for pre-packaged greens because we don't know what's edible in our own yards; a time when it must be explained to tourists that wild bears and wolves and bison in Yellowstone Park are dangerous. We have domesticated ourselves. And we gaze longingly at the foreign concept of naturalness no differently than a lioness born in a zoo gazes wistfully at the world through the bars of her enclosure.

But our ultimate place in nature is stranger still. It is the biggest myth the modern mind can weave around itself that we modern humans are not a part of nature. It is true that we may feel that way, and with good reason: those of us who grew up with recycling jingles and Captain Planet cartoons have learned to see humanity as a separate — and harmful— force, oppositional to nature.

But we are still animals born of this earth. We can never really become disconnected from it. We may have divorced ourselves from our former place and role in nature, but we can never truly remove ourselves from nature, not totally. We are biological beings that live and grow, harvest and eat, reproduce and die. We are not removed from the ecosystems we inhabit; conversely, we are heavy players in them. We have not lost our place, but we *have* changed our roles.

Therefore, the question of reclaiming that naturalness must be examined with new eyes. It is not a matter of regaining something that was lost, but rather of understanding something within ourselves that we have forgotten — or were never taught to see to begin with.

We live in a time in which our lives run counter to our innate instincts— and subconsciously we bristle. But we can be taught how to reconcile our modern lives with our primal identities. *Domesticated animals do not cease to be animals.* And our essential beings, our true and natural humanness, is to be found in our animal selves.

Introduction:
The Modern Totemist

The two most important questions to ask yourself in this life are: *Who are you?* and *What do you want?*

The truism *know thyself* is likely as old as thought itself, yet untold generations of men and women have wrestled with understanding it. These existential questions are among the most profoundly difficult to answer, and yet are so simple they are ironically something someone might casually demand of you if you entered the wrong building. To begin to address these two critical questions is the first step toward attaining wisdom; perhaps accepting that you may never fully know is the key to attaining it.

And it seems that every new religion, philosophy, lifestyle, attempts to put humanity in its place— this is your role, this is your handicap, this is your purpose, this is your path to grace.   Yet, a good many of them make the same fundamental mistake in assuming that peace, fulfillment, purpose — *wisdom*— can be attained from the outside inward.

Who are you, and what do you want? These questions strike at the fundamental core of the self. The journey to uncover that true unblemished identity can, by design, only be an inward journey. Even as others who have done the same before you may offer their guidance, it is a quest unique to every human soul, every life, every experience.

Only you can decide the answer when it is you who asks the question.

And so when one first steps into that profound, spiritual, existential journey towards wisdom, it can be counterintuitive — and counterproductive — to be told to look outside the self for knowledge, for power, for grace, for that flash of enlightenment. Bless me, O Lord, for I have sinned. Give me courage, Odin, that I can fight on. Empower me, Diana, that I might work my Will. Guide me, Buddha, that I may find the light as you have.

When your goal is to reach the top of the mountain, then pray to the spirit of the mountain. But when your goal is to reach your own heart, then pray to the spirit of yourself.

The spirit of the self, the true and essential nature of a person, is found within the animal totem.

Unlike many other paths that would point you towards their truth, the way of **totemism** is the journey to know the essential self— and to come to know it from the inside out. This makes modern totemism unique among many others along the contemporary religious and philosophical options. Even among the many bright colors of the metaphysical, new-age, and neo-pagan cultural spectrum that champion the virtues of choice and unique personal truths, we see this problematic pattern. There is still focus on empowerment and enlightenment through the external agents of gods or spirits, of energy or magick. Pagans try to create change within their lives by changing the external world and circumstances, and not change themselves.

Little, if any, effort in contemporary western religion is put towards understanding the source of our own desire for change. Even less work is put towards changing our own behavior to make such supernatural interference unneeded or unnecessary.

The path of the totemist is the path of knowing the self— a way of deep reflection, of deconstructing and examining all aspects of the mind, the heart, and the soul. Through complex self-analysis, we come to know, and therefore understand, the various conflicting and harmonizing thoughts, instincts, and reactions within ourselves. These are the inner-voices of the mind, perceived of by the artistic human soul as our essential animal selves. You will meet your courage, and your fears, the tiny voices within you that influence the thoughts you have and the decisions you make. You will meet your darkness, and your light. And you will befriend them.

The totemist knows that your animal self is the bedrock of your identity, it is essential to your being. It is not to be changed, or absolved while others parts are praised, or even ignored— it simply *is*. And those animal parts of you — all parts of you — are to be respected, utilized, and loved simply for what they are.

Know thyself, understand and love thyself — and you will know wisdom.

PART ONE
The Path of the Totem

Chapter One:
What is a totem?

What do we mean when we say *totem*?

When we are faced with all of our preconceptions of the idea— from history, modern use, and fiction combined— it might leave us to reconcile a rather wide variety of ideas. For clarity's sake, we must first discuss several related— but distinct — variations on the term *totem* the reader may have previously encountered.

Within our personal system of totem use that will be discussed throughout this book, a **totem** is: *a manifestation of the essential self or spiritual self; a permanent, personal* *tutelary spirit taking an animal form often relatable to an aspect of its bearer's character or personality.*

The totem is your spiritual essence, your soul, shown to you in its more pure animal form. It can be understood as both an aspect of the self and at the same time as a separate entity that connects the self to whatever higher plane of existence you understand, as the true or pure essential self is always connected to the divine, (however you individually define divinity).

Anyone who has previously researched the topic of totems will find that the "dictionary" definition of a totem is quite different, especially compared to what we hear discussed within a neo-pagan context, and that makes such research a bit of a challenge. Most people begin casual research with Wikipedia, and as its credibility has improved dramatically since I was a student, that is likely to be someone's first exposure to the formal or dictionary definition of the term. As far as its entry reads this morning, that definition of a totem is: "a spirit being, sacred object, or symbol that serves as an emblem of a group of people, family, clan, lineage, or tribe." Obviously, there are some significant differences here compared to our tradition's definition.

Herein lies the source of a majority of the confusion encountered when discussing and researching this topic, so take heed: the term "totem" is used differently by contemporary pagan totemists than the (former) meaning of an **anthropological totem,** which influenced the dictionary. It also has its own meaning to some Native American and other indigenous traditions as well.

As anthropology was my field of study, I feel comfortable pointing the finger in their direction, though the same mistakes were made in related fields by historians, ethnographers, sociologists, etc. You see, in the past, these scientists would observe the beliefs, traditions, and practices of many different cultures and notice broad similarities between them, and with the intention of clarity, would use the same word to describe those points of similarity. Unfortunately, this was abundant with problems.

For one, it had the unfortunate side-affect of glossing over many very real and important differences between cultural traditions, and in some cases became a vehicle for ethnocentric superiority when used to paint all "primitive" cultures with a single broad brush. Thankfully, contemporary anthropology is doing better now that it knows better, but it has only been "doing better" for about the last 15 to 20 years, so a vast amount of anthropological literature using language in this way is still in circulation. And unfortunately, many other authors, such as reporters and journalists, continue to use language this way.

But another problem arrises in the fact that often the word anthropologists would pick for such a broad concept had its own separate, distinct meaning— creating a situation such as with the word totem where we have numerous different definitions for the same word: a "traditional" meaning, an "anthropological/scientific/dictionary" meaning, and a "contemporary" meaning, which is how the majority of people use and understand the word. All of these definitions are equally valid— but it confuses the heck out of people, to say the least. For this same reason, we have the exact same problem with quite a lot of words common in neo-pagan culture, such as the words shaman, witch, smudge, heathen, and pagan itself. 1

But to get us back to our kind of totems, quite confusingly, to search the true scientific and historic records for what is *intended* when neo-pagans speak of "totems," you will need to search for "tutelary spirits" or "spirit guides," though you will find as often as not that such entities do not appear in animal form. A search for "animal totem" or "personal totem" will produce information more similar to what we deal with in this book, but keep in mind that most all of what you will find will be modern ideas. There are a lot of people out there who work with animal spirit magick and call it "ancient" or "traditional"; there is nothing ethically wrong with what they believe, just keep in mind it's almost entirely modern **fakelore** (or a false idea being passed off as genuine folklore).

The fact is, there is surprisingly little information from the historic and anthropological records regarding personal animal totems, on par with our kind of totems. Especially when compared to our expectations, these kinds of totems are surprisingly uncommon among ancient and/or traditional cultures. There was some use among Native

---

1 The problems in the words *witch* and *witchcraft* are even more complicated, as we find it used often in a fourth context: by other religions. If you Google the word "witch," the article could be referring to the ancient wise-women of Great Britain before the Roman conquest (the traditional use); it could be referring to someone accused of sending supernatural harm or misfortune with ill-intent, never minding if they are a Vodun Mambo or a Q'ero Doña (the older anthropological use); it could simply be referring to a practitioner of modern Wicca (the contemporary); or it could be referencing someone supposedly under Satanic influence (perhaps a Christian, Islamic, or even Buddhist source). Certainly, anyone who is or who loves someone who identifies as a Witch can appreciate how troublesome such complicated etymology can be.

American cultures, such as among the Ojibwa (where we get the word) and several Plains Tribes such as the Lakota-Sioux. But despite our ignorant expectations that every Native American had a personal animal totem, these totems tended to fall more along the lines of that old-timey anthropological definition as espoused by Wikipedia, in that the animal spirits in question either represented a family line, an extended clan, or other family group rather than only an individual. Within our modern totemism tradition, we would refer to this as a **group totem**. More often than not, most references you will find to personal "Indian totems" are contemporary or modern ideas, either coming from the tribes or (more likely) from outside of them, and do not necessarily represent any traditional or ancient beliefs.

Also within (mostly) contemporary Native American ideas, you will find mention of *temporary* animal spirit guides, or situations in which an animal spirit communicates with or works with a person for a limited time or for a single issue, though such a situation also occurs in the mythology of many other cultures, including the Celts and the Romans. Such a *temporary* tutelar spirit will be defined in this book as a **spirit guide**. For our purposes, this is not a totem; the interaction is limited, the entity comes from outside of the self, and it does not represent an aspect of a person's own identity or soul. But others, including anthropologists, would define this as a type of totem.

Now, even as I put some effort into convincing the reader that a practice need not be derived directly from any ancient belief system to be valid, it is nevertheless exceptionally helpful to be able to categorize our idea of the personal totem within the spiritual context of what is widely known and believed within the neo-pagan community and western culture as a whole. After all, I would wager my reputation that anyone who buys this book already has an idea in their head of what a totem is, and just wants to learn more. Yet as I have suggested, the concept of the personal animal totem seems surprisingly rare among ancient traditions, at least compared to our expectations. (I suspect we have fiction to blame for that; *Clan of the Cave Bear,* I'm looking at you.)

So how do we reconcile these concepts?

The answer lies in looking beyond the simple animal face of the totem and for the moment seeing it instead simply as a personal, protective or guiding spiritual entity (without predefined form). Then we begin to see the universality that helps bind the idea to the greater fabric of human spirituality. In other words, the simplified concept of the **tutelar spirit** — the "spirit helper" or "guardian spirit" — is much more prevalent across the cultures of the world and across time— it is simply found as guardian angels or other pseudo-humanoid spirits, perhaps ancestral guides, or as spirits that have no known form at all. As one example, we can look to the Greco-Roman *daemons*, who were lesser deities that were individual guardians and teaching spirits.

It is this idea that the reader should keep in mind throughout this book: that every person innately has some higher spiritual aspect to themselves that manifests as separate, sacred entities. The practice of understanding a tutelar spirit in an animal form might be an unusual idea, but the broader idea itself is certainly not, and can be found cross-culturally. [2]

We are working with personal animal totems in this book. These are aspects of the spiritual or higher self, and therefore they are with a person always, and do not change

---

[2] And though they are fiction, the personal totems from Jean M. Auel's *The Clan of the Cave Bear* and the animal "daemons" from the Phillip Pullman's *His Dark Materials* series hit pretty close to the mark, and do so for the reader precisely because of this underlying cultural concept.

within their lifetime. Within the system we use, every person has a total of nine totems, each corresponding to different aspects of personality and psyche.

The Nine Totems are:

- The **Primary Totem**, the one face reflective of the entire essential self
- The **Lord Totem**, our masculine and assertive (or passive) nature
- The **Lady Totem**, our feminine and passive (or assertive) nature
- The **Air Totem** in the East, our intellect and mind
- The **Fire Totem** in the South, our impulses and passions
- The **Water Totem** in the West, our emotions
- The **Earth Totem** in the North, our body
- The **Light Totem** that is Above, our ideal self
- The **Dark Totem** that is Below, our dark side

We perceive of these as being metaphorically oriented around or orbiting a person, who becomes the point in the center, a position shared by the Primary Totem. The Lord and Lady totems are found just to the left and right side of the person, overlapping the center position. The elemental totems are oriented to the six cardinal directions, often to the directions as described but just as often in a unique pattern, creating a sphere around the person.

Each of the nine will be given a more in-depth treatment in subsequent chapters.

Chapter Two:
What is not a totem?

As I mentioned before, there is a related but separate concept from the totem that I have defined as the *spirit guide.* Spirit guides are what is most commonly confused with totems, both conceptually and in practice. Throughout our lives, people are often visited by spirit guides in a variety of forms, including animal; they come to us to help us through a challenging time, to teach us a specific lesson, or to otherwise assist us with a special situation to which our totems may not be well suited to handle. While they can fulfill a similar role of guide or teacher, they are not considered totems as they: 1) come from outside the self; and 2) they are with us only temporarily (although that can mean anything from minutes to years).

There are a few other ideas that are easily confused with a totem as I've defined it. Most people would agree there is a difference between divinity itself and a pathway or connection to that divinity, which is the totem as the face of the soul. That is to say, totems are not gods, which most people would agree are higher entities than human souls. However, it is worth pointing out that most deities, especially pre/non-Christian deities, are often associated with an animal energy. For example, in the Hindu pantheon, the gods usually have a unique animal "mount" they ride, connecting the goddess Saraswati to the Swan and Ganesha to the Rat. The ancient Nordic gods also have strong connections to animals, linking Freya to the Skogcats that pull her chariot and Odin to his messenger

Ravens. Any entity considered to be a deity is not and cannot be a totem, but if a person feels a strong affinity for a god or goddess, it is worth considering that this *may* be a sign of a totemic connection to their associate animal. That is to say, a person with a special connection to Skadi *may* have a Wolf totem, and the totem could be facilitating the easy relationship with the goddess.

Along a similar vein, pagans can also form a strong connection with an individual, live animal. Those with a connection to witchcraft traditions might call this animal their *familiar*, though the term is not universally used. For purposes of this book, a **familiar** is an individual living animal with whom a person shares a metaphysical or spiritual relationship. Just like with deities, a familiar is not a totem, but such a relationship may be hinting at a connection to related totem animal energies. That same person with a Wolf totem may form a strong spiritual bond with a favorite german shepherd, for example.

This same type of association with a single living animal also applies to meaningful wild encounters, and can potentially be pointing towards a totem animal of a related type. Now, this is important: our totemic path is in no way a system of geomancy, wherein signs or symbols are interpreted in every wild animal sighting. Animals have their own lives, and almost always there is no metaphysical message to be found in their actions. The word "meaningful" is of critical importance, and only interactions that have a strong significance in your life should be considered a sign of a totemic connection. One often encounters in literature the idea that living through an animal attack is a sign of it testing your ability to bear that animal as a totem. Other interactions that simply feel spiritually significant can be valid. Just exercise common sense in your interpretation, and don't try to force a relationship with the first wild Crow or Squirrel you run across.

It can be easy to confuse all these things with totems, and we will extrapolate in later sections on the process of discovering and more definitively defining one's true totems.

Chapter Three:
Archetypes and Carl Jung

The contributions of early twentieth-century psychologist Carl Jung have had noteworthy influence on contemporary neo-pagan thinking, despite just how few pagans are aware of it. I feel it exceptionally important that he be given his due. All things considered, his theories of the collective unconscious, dream and metaphor interpretation, and his infamous archetypes make him as much a "founding father" of the neo-pagan movement as Gardner and Valiente, Budapest, or Starhawk.

Among other things, Jung suggested the existence of the human **collective unconscious**, or the idea that all human minds have the same unconscious structures, influencing how we understand and contextualize our experiences. These structures are instincts and **archetypes**, or unconscious, universally understood symbols that supersede all learned, cultural symbology. These archetypal symbols and patterns, he argued, can be seen expressed in humanity's varied forms of art, religion and myth, and dreams and imagination throughout the world. The archetypes affect and influence all humans unconsciously when they break down and try to understand their experiences.

Bedrock concepts of neo-pagan thinking such as "The Earth Mother" concept (which is equally present in Rome's Demeter and Peru's Pachamama), and of "The Triple Goddess" (seen everywhere from the three faces of Brigid to the major phases of the moon), can both be traced directly back to Jung's archetypes. He coined many, but some other faces familiar to pagans include: the Sage/Wise Old Man, the Crone/Old Woman/Witch, The Tree of Life/ Axis Mundi and the Three-Layered World, the Trickster, Water of Life, and the Tower— and the idea that there are light vs. "shadow" versions of all of these. (To be clear to the indignant pagan, I am not suggesting that these concepts were *invented* by Jung; rather, he pointed out that these patterns exist across cultures, named and defined many of them as we use them today, and suggested a reason why these patterns exist.)

Contemporary psychology is critical of much of Jung's work with the concept of the collective unconscious and related ideas. Even as the *expression* of these patterns is easily observed throughout human culture by the anthropologist, these shared patterns do not necessarily prove or disprove *the cause* of them as theorized by Jung. Further, modern psychology is generally set on the idea that dream images are largely random, and that attempts to "force" profound meaning into them through Freudian-style psychoanalysis that Jung was quite fond of is not a productive path to understanding (or healing) the self.

Generally speaking, today Jung's ideas should be taken with a heavy dose of the proverbial salt. But regardless of how it is understood and accepted today, the work of Jung (and his contemporaries such as Freud) has had lasting influence on the way contemporary, common western culture *thinks* of the unconscious mind and the corresponding symbols and images it generates.

But more importantly to the topic of this book, Jung's concept of the universal archetype provides good language to describe what the religions of neo-paganism teach and understand about concepts of divinity and the spiritual or metaphysical world. Most pagans have encountered difficulty explaining in a satisfactory way the "one vs many" problem to die-hard monotheists; how can one person worship the Norse gods and another the Celtic gods, and yet both pay homage to "The Lord and Lady" as though there is no discrepancy? The answer, "all gods are faces of the same divinity" carries with it an undertone of Jung's archetypes, if it is implying that Odin, Jupiter, Indra, and the Dagda are all expressions of the same "warrior king and father" template to describe the same masculine divine energy.

It is also important to point out that Jung also defined an archetype that bears many profound similarities to the contemporary totem: the **animus/anima**. According to Jung, this archetype represents within an individual's mind the totality of their unconscious self, or that which is the inner, hidden, or unexpressed self, taking a variety of forms either animal or human. Being a product of his time, Jung initially only defined the animus as the unconscious and un-actualized masculine qualities within the minds of meek women, essentially making the animus a manifestation of all the strength and power they could have had— or wanted to have— had they been born male. (Remember, Jung was a contemporary of Freud, who legitimately believed penis envy was a real problem affecting women.) It was only later that he felt compelled to create the mirrored concept of the anima, representing the unconscious and presumably repressed feminine qualities within the minds of men.

Nevertheless, if we put aside the short-sighted prejudices of the time period, Jung's animus/anima archetypes still bear a remarkable similarly to our contemporary totems. The totem is the true self, and yet it is also the inner, unconscious strength and potential, that which you can be but are not; the opposite of the self, the shadow or hidden self. It also happens that the Primary totem animal is almost always the opposite sex of its bearer. And the Lord and Lady totems (within everyone) are the seat of all masculine and feminine tendencies, expressed in their bearer's bodily form or not. Jung's animus/anima doesn't fit our totemic model exactly, but it's easy to see how someone else looking at the same soul of humanity was seeing similar patterns emerging.

All of this is important as we delve further into what a totem truly is, as the natural landscape that houses the animal self is, for the most part, the same unconscious template of the mind discussed by Jung. The only important distinction I must make between his presentation of it and ours is that ours accepts far more that our minds are shaped by cultural programming, by the many influences that impact our growing and malleable minds throughout a lifetime. Jung understood it more from the perspective of biological racial memory and very basic animal perception of the natural world, as something all people are born with and then build on, rather than as something that is mostly learned, as we believe.

At any rate, while it is important to point to the origins of ideas and their areas of similarity, I mention right now that our totemic tradition takes the issues of personal introspection to a deeper place than even Jung may have intended. Strap in, it gets bumpy.

Chapter Four:
What does a totem do?

In a practical sense, the totem has many roles. I have seen that different people each approach their totems in slightly different ways. As is required to say in neo-paganism, no way is necessarily "wrong." However, I hope to make the case to the reader that there is logic and purpose to our system of nine permanent personal totems, as that system provides a framework for a multitude of practical benefits, from balanced personal introspection; a source of inspiration, healing, strength and growth; to metaphysical work and *magick* (the process of focusing energy on a specific task by willpower to affect change.)

From a psychological perspective, totems provide us with a unique opportunity to see ourselves objectively, and to converse with and learn from our real, honest, true selves. As the saying goes, it is impossible to see ourselves as others see us. But when you are able to perceive of your true self as a separate entity from yourself, you gain valuable perspective on your strengths and weaknesses, your skills and talents, your habits and behaviors, your instincts, and in a greater sense how you uniquely interact with and fit into the world.

When combined with the disciplines of meditation or shamanic journeying (see Part Five), the psychological benefits of interacting with one's totems take on even more productive dimensions. After all, one might wonder if simply envisioning an aspect of your personality with a furry animal face wouldn't just parrot back at you ideas you already knew you had (parrot pun totally intended). But by way of basic mental discipline, you can teach yourself to enter a state of focused relaxation, receptive to ideas from your totem that will be experienced as novel and new. You can understand the mechanics of such interaction however you wish. (Is this an interaction between yourself and a spiritual entity, or a way to access aspects of yourself you couldn't see before?) Ultimately, the result — and the benefit — will be the same: if you are open to communication with your totems, you will hear or see valuable *new* ideas, lessons and messages, confirmations and challenges — all of which would not have been accessible to you otherwise, when viewing yourself as a singular, solitary entity.

Further still, practitioners of magick or energy manipulation will find their nine totems provide easy access to the various types of energies they represent. For example, summoning the energies of Air becomes easier and more natural when one calls upon one's Air totem to facilitate the connection. The masculine and feminine aspects of divinity are accessed in the same way through the Lord and Lady totems.

Yet, even with metaphysics put completely aside, the totems retain their value. One does not have to associate the Fire totem with the magickal elemental energy to see it as representation of the passionate and impulsive aspect of one's character. For example, a man may discover he has a Primary Bison totem. It might have never occurred him how critically important it is to his own mental health that he be surrounded and supported by loved ones until his Bison totem, a female, taught him about the importance of the natal herd as formed by closely related Bison cows, and so he could grow in his understanding of his own emotional needs. And more, that man would likely find reflected in Bison other things about himself he never knew or understood before, such as his need for open spaces and unrestricted freedom, his strength to deal with nearly any disaster (provided his herd is with him), his great competitive spirit compelling him to lead others, his proclivity to rise too easily to offense or challenge, and though he'd likely fear no one, perhaps he'd find an explanation for his instinctual mistrust of loners — or people with large carnivore totems.

Chapter Five:
Why Animals?

I previously mentioned that the concept of the personal guardian spirit transcends most cultures, and the varying form of those spirits is its largest area of divergence from our concept of the personal totem. This raises the very important question of why this manifestation of the higher or spiritual self is seen by totemists in an animal form— or even if it must be seen as an animal at all.

It is important to remember that we are dealing with something that has no physical, observable form; whether understood as a spiritual entity, a metaphysical form, or a complex idea, there is nothing for the physical eye to see in a totem, and we deal instead with the image that the mind, the inner eye, decides to put to it.

So when we decide to look at a totem as I've defined it, as something that is both an aspect of the self as well as a higher and separate entity, our minds will conclude we are dealing with a form of *human-like* but *non-human intelligence*. Each totem is an aspect of or one part of a whole human personality, and is therefore a simpler and incomplete form of human intelligence that is yet still human. In either case, the mind is tasked with putting a face on something that has no face, and with categorizing something that is at once not fully human but still human-like.

For the modern person, animals are by far the best and easiest form for the mind to turn to. We see animals as intelligent creatures with characters less complicated than our own, with a great deal of variety; we have many things in common with them, but they are not the same as us. And our cultural tradition of anthropomorphizing animals (that is, ascribing them human qualities) through the fairytales of our culture, cartoons and animated films, allows us to quite easily accept animals as complex thinking, feeling, even talking individuals with intelligent opinions; we are able to see even the largest and toothiest of them as non-threatening, something our ancestors likely had more difficulty with. We accept animals well as the face of non-human intelligence.

I have often wondered if perhaps this is why many older cultures specifically did not use animal faces for their personified higher, spiritual selves. We like to imagine that all ancient people lived as one with Mother Nature and saw all of her creatures as their brothers, but this is not necessarily true. At the very least, no one expects this of post-agricultural societies, those that had begun to firmly draw the line separating "civilization" from "the wild." In fact, it is more than likely that any culture that on the one hand had conceptually separated itself from nature, but that on the other hand was still very much vulnerable to the whims of nature, would have had difficulty seeing animals as worthy of the role of a personal totem, as animals would be aspects of that un-civilized and therefore unworthy "wild." And this is largely what we see among many of the dominant cultures from about 5,000 years ago to the present; from the Greeks to the Norse to the Egyptians, Mongolians, and Christians: animals may or may not have been respected as worthwhile, but they were seen as definitively *less* than human in the grand scale of things. It's no wonder to me that they perceived their guardian angels as humans with wings, because only something with the form of a man could have intelligence and character worth listening to. But I digress.

Ironically, it has taken the complete disconnect from nature that we experience in the modern world to take us full-circle to a place where we can respect animal intelligence as different from but as worthy as our own. After all, how many of you reading this have ever been almost eaten by a tiger? You have no reason to see them as anything other than romantically beautiful creatures. Most of us have little to no experience with the majority of animals, and when we do it is under limited and partially-protected circumstances such as in a state park or wildlife refuge.

Whatever the unconscious inspiration for it, it is our assertion that animal form is the best face to put to a totem. When we put cultural bias (or cultural preference) of the value of animals aside, we are still left with the fact that our totems are not human. That is, they are a higher aspect of you, yet separate aspects of you, but are not an exact mirror-image of you. As such, a human form for a totem is an incorrect fit because a full human personality is not only too complicated for the job, it would be too similar to the form in which you already perceive yourself. For something that represents a primal, innate, natural, instinctual aspect of your soul, it makes sense to understand it as another animal child of Mother Earth, more at peace with their existence and un-compromised by doubt or confusion, providing a pathway back to our essential beings. A winged man in fancy robes doesn't even exist on this earth; it is a lesser path to the essential nature of the human being.[3]

---

[3] To clarify, I am not saying angels are not worthy beings or that they are ineffective as spiritual teachers; far from it. Rather, I am suggesting they are not a good fit as a face for our essential selves due to their category as purely spiritual beings rather than terrestrial animals.

Lastly, another fine reason to understand your essential self in animal form is the fact that animals belong to no one people or cultural tradition. As I mentioned previously, while some specific practices may be the sole right of a cultural group that is not your own, animals themselves simply belong to the earth— and therefore, their magick belongs to all of humanity. If someone, for a wide variety of reasons, wishes to communicate with the etherial, metaphysical, spiritual world directly — rather than through the lens of one culture or another— then animal magick carries no such cultural baggage. If you are the sort of pagan who prefers to simply revere "The Earth Mother" and "The Sky Father" or "The Horned God" as opposed to tying yourself to the pantheon of one ancient culture or another, you may understand exactly what I'm getting at.

Now, all that being said, it is nevertheless true that many modern people are still unwilling or unable to accept their totems in animal form. The myth that humanity is superior-to and separate-from the rest of the circle of life is still very pervasive and affects the minds of many people. Therefore, it is important to point out that people's totems can very often show themselves in a non-animal form, for a variety of reasons.

Ultimately, what is most important is that a connection is made and the message is communicated; more often than not it seems the totem is more concerned with being *heard* than with being *perceived* in one form over another. I have known many people within the neo-pagan and metaphysical community who have gotten through life perfectly fine interacting with their true, essential animal selves by seeing them as angels, ancestors, or even different types of dragons. In my opinion, this only creates more opportunities for misunderstanding between the person and their totems, but it is better that they connect to them at all.

I will get further into the "why" of the animal form in the chapters on discovering your totems, and later, on discussing the place of metaphysical animals in totemism, but know that a big part of the relationship is that a true animal is connected to a living form, and that is a very important component of its role as the "bridge" between you and your higher self and divinity. That is, dragons are at best metaphysical entities, and they have no basis for understanding life in a meat body like yours the way a true animal would.

Chapter Six:
The Essential Self

As a final thought before we get into the meat and potatoes of utilizing our totemic system, I feel it necessary to address with a little more clarity the concept of the essential self — or rather, the concept as the totemist would define it. The astute reader may have noticed that I have referenced the "higher" or "divine" nature of the self and then used such terms interchangeably with "primal" or "animal" self, intermixed with "essential self." And in fact, to one who has sought to embrace and understand all aspects of the self as sacred — that is, to the totemist — those concepts are all one and the same.

And I understand further that many people would not understand these ideas as synonymous, at least not initially. There is an extensive back-log of cultural baggage that hangs in the backs of our minds that still insists that what is "animal" or "of the lowly earth" is antithetical to, or the opposite of, that which is "higher," "civilized," or "heavenly" — and is therefore not sacred and not divine. And so we tend to associate the idea of "the animal" with that which is base and brutish, unsophisticated at best. The idea of embracing "the animal" can even feel anti-spiritual or sinful, especially to those who view life as a challenge to *transcend* or reject in some way the reality of these earthly forms into which we were born.

That sort of transcendence is not the lesson of the totem. All of you is your divine self. You are who you are, and that is sacred— including (and especially) the "animal" aspects that perhaps others have tried to tell you are invalid or wrong. Instead, the true lesson of the shining pagan heart is that nothing of this earth, including you, is inherently good or evil; morality is a result of the choices we make, the actions we take, and of how we use what we are given and respond to our experiences.

But it is also true that the human mind is very good at forgetting the things that it has known inside of itself all along. That is why, for the sake of clarity, in this book I do draw a distinction between "the self" and "the higher/animal/essential self." Many people envision where they are now and where they'd like to be after their period of learning as two different places, two separate ideas, and conceptually this results in the idea of two separate selves: that form which exists bearing the full weight of every cloud of confusion and uncertainty, and that form which is pure and unclouded by confusion that we hope to become.

But that is, at best, a trick of grammar. You are who you always have been and always will be: yourself. Your **essential self** is simply what you are when you are able to clearly know yourself.

PART TWO
Structure and Definition

Chapter One:
Why Nine?

If someone has looked into the works of other modern totem workers, it quickly becomes apparent that everyone has a different answer regarding how many totems you actually get. Some who style themselves "traditionalists" (whatever that means) or "old school" may insist that you only get — and only need— a single totem. Others take the complete opposite route, suggesting that multiple totems will come and go throughout a person's lifetime and you will simply receive as many or as few as you need.

I hope to make the case for the logic of our structure of nine permanent totems per human life, (though it will also include limited interaction with any number of temporary spirit guides.) As stated before, the nine totems are:

- The **Primary Totem**, the one face reflective of the entire essential self
- The **Lord Totem**, our masculine and assertive (or passive) nature
- The **Lady Totem**, our feminine and passive (or assertive) nature
- The **Air Totem** in the East, our intellect and mind
- The **Fire totem** in the South, our impulses and passions
- The **Water Totem** in the West, our emotions
- The **Earth Totem** in the North, our body
- The **Light Totem** that is Above, our ideal self
- The **Dark Totem** that is Below, our dark side

Now, anyone familiar with the basics of neo-pagan practice will immediately notice the four cardinal elemental energies, often used in Wicca or in other paths that cast circles. Further, the addition of Above and Below makes the set echo the Six Sacred Directions (utilized within several modern paths of Native American religion, including the Lakota-Sioux and the Diné/Navajo), and also suggests a connection to the widely used Medicine Wheel (See Fig 1A). When we remember the evocation of the Lord and Lady deities in a Wiccan circle, we bring the Lord and Lady totems into the picture.

There is a reason why our system of totemism has borrowed from these concepts: they work. That is, magickally speaking, they provide a functional and

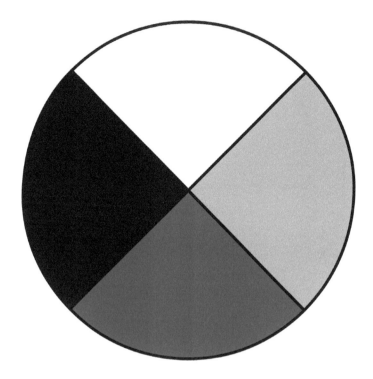

Fig. 1A: Native American Medicine Wheel

balanced framework on which to represent the full spread of characteristics of the essential self, as I will explain.

In this instance, this connection to antiquity is important only because it underlines that the practical application of these ideas are very well used and well established. The idea of four essential elemental energies of nature is tied intimately with the concept of the Four Humors, and those ideas go all the way back to the Middle Ages, if not Hippocrates' Greece. And if we take images of so-called solar crosses (or a cross within a circle) (See Fig 1B) found

Fig. 1B: Celtic Solar Cross

in ancient rock art as representational of the Celtic Sun Wheel, or a Native American Medicine Wheel (depending on location), then this idea could potentially extend back to the stone-age— on more than one continent!

Over the centuries, knowledge and inspiration caused these elemental energies to be placed around that cross shape in relation to each other in a way that is balanced and sequential. And more importantly, in a way that the characteristics associated with each element fit well within the context of our collective unconscious. It makes sense to some deep part of our minds that Fire is a good metaphor for hot blood, and we'd have a more difficult time associating lust and rage with water or wood or sand. And it makes sense that Fire is positioned on the opposite side of the cross to Earth and the body, as heightened and passionate impulses run oppositional to concerns of safety and bodily preservation. (Air/intellect and Water/emotion have a similar antithetical relationship, as do the best and worst aspects of ourselves.)

Now, many people can and do choose to associate the characteristics and/or elements of the six "elemental" totems in a different way than how I have described. For example, in the system of the Lakota-Sioux, they recognize Earth, Fire, Water, and Wind, and they ascribe relatable but notably different characteristics to each of these elements (compared to Wicca), yet they work just fine as templates for the elemental totems. And let's not even get started (yet!) on how someone may define what is "femininity" and "masculinity," and how those concepts are related to assertiveness and passivity. Even within an entirely neo-pagan conversation, you will find diverging personal opinions regarding the finer distinctions separating one from another.

When we consider all that varied opinion on the characteristics of the elementals, it makes the relationship of each of them to a cardinal direction more tenuous and malleable than of the element to the characteristic. For example, my other half prefers to assign Fire to the East and therefore Air to the South, but by the way he has come to know and understand the characteristics of the elementals, this spread works better to his mind.

Ultimately, if you can make a case for why an alternative system works better for you than what I have presented here, that is perfectly respectable and none of my business. I do ask, however, that you wait and entertain our system first, and I promise that afterward you'll have a better place from which to make your personal alterations.

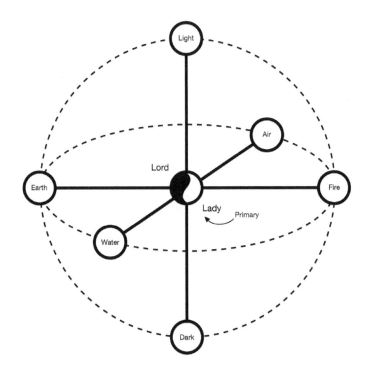

Fig. 1C: The Sphere of Nine Totems

Now, despite all this, I have implied that it is more important that a person recognize a full nine totems and the three-dimensional structure they imply over how they understand the characteristics and elements align to the various directions, and there is a good reason for that: mathematical alignment. Allow me to explain.

When we place a totem at each of the cardinal directions as well as up and down, we imagine the person (as well as the Primary, Lord, and Lady totems, which all overlap) in

46

the center. From one way of looking at it, they form a sort of sphere around the person. But from another way of looking at it, if we draw lines connecting each totem with its opposite, we have set the person (and the center three totems) at the intersection of three lines. (See Fig 1C)

The intersection of these three lines is not by accident. In mathematics, a known point in space can be plotted on a line graph and requires three values: a value for the X-axis (representing distance from left to right), a value for the Y-axis (representing distance from up to down), and a value for a Z-axis (representing a value from forward to backward) (See Fig 1D). These three basic dimensions are what is necessary to define where any given point in space exists.

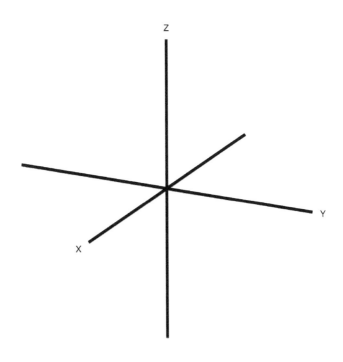

Fig. 1D: X, Y, & Z Axis

When applied to our totemic system, we are metaphorically defining the individual person as a unique point in space. If we take each of the two totems represented on a line axis, and remember that they represent characteristics and energies that are oppositional to each other, the place where they intersect is the point of value on that line. When the intersections of all six elemental totems are considered, we end up with three values defining a single point, or a distinct place in known space. And that point is where a unique individual person exists, both in the physical world and metaphysically at the intersections of the elemental energies. The totems represent who you are, *where* you are, and how you fit into this life.

More specifically, your totems become the values that define where you as a unique individual fall within the grand scheme of potential human character. When considering the characteristics of Air (intellect) and Water (emotion) as the two extremes, where you as an individual find your balance point between them is represented by the characters of your Water and Air totem animals, which both live within you. They express just where you fall along the scale of leading more from the head or from the heart. If totems didn't interact with you or with each other (especially their opposite) in any meaningful way, there would be less need for any specific number of totems. But we do not understand being brainy as simply being *different* from being emotional: we see it as the opposite. If a person leans more toward one, they lean away from the other; their energetic relationship is entwined along a single axis.

This is why we must have nine totems. It's why it just doesn't work as well to insist on having only three elemental totems, following the Druidic pattern of Earth, Sea, and Sky; nor does it work to have five based on the traditional Chinese elements of Fire, Water, Air, Wood, and

Metal. Or to have any other combination that someone may propose.

To define the point in space that is *you*, you need three points of data along each of the three dimensions, with each point understood as having its own two variable values of increase or decrease, totaling six places of variability. Or, more simply, it establishes where you are from left to right, from front to back, and from top to bottom — adding up to six totems. When combined with the center point, understood to have two sides or halves, that adds up to nine totems.

This system of describing our characteristics echoes color theory, which organizes all colors into the color wheel and is used both to describe hues in relation to painting and relationships between colored light. It establishes among other things that complimentary colors, or colors that appear opposite to each other on the wheel, will cancel each other out (when we are dealing with light) or will either match dramatically or clash hideously (when we are dealing with art). Elemental totemic energies that sit across from each other in your totemic sphere have a similar relationship, and finding a balance point between oppositional drives or internal influences pulling in different directions is a matter of taking equally a moderate amount of both extremes.

We will get more into the mechanics of such use in every-day life after each of the nine are explained in more detail. But more than simply defining your character over-all, you will find that you will "shift" closer to some of your elemental totems— and therefore away from others— as your moods change and as you act from various aspects of your personality. That is, if you are in the midst of an emotional crisis, you are "closer" to the influence of the Water totem and "farther away" from the Air totem. And finding your way back from that extreme of Water and emotion to a sense of balance in the center becomes a job for the rational mind, the Air totem.

Chapter Two:
The Primary Totem

The first time I met my Primary totem I didn't recognize him for what he was. I was in a deep state of trance and conducting a shamanic journey at one early point during my college years, and I was suddenly in the presence of a huge black cat. When I asked him who he was or what he had to do with me, he hesitated and eventually supplied the answer: " . . . I am your dark side."

Of course, it was not until some time later that I understood the true nature of our relationship: that the black Jaguar was my Primary totem. And as is typical for entities that inhabit the spirit, the answer he once gave me was not "wrong," technically speaking, but was clouded in double-meaning and artistic exaggeration, and was not as full or exact as it could have been — or perhaps it was exactly as direct as was necessary at the time. An adage between shamans no doubt as old as the discipline itself would lament that spirits always speak with a shadow on their tongues.

For some, understanding the relationship between a totem and its human bearer is a simple thing. In fact, it is surprisingly common to find people who know exactly which animal is their totem (even as they might call it a "power animal" or "spirit animal") despite the fact that they may have no interest in the magick of totemism, are followers of religions that don't recognize animal totems, or who otherwise live without religion at all. For some, the feeling of kindred that is evoked between themselves and a particular animal is strong and undeniable, and their relationship to it needs no clarification.

But with others, even those who may be willing and seeking a totemic connection, the path to that epiphany is longer and complicated, with twists and turns of cognition. Is the Primary totem animal a reflection of the self, like a mirrored image, reflecting the strongest and most obvious characteristics of the person? Or is this totem a reflection of the hidden self, the contrary or opposite self, representing that which a person might be but is not?

The answer, in fact, is both. The Primary totem is at once a reflection of our most essential qualities as well as a window into aspects of the self that may or may not be presented in our everyday personalities. Properly, we will define the **Primary Totem** as: the animal that is directly reflective of our entire essential selves.

Carl Jung posited the idea that we can potentially encounter two different archetypal personalities within our minds that both represent our own self-image: The Self and The Persona. The Self represents who we think we are to ourselves, the part that we might think of as the "real" us; The Persona represents the face that we show to others, or who other people would say we are, which can often be quite different from The Self.

The Primary totemic energy, by way of our our discipline of totemism, encompasses the concepts of both The Self and The Persona. (And coincidentally there are no direct parallels between Jung's personal or identity archetypes and our system of nine totems.) But Jung's concept of these two different "faces" for the self can help us over the conceptual speed-bump of how the Primary Totem can be at once "the true self" and "the opposite of the self." Not every aspect of who you truly are makes it through the twists and turns of your willful and rationalizing brain to crest the surface into your public personality and your every-day life. In a way, you could also say that the Primary Totem represents "the rest" of the self, as every person shows the world some but not all of who they really are.

For some people, there may be very little that is kept hidden, and these "authentic" personalities are the sort who may find it difficult to see the Primary Totem as the contrary self. Conversely, the sort of person who crafts a very neat public face for daily use and who puts that "mask" away once safely tucked into their solitude may find it more difficult to digest the idea that both identities are a unified concept represented by a single animal.

In my case, when my totem chose to first show himself to me, I was at a place in my spiritual journey where I was feeling considerable concern over making the "right" or most ethical decisions regarding my spiritual beliefs. I was asking some very fundamental questions and venturing away from the more well-defined religious boundaries of my childhood onto the shakier ground of the "unaffiliated" seeker; I was beginning to discard aspects of Christianity and cobble together the mixed bag of ideas of a new and green-horned eclectic pagan. On the one hand, I could no longer force myself to claim I believed in things I intellectually knew to be untrue. But on the other, I was afraid of leaving behind the comforts of faith — and at some level still fearing the threats aimed at the heretical rebel, even as I knew at the time both in my mind and my heart that such threats were baseless.

When you are at a place in your life where part of you simply knows what you will do, who you are, or what you know is true, that is the voice of your Primary totem. And it is amazing just how often we avoid this knowing, or are unable to see it altogether, because of our own fears, doubts, or past learning that clouds our ability to accept who and what we are. All things considered, the nature of your Primary totem can be more "you" than you yourself are, if you deny it. I knew, in some deep inner place, that I was a pagan even before I began to research the details of exactly what one was; I knew even before I had learned a word for it. The part of me who knew this from the beginning had to work with the part of me that needed to take the longer road to understanding, and so at the time that first part of me could be perceived in no other way than as wildly and tantalizingly dangerous: the dark side.

Now, at this point I would like to re-introduce another bedrock concept of the Primary totem I mentioned earlier: that the animal is almost always the opposite sex of its bearer. Now, I understand that making assertions concerning gender, sex, and personal identity in the same sentence is a dangerous occupation these days, and doubly-so within neo-pagan culture that is preoccupied with all-encompassing acceptance to the point of obsession. You will hear me discuss gender further in the following section on the Lord and Lady totems as it carries even more importance there. But suffice it to say, it is true that the gender roles of "male" and "female" in the human animal are culturally ascribed and are indeed variable and malleable. *But* within the region of the unconscious mind concerned with archetypes, divorcing gender roles from the biological sexes assigned to them is difficult, if not impossible. That is, it is right and good that we allow individuals the right to self-identify, but that doesn't change the fact that all human minds have internal concepts of "maleness" and "femaleness" and we tend to divide people into one category or the other without conscious choice — even those who are comfortable understanding gender as a spectrum are still using "maleness" and "femaleness" as the two metrics. Or in even simpler terms, the *concepts* of "male" and "female" exist within our minds, and it is that unconscious template of the mind that we are concerned with as that is what shapes our perceptions of totems.

With this in mind it becomes important to include sex in our understanding of our Primary totem's role as the opposite of the self, the hidden qualities of the self, or "the rest" of the self that is not a part of the self we show the world. If someone identifies as "female," that (usually) means she identifies as "not a male." Keep in mind that gender is an entirely human contrivance— that is, gender is the role you are expected to play in your society, and not biological sex, even as we assign gender roles to individuals based on their sex; and technically speaking, animals don't have genders, only sexes. But our unconscious templates in our minds do a fine job of combining sex and gender into the male/female binary, and conceptually it becomes extraordinarily convenient — even necessary, according to our individual paradigms— for us to see our contrary selves as the opposite sex.

Yet, as intelligent people we also understand that any and all qualities of personality can theoretically exist in men, women, and those in-between. In a more artistic sense, I think we would all agree there is no functional difference between a male and female human *soul,* and sex is merely an issue of the meat conveyance that houses it. But in recognizing this, we arrive at the same place as before: even as we often see the Primary totem as the opposite of ourselves, in truth they simply *are* ourselves. A person may be a woman in this life and in this body, but an open mind recognizes that the entirety of the essential self cannot fit into our limited mental template defining the sex/gender binary, and that on a spiritual level that person has both femaleness and maleness within her— as all people do. And all individuals can vary as to how much of each (or neither) is present within their personality, and therefore how much (or little) of either is therefore reserved for the shadow self in the Primary totem.

Coincidentally, the very same argument is put forth to explain why the faces or archetypes of divinity tend to come in pairs, a male and female partnership, not just to pagans but cross-culturally, and especially to Hindus. The argument is that true divinity is neither male nor female, and is also both, but limited human minds are uncomfortable accepting a face of God that isn't a man or a woman because that's all we know. So the best solution is to humanize divinity by representing it as a complimentary human married pair. Your relationship with your Primary totem functions in the same way, and together you and your totem represent a whole essential personality with both a male and female face.

Chapter Three:
The Lord and the Lady Totems

Within our path of totemism, the Lord and Lady totems occupy a unique area of the mind. On the one hand, we recognize them as separate entities from the Primary totem. The idea that we are now dividing the essential self into two halves implies that each is a less precise representation of the self, and therefore more distinct from the true, primary self. Yet on the other hand, I have stated that the Lord and Lady totems should be perceived as aspects of the center, that they plus the Primary together should be accepted as the three "center" totems, and so directly representational of the essential self by occupying the center point on our line graphs. In fact, the Lord and Lady totems occur mid-way between these conceptual points. Yes, we have begun to "divide" the self into separate aspects; yet the Lord and Lady totems remain far closer to our concept of the pure essential self than any of the elemental totems, which are comfortably representational of only limited parts of our characters. They are, in their way, a bridge between concepts, and in this case the Lord and Lady totems occupy the gray space between there being one and many voices within your head.

Now, as part of an (unintentionally) ironic effort to make art imitate life, I need to interject with a little issue here: my other half (that is, my *other* other half: my husband) understands the Lord and Lady totems in a way that is both supportive of, but in opposition to, the way I do. For me, their primary function is to express the masculine and feminine energies (and tendencies) within a person; following the mythology of modern neo-paganism, the concepts of ideal maleness (i.e. The Lord) and ideal femaleness (i.e. The Lady) also serve as the gatekeepers of dualistic energies (light/dark, active/passive etc), but they are secondary characteristics of them. But for my husband, it is the opposite. Following a pattern more similar to the Chinese *yin/yang* or the Hindu *shiva/shakti*, for him the *primary* function of the Lord and Lady totems is expressing the qualities of dualistic energy, and their connection to sex/gender is *secondary*.

To save you from too much extraneous reading, needless to say, we've gone rounds on this. Neither of us can emerge victorious in the argument because both understandings are right— at once. To our path of totemism, the **Lord totem** represents the totality of your concept of ideal maleness *and* the face of your active (or passive) energy, and the **Lady totem** the totality of ideal femaleness *and* the face of your passive (or active) energy. Both exist largely according to your personal paradigm, and whether their sexes or their dualistic energies are the primary and most prominent characteristics for you is something you may need to work out for yourself. I will explain both positions and then, gods willing, mix oil and water and unify them.

by Sex and Gender

By my understanding, the sexes of the Lord and Lady totem are important aspects of their personas. Now to repeat: biological sex is a related but separate concept from gender, where sex is referencing the biological form of the body while gender is referencing the uniquely human idea that each sex carries with it a predefined role governing behaviors and one's place in society. Further,

58

even as we may intellectually recognize that gender definitions are fluid and that no specific personality characteristic can be found solely in men or in women, we nevertheless must reconcile with the part of our minds (perhaps Jung's collective unconscious) that combines all we know about both gender and sex into the basic binary concepts of "maleness" and "femaleness" that are distinctly different from each other. To recognize the existence of these archetypes within ourselves is not the same thing as taking an inflexible social stance of rigidly defined binary gender identity. As I said before, even the modern concept of gender as a spectrum still uses "masculinity" and "femininity" as the points of reference from which all other positions are measured.

The issue of gender I am taking such great pains to unpack is consequently a pressing cognitive problem and therefore a hot topic of debate in modern neo-paganism. First and foremost, this is because our granddaddy tradition of Wicca states clearly that divinity is best seen as two complimentary but contradictory forms, the Lord and Lady. Wiccan teachings emphasize that a meaningful reaction of creation — that is, magick — is a result of the Lord and the Lady coming together. These two divine forms are echoed in nature, as the ever-evolving relationship between the Lord and the Lady is what drives the birth of every new year each spring and the cycle of seasons; their complimentary magick is echoed when the physical representations of their forms come together and a man and a woman make a child. The reconciliation of these bedrock ideas with contemporary inclusiveness and modern understanding of the full rainbow of human sexuality and gender identity obviously creates its problems; how we define the roles of LGBTQ people within a tradition built upon the metaphor of sexual reproduction creates even more.

In the past, the suggestion has surfaced that perhaps the road to reconciliation for pagans may lie in accepting the concepts of the Lord and Lady as energies or ideas only (again, similar to the Chinese *yin/yang* or the Hindu *shiva/shakti*) instead of as personalities with human faces. Nevertheless, there is comfort in those human faces, in turning an energetic pattern of nature's function into a mother and father who are making decisions and who are "in charge" of this madness called our lives— and more importantly, in unifying these energetic concepts with the myriad of gods and goddesses from throughout human existence. The simple, basic, unconscious aspects of our minds really like — dare I say, need — to "put a face" to these things to bring them to our level where we can relate to, understand, and ultimately love them. If we didn't do this very thing, after all, we would have no need of totem animals. Ultimately, I feel asking people to give up the Lord and Lady as personalities, as gods, might even be counterproductive to their effort to find wisdom, even as I can think of no other way to suggest reconciling the issues of gender identity within the tradition.

So along the same lines, it has been both my personal experience and observation that doing the same to the Lord and Lady totems, that seeing them just as expressions of dualistic energy, is incorrect. I have found the concepts of "man" and "woman" (or even "mother" and "father") exist at a deeper and more primal level of the subconscious mind than any understanding of dualistic or binary energy forces. Westerners will grow-up exposed to these binary energies through metaphor in fiction, but they will not feature nearly as prominently in our unconscious minds as direct life experience resulting in ideas of maleness and femaleness, mother and father, man and woman.

Further, our totems exist largely to help us understand ourselves and most people will expend far more mental energy throughout their lives trying to reconcile the differences between the sexes than they ever will the difference between *yin* and *yang*— especially if the exhausting amount I've already said about sex and gender can be taken as any indication! In short, taking the primary factors of gender and sex away from the Lord and Lady totems inhibits their very function. I, for one, have found that my Lord and Lady totems are actually more similar in character than they are "diametrically opposed" to each other (a Lion and an Elephant matriarch — both large, strong, sole leaders of an extended family unit), and I've found this is not an uncommon thing.

For *me*, the Lord totem represents the totality of your ideal maleness, your ideal man or father, and your Lady totem is your ideal femaleness, you ideal woman or mother. Combined, within yourself, they represent the influence of that which taken *together* represents the full potential of a human personality: your essential self.

by Dualistic Energy

There is a force in nature that creates and changes, that moves, that is expressed energy, that is constant action; opposite to that is the force of preservation and reservation, that prevents rapid change and creates constance, that saves energy, that is protective and as still as nature will allow. They work against each other, and yet, they work together, and their interaction is what drives creation itself. These concepts have been noted and named by almost every culture and can be broadly understood not only in a spiritual context— the light and dark, order and chaos, the active and passive— but also a scientific one: as potential and kinetic energy.

If we look to the binary energies of traditional cultures— for example, *yin/yang* and *shiva/shakti* as we've been discussing— it's easy to see that while the concepts themselves are constants, different human cultures assign "maleness" or "femaleness" to them arbitrarily. In fact, in those two examples, they are almost completely opposite to each other: the masculine Chinese *yang* energy is the "spark" of life, the push of power and the generative force, and the agent of change— while in Hinduism most of those same qualities are ascribed to *shakti,* the feminine force. The gender assignment is all but totally arbitrary, and more likely than not, it was assigned based on base characteristics of the traditional gender roles of their cultures of origin— roles that for contemporary pagans will be all but meaningless.

In neo-paganism, these energetic forces are often described through the characters of the Lord and Lady; traditionally the Lord is active/chaos energy and the Lady is passive/order energy. While it is true that many contemporary pagans choose to use the Lord and Lady as more generic (and culturally unattached) gods and goddesses for their personal study and worship, it should be carefully noted that this was not their original intent. In traditional Wicca, the "Lord" and "Lady" were simply names given to the dualistic energy forces, in the same way the Hindus named them *shiva* and *shakti.* Instead, each of these forces were understood to embody and empower all the various gods and goddesses out there— as well as people— in varying amounts, but they were not the gods themselves.

Therefore, the Lord and Lady totems, along the same lines, are first and foremost a matter of the active and passive *energy* within you. This is according to my husband's opinion, which consequently carries even more experience with totems than mine.

Now, while contemporary pagans acknowledge that the male ejaculates while the female gestates, and that in many traditional cultures (which naturally inspired neo-pagan thought) the man hunted and planted while the woman baked and reared young, for many that is hardly enough to justify assigning those creative energies to any gender, considering how complicated people are. My husband believes that over-complicating the energetic concepts to fit modern notions of gender is unnecessary, as their connection is far more to basic animal sex rather than human gender. However, as he respects that everyone's inner, unconscious understanding of these things can and will vary, he recognizes that the sex/gender assignment for our totems may go in either direction, and that the male Lord totem could sit for either the person's active *or* passive energy, and vice-versa for the Lady. He would even go so far to say that a person could just name *Yin* and *Yang* totems if they prefer to keep the enormously complicated notion of gender identity out of it.

Complimentary and Oppositional

And so in this roundabout way, we come back to the Lord and the Lady totems. At this point, some may be nodding in agreement at the complexity of the issue between sex/gender and the dualistic energies, while for others this concept may seem infinitely simplistic, and they may well be pulling their hair at my insistence on overcomplicating it. It is literally just that simple and just that hard.

Neo-pagans will be more familiar with the Lord and Lady/dualistic energies debate, and so may be better suited to understand how the concept can encompass both ideas at once. Yes, in the beginning, it was a simple thing for the first Wiccans to understand "the Lord" to mean the active, generative force in nature, and to have no trouble blending this concept with a god-form that was the father and progenitor, the archetypal male, because Wicca was invented in the 1950s and gender roles were far more defined and codified back then. Today, pagans have to find their own way to their own understanding, though I will suggest that said understanding almost always comes from the realization that all people *and* all gods and spirits have some of both of the dualistic energies within them in varying amounts. And perhaps if you're going to worship a Lord and a Lady as fully-fledged gods, it might be wise to acknowledge the dualistic energies they rule as related but separate concepts.

As far as your Lord and Lady totems go, take solace in what I have been saying all along: that your totems are already set within you, as they are, and the work that lies before you is in the discovery. Therefore, if you have been reading along and naturally agreed more with my way of understanding, or with my husband's, or have possession of a workable combination of both, proceed with confidence that your own totems will likely mirror this.

At any rate, this conundrum of definitions does make providing too many descriptive *qualities* of these totems a problem, as well as their roles within you. However, a person's parents often have a heavy influence on the development of these archetypes — and if not the mother and father, then whichever male and female role models you had in childhood. There are some observable patterns in the distribution of certain qualities, due to our shared cultural experiences: the Lord totem has a better chance of being the protector, for example, because many of us are comfortable thinking of that as the father's job, and because that incorporates the active energy. But that is not always the case; as it happens, both mine and my husband's Lady totems represent our *active* energy, and my Elephant Lady totem is unquestionably the protector. Nothing about the temperament, characteristics, strengths, influences, or otherwise the qualities of *your* Lord and Lady totems are written in stone.

To our path of totemism, the **Lord totem** represents the totality of your concept of ideal maleness and the face of your active (or passive) energy, and the **Lady totem** the totality of ideal femaleness and the face of your passive (or active) energy — and that which taken *together* represent the full potential of a human personality: your essential self.

Chapter Four:
The Elemental Totems: Earth, Air, Fire, Water, Light, and Dark

The Four Humors

Whenever I have introduced the idea of the elemental totems to practicing neo-pagans, they are easily taken as a given by people who are used to utilizing elemental energies in every-day practice. Even as there may be some disagreement on the specific way I personally define the elementals, pagans require little to no explanation as to what they are or why they need to be here. Therefore, a larger part of my explanation of the elemental totems is more likely aimed at those readers who are not pagan.

However, I am not implying that pagans may skip this sub-chapter; discussing what we already know is required to gain a deeper understanding of it. And aside from that, it may not be immediately apparent to a pagan just how the elemental energies relate to the totem animals representing them, or how they in turn play their larger part in influencing the functionality of the essential self.

To begin, the concept of fundamental earthly energies which serve to make up the entirety of the natural world is a concept that in the West goes back at least as far as ancient Greece. When we consider Chinese traditional medicine and their similar elemental forms, the idea could be many thousands of years old. Today, we have the benefit of knowledge of atoms, molecules, and a whole periodic table of elements we know to make up the physical world. However, it is worth knowing that until the advent of modern science, even the most educated minds of the time across many advanced ancient cultures perceived the natural world as being composed of only four or five elements: Earth, Air, Fire, and Water in the West, while the Chinese bisected "Earth" and went with Wood and Metal. Each of these elements was said to have certain "qualities" that differentiated them from one another, and of specific importance was whether they were hot or cold, and wet or dry.

These ancient scholars, in turn, utilized their theory of elements in other aspects of science known at the time. In the West, elementals had strong influence in both alchemy (the grandaddy of chemistry) and more importantly in medicine. The four elements gave rise to the theory of the *four* **humors** (often spelled "humours"), or the idea that a human body is composed of four essential fluids called humors: yellow bile, black bile, blood, and phlegm, each of which corresponded to an element and shared its hot/cold and wet/dry qualities. Illness was believed to be a result of an imbalance of the humors, and healing was a matter of restoring the balance of them.[4]

Those four humors, in turn, gave rise to a sort of primitive psychology that defined the ***four temperaments***, or four basic personality types that were each a result of whichever humor was most prolific in an individual: melancholic (quiet and analytical), choleric (moody), sanguine (optimistic and sociable), and phlegmatic (peaceful and content).

---

[4] Consequently, such bizarre practices as blood-letting make slightly more sense when understood as an attempt to balance the ratio of blood to the other fluids in the body to restore equilibrium.

The concepts of four elements, humors, and temperaments have all been discarded from modern science. Today, they occupy some small role in various types of holistic medicine and some forms of metaphysical healing. And of course, the elementals alone remain as metaphors of metaphysical energy types in neo-paganism. Over-all, the modern person is left with the impression that these ideas have little value remaining, and for the most part I would agree.

However, few people understand that the four humors have actually remained a very prominent part of our modern lives without us even noticing: through fiction, and in a larger sense, through a great many creative arts. The "qualities" of the four humors, and through them the four temperaments, have remained up until this day such a standard part of modern story-telling that even writers might not even understand they're using them.

To illustrate, I want you to recall the main characters in your favorite book or television show — or in any modern story, for that matter. More often than not, the characters can be divided into personalities best illustrated by the compliment of your average boy-band: the leader, or the brave and headstrong one; the clever, neurotic, or nerdy one; the sweet, shy, silly, or perhaps simple one; and the tough or moody "bad boy" one. Some casts of characters may have more than one of a certain type, or they may get away with omitting one, leaving the simple character behind to guard the castle or pilot the ship, or even casting the moody one as the villain instead as one of the heroes. But once seen, the pattern cannot be un-seen: the four humors are in everything we love.

Especially in the modern West, all of us grow up constantly exposed to fiction that is cast with this same spread of characters; we get very used to the idea that you need one of each of these "types" to have a strong team with diverse but complimentary personalities and skills. In real life we see more often than not that people surround themselves with friends whose personalities are similar to their own. But in stories, we take it as a given that these four types depend on each other, and might even be necessary, to form a strong and productive friendship and drive a plot forward.

And here is where things get interesting in regard to our totems. The four humors may not be a part of humanity's collective unconscious, but when everyone within a large culture is exposed to these archetypes since childhood they can exist in an unconscious place almost as deep. If we are tasked with dividing our essential self into its more basic qualities, the metaphors of the humors — or rather, the superhero team, the sitcom friends, or the wizarding school houses — is unconsciously readily available to us. And it provides a working framework that balances the often-conflicting sides of the self in a way that makes them harmonious and functional.

Time has lost the connection between these four "types" of personalities and the original bodily fluids that inspired them— thankfully! But we did not lose the metaphorical connection between the personalities and the original four elements we started with. However, it should be noted that through many hundreds if not thousands of years of filtration through creative minds, it is true that the modern associations between the elementals and their corresponding personality traits have meandered somewhat from their original templates. However, the fact that the humors inspired these modern templates is inarguable. A headstrong person is a "hot head," well represented by fiery metaphor, while the "air-headed" absent minded professor is often at odds with their unpredictable and "stormy" moody counterpart. And the unshakable strength and gentle humor of the "down to earth" character is often what draws them together in time to save the day.

The Totems

Taking all of this business of the humors in mind, we begin to look at the four elemental totems within our path of totemism. As is the case with the qualities of "masculinity" and "femininity" ascribed to the Lord and Lady, there is room in the elemental totems for individual alterations and adaptations based on your personal relationship to the elemental metaphors and your experiential paradigm. But taking into consideration that everyone understands what sex and gender are but only pagans generally understand the elementals, in the interest of clarity I will describe them the way I personally understand them, and you can either agree or take it on your own from there. As I explained in the section on why it's necessary to have nine totems, what is most important is that your final product is both balanced and comprehensive, and not necessarily exactly like mine or anyone else's.

Another point to take into consideration when searching for your elemental totems: unlike the previous totems we have discussed, all six of these can be either male or female. It's true that the elementals, both to neo-pagans and according to the traditional humors, do have maleness or femaleness associated with them (earth and water are feminine, while fire and air are masculine). But the human concept of the sex/gender binary has relatively little to do with the human characteristics dealt with by these elemental totems. Often I have seen that people with a generally healthy relationship to gender will have an even split, three male and three female. But it is also worth noting that you might not know at all, initially or ever, as many animals do not have obvious outward displays of their sex in either appearance or behavior, such as with Cougars or Tigers.

On the other hand, with other types of animals there can be an enormous difference between how the males and the females behave, and so knowing whether you have a Lion or a lLoness as your totem can make a world of difference. The sex of the animal is only important in defining the behavioral qualities of the animal if there is a difference between the sexes to be found, and has little or nothing to do with how that sex affects your corresponding personality traits.

The Earth in the North

The Earth totem is first and foremost representational of the body. Initially, we may not necessarily think of the body as contributing to a reflection of our personalities. However, the influence of the physical contributes its fair share to the metaphysical, and there is a noteworthy aspect of the self who is concerned with our well-being as physical creatures — who after all must remain in these bodies to continue to participate in this life in the first place. But Earth is also the part of our personalities that has the most constance; the **Earth totem** is the part of the self in charge of holding steady in times of crisis, the part that defines what an individual finds comforting and secure, and the part that decides what is most essential to life when taken against all else.

The Earth elemental is generally thought of as the one that is the most permanent, (or as permanent and slow as is possible in nature, which is always changing at least a little bit as it moves forward in time) with the greatest resistance to change. That doggedness manifests equally as a stubborn refusal to learn and as steady and secure faith. Earth is slow to create change, yet its affect is relatively constant, and its concerns are largely turned inward. It is the element of the hearth and the home, of beginnings. All life begins and ends with the dust of the earth, and so too does all magick— and all creation — begin with the earth elemental that provides the sturdy foundation that supports and nourishes all other life.

Within a human personality, the Earth elemental gives the Earth totem the role of the "brother's keeper," best compared to a babysitter or a designated driver; depending on what you're trying to get away with, the Earth totem can seem like a buzzkill or like that precious rare responsible friend you'd trust to look after your pets while you're on vacation. When you get into trouble, your Earth totem is the one you can phone at 3am to come and pick you up, no matter how drunk you are or where you ended up. Not only will they always come for you, but they will always be there for you with a cup of hot chocolate and a shoulder to lean on. And no matter how many times you screw-up, or how often you lose your way in life, your Earth totem is the character who will seem genuinely unmoved and unaffected by your drama. Don't make the mistake of assuming them to be dull, slow, or boring; rather, they possess a great strength of character and have immense faith in their own core abilities. Your Earth totem is that character who will agree to go along on any crazy adventure with a shrug and a smile, and who will make it through easily so long as they have a few essential tools— whether that be a med-kit, a sword, or a sandwich. On the rare occasion that the Earth totem is moved by something, it pulls with it the force of mountains; its fear is paralyzing, its love all-consuming, and its wrath volcanic.

What do you need from your life to feel secure? What level of creature comfort do you require? How do you define what is home, and how difficult is it to be away from it? How important is your physical appearance, your level of physical fitness and the activity you get, what is important for you to feel healthy? Stripped of all else in the worst kind of emergency, what would you feel is essential to your survival, your happiness, and your long-term well-being? All of this is the domain of the Earth totem.

The Air in the East

The **Air totem** is predominantly in charge of ideas, intellect, and creativity, of what we in the West comfortably define as "the mind," even as we recognize that all impulses come from the brain and not just the thoughts alone.

Depending on your personality, the Air totem can be quite unemotional, professional, even stern; but it can just as likely contain a great deal of colorful silliness. Air is the elemental of both rational logic as well as aimless creative fun. Air can cause change quickly, in sudden gusts and bursts, as well as slowly and methodically, blowing one grain of sand from the canyon at a time. Similarly to Water in a physical sense, it fills all available space it is given. Air can also change itself quickly, and can sometimes lack a sense of stability or constance; new ideas blow into the mind as easily as they blow out again. But this can be deceptive, for it usually takes long periods of time for Air to truly have the ability to carve sculptures in mountains, to make meaningful and lasting changes in the world— with the notable exception of the occasional tornado! Most of the time, it can only affect great change when applied with patience, persistence, and most importantly discipline— the domain of Earth—and without that discipline it is far less productive. Flightily creativity may think of a hundred new things before breakfast, but to saddle that creativity is the only way to make that idea come to life.

The Air totem as a personality can vary considerably depending on your relationship to your own intelligence. For some, the Air totem is the hard logic, the one with its nose forever in the rule-book, wagging a finger in the air and proclaiming that the plan can't work. For others, the Air totem is the one being scolded by that first character, the one whose unconventional idea seems to defy all reason — until it works. In either case, the Air totem is the one who brings the glut of ideas to the table, and isn't necessarily always the one most qualified to make a decision as to which is the best one to use. And if it is put in charge, Air will always be troubled by indecision and will often second-guess itself, unable to see the forest for the trees— keep in mind the mental image of wind blowing leaves in one direction and then another for a sense of how easy it can be for the Air totem to see things from multiple angles, to debate from opposing sides of the same issue. As such, it can sometimes be easy to dismiss the Air totem as lacking a sense of responsibility or even trustworthiness, as the absent-minded doctor, as a well-read nerd with no real-world experience, or as a goof-ball with no ability to take things seriously and pay attention. But in fact, Air only appears so flighty because it is taking-in the issue from every conceivable — and possibly inconceivable— angle, and in the end its decision will likely be better thought-out than any one else's.

Consequently, Air can also be deceptively moral. That is, I have observed that many people keep their sense of ethics within their Air totems— even as to some that may seem like an emotional issue based in empathy, the domain of the Water totem which is the realm of emotion. Logic is comfortable with rules, even of ethics, even as it may equally enjoy debating the parameters of them. And keeping ethics as the charge of the free-flowing Water totem can turn out to be just as flighty, untrustworthy, and ultimately corruptible as what we erroneously expect of Air. Ultimately, most people need more concrete ethical rules based on reason, not "the feels."

Crossing the Air totem can be a literal hit or miss — the new idea may pass by with disinterest, or it may change Air's existing opinion. But there is also a chance the intellectual challenge may insult a person's deeply held morals, sense of identity, or even world view. In those cases, the Air totem can be a formidable enemy— or weapon. (We've all been to the Internet and seen the comments section of almost any article!) Keep in mind that one traditional symbol of the Air elemental is the sword, and when Air goes to war it knows exactly where to cut to cause the most damage.

How do you problem-solve, how do you create solutions? How do you best learn new ideas, learn new ways of doing things, and how easily can you invent new ones? How do you make yourself remember what you already know, and tie it all together to create context and meaning? When taken at its core, how easily can you entertain a point of view that is not your own? All of this is the domain of the Air totem.

The Fire in the South

With the Fire totem, we can encounter some difficulty in its explanation: the defining characteristics of Fire and Water are both what we usually consider "emotions" or "feelings," and differentiating between the two can be a subtle thing. For our purposes, the **Fire totem** is best defined as reflecting your passions, infatuations, and impulses that are fleeting in nature— as opposed to true "emotions" which have more depth, connection to past experiences, and longevity and which are ascribed to Water.

Fire's concerns are turned outward and it is quick to cause change. Essentially, Fire is everything that Earth is not; we can think of Earth as being the face of permanence and resistance to change while Fire is the face of change with very little permanence — or even substance — at all. Where Earth is all about "just being," Fire is absolutely all about "doing." Just to exist, a fire has to be burning something, has to be changing one type of matter into another, and once no more change can take place it burns out — and ceases to exist. Fire is the essence of regeneration, when a forest fire opens a giant sequoia pinecone to release the seed of a new tree. It is the essence of renewal by destruction, or reincarnation by death, when that fire burns away the whole forest that died from lack of rainfall so that new sequoia can grow in its place. Like Water, it cleanses. It is change, chaos, movement. In its most abstract sense, the Fire elemental is almost more a verb than it is a noun.

As a personality, the Fire totem is very much concerned with "the now." Regardless of how many successes or failures you've faced, the past is the past and has little to do with today; tomorrow hasn't happened yet and anything is possible. As such, the Fire totem is everything within a person that acts on impulse and without inhibition, that reacts to a situation without much or any forethought— or much or any emotional baggage. When acting from a place of joy, love, or fun, the Fire totem can be a passionate adventurer; when acting from anger, fear, or other hurt it can be moody, brutal, even violent.

The nature of Fire reactions cover the full span of human experience, both positive and negative. As such, there is a great deal of variance in the "normal" personality of Fire totems, as a great deal depends on your personal proclivity to first react to situations in one way or another. If you are the sort of person who sees every bend in the road as a challenge to better yourself, your Fire totem may likely appear a brave and headstrong hero— or perhaps the sort to get you into trouble in the name of having a good time. If you are more suspicious of the intentions of others, your Fire totem might appear defensive and have a bad habit of snapping at people.

The sudden influence of the Fire totem can be overwhelming if it is strong, but remember that your reaction is temporary and impermanent. The key is to enjoy the spark of life it brings without letting it overtake your better senses. The Fire totem's impetuous nature, almost innocent in its way, is what influences you to live life to its fullest and is the source of fun in its purest sense. This totem is your friend who will phone you at 3a.m. to take you on an adventure, the totem who never can resist a "keep out" sign. If the Earth totem is the friend you call to bail you out of jail, the Fire totem is the one in the cell with you saying, "We messed up." Of course it's safer not to go with him on his crazy schemes, but what kind of life is that? Of course he makes terrible decisions when he's drunk, but you would have never ended up on that fishing boat to Nova Scotia without him.

Yet as much as one person's Fire totem can seem to vary from another's, all of them share the same core trait that not only binds them all together, but gives them their greatest ability to change bad habits and adapt in new ways: impermanence. To exist, a fire needs fuel to burn; our Fire-based reactions will occur as a result of certain stimuli. To douse an unwanted Fire reaction, change the series of events or behaviors that led to it (scatter those sticks, kick dirt into the flames). If you want to start a Fire reaction on purpose (that is, form a new habit, start a new discipline, or have a different reaction to certain circumstances) then you can build one by repeating a series of behaviors that lead to it until it becomes habit. The permanence of Earth is necessary for self-discipline, but equally so is a purposefully cultivated Fire-based reaction of focused attention and enthusiasm. For that reason, your Fire totem is important to take with you into meditation, perhaps even more-so than the other totems.

But don't let the hotheaded Fire totem confuse you into thinking he's just a good time. Air might be responsible for generating ideas, but without the enthusiasm and energy that Fire brings, that idea will never get off the ground. The Fire totem's entire nature is to continue to motivate you, to keep you moving towards new goals and new interests, to keep you going. Without it your life wouldn't just be boring, it would be so stagnant it couldn't rightly be called a life at all. While the Earth totem answers the question of what you feel is essential to survive, the Fire totem defines what you feel is essential to *live*, to continue to laugh and to cry and to be fully human. And the innocence of hope, consequently, is entirely Fire's doing.

What is it that really moves you? What makes you get up and dance, get up and fight, or get up and chase after something you want? What makes you scream at the person you love? Or be obsessed with a thing you can't have? What makes you act when you know you know better? And what makes you a better person for it? All of this is the domain of the Fire totem.

The Water in the West

The **Water totem** is defined as the totem of your emotions, of your "feelings" that have more depth, connection to past experiences, and longevity than the impulses of Fire. In every way that Fire is defined as a reaction occurring without much forethought, Water emotions have "a good reason" for occurring, a connection to your life history, your ideas, and your memories. While both can be strong sensations, it is fair to say that Water emotions feel "deeper" than Fire emotions. They have more substance and are processed by our minds in a different way than fleeting flashes of passion.

Like Fire, Water cleanses. Like Air, it can fill all available space and can cause change slowly and methodically or in a sudden rush of violence, by building a stalagmite one drip at a time or shifting the very earth in a violent flood. More often than not, however, it follows the path of gravity and settles for the lowest and easiest places to pool in the landscape, making Water personalities usually deeply understanding, tolerant, and able to cope with the world around them. Water is the most talented shape-shifter and is able to accommodate nearly any change in its environment— it can fill any vessel, freeze into ice to become like Earth, evaporate into steam to become like Air, even boil to burn like Fire. That shift might appear chaotic, but in reality, it is only a sign of its innate adaptability; the sudden tears may make the Water character appear weak or unstable, but that is simply an outward sign of their strong ability to process their experiences and cope with life— and to help others do the same. Ultimately, Water in its pure state is clear and transparent, open and hiding nothing— unless it has been muddied or churned.

But it is not unfair to say that the Water totem is that friend whom you knew had secrets even before you got to know her; she has layers that require compassion, trust, and patience to unravel and fully understand. It is a mistake to label her unintelligent— or hysterical. In fact, Water is profoundly intelligent in a way that is best described as "clever," as it carries with it an undertone of crafty shiftiness like a fox or a raccoon, and that likely comes from its ability to intuitively read anybody or any situation and manipulate it to its advantage. Depending on your own comfort with that side of yourself, your Water totem can be a deeply loyal friend or someone very difficult to deal with — or both at once. You can trust her if you like, but what's the fun in that?

Humanity has had a strange relationship with the Water elemental and its associated characteristics. At the onset, I think most people would recognize an entire rainbow of different emotions in people, and understand a diverse spread running from positive to negative and everything in between. Yet, when we label a person "emotional," we seem to automatically associate them with only the negative ones — we call them unstable, biased, weepy, fearful, irrational, even untrustworthy, secretive, a loose cannon whose motives are always in question. Rarely are we comfortable calling someone "emotional" as a result of them being happy all the time.

Out of the four humor-inspired characters we see in fiction, modern authors seem far more likely to cast the moody "water" character as a person of questionable loyalty, if not the villain outright (even as that makes said villain a critical and enjoyable part of the four humor character structure). Air characters make fine villains, yet their deference to logic and reason as often as not makes them vulnerable to "seeing the light" in the final act, to being talked-out of their evil scheme if it can be explained to them where they went wrong. Water, unfortunately for our heroes, doesn't have this weakness, and we all recognize at some intuitive level that emotional motivation is difficult if not impossible to disrupt; we are more protective of our feelings than our ideas and are more likely to ignore suggestions that they are misplaced.

There may be some room in this argument of common perception to consider the influence of the biases of the past, as traditionally logic and rationality were thought to be traits more suited to (superior) men while mysterious and uncontrollable emotion was the domain of the hysterical woman — casting it in a gigantic shadow of suspicion and doubt even today. Over-all, however, I feel that rejecting our feelings in the face of "superior" reason is a problem faced by both modern women and men, and so too is seeing emotions as "lesser" in the face of reason. (Thanks a lot, Mister Spock!) It all results in a cultural continuum that unfairly sees the Water-heavy personality (of any gender) as unstable and therefore untrustworthy in a crisis. (Damn it, Jim! I'm a doctor, not a philosopher!)

Still, there are numerous ways in which we individually relate to ourselves and each other that unconsciously emphasizes this tendency to vilify Water. For example, we are far more likely to express positive emotions in a casual way while keeping our darker emotions to ourselves; the feelings we internalize and let fester are far less likely to be positive. And we know we are more likely to carry around deeper feelings and opinions of people or events if those opinions are negative, something painful like anger or guilt or regret, making the association complex and multidimensional in the way a purely "happy" opinion usually is not. We know we are more likely to form strong memories of our bad experiences at the expense of good ones, even as that's simply a safety mechanism to avoid making the same mistakes.

All of this adds up to mean a person who runs heavy with deep, complex emotions is seen as having deep secrets and shady darkness within them. The metaphor of water works very well in this case: shallow waters bubbling over stones in a creek are lively and positive, while whatever is under the surface in deeper, darker places is rarely simple.

If crossed, the Water totem can be a dangerous enemy. Fire can easily burn out, Earth is difficult to move in the first place, and Air can blow past just about anything, but once Water makes something wet it takes time to dry-out. This is the character with a long memory and likely troubled past, who still feels pain from wounds endured years ago, and the one who holds grudges. And though both Fire and Air can cleanse something and come away unchanged, Water cannot wash a thing without taking that dirt into itself, making the Water character the emotional empath, the one who comforts others by taking on their pain. As the emotions of Water are a result of our experiences they can be difficult to change if they run deeply; we feel they are supported by "real" or "important" reasons, and just "letting it go" requires ignoring those reasons.

When you feel anger towards someone who stepped on your foot in the elevator, the feeling comes and is forgotten just as quickly; that is Fire anger. But when you nurse a dislike for someone, let it ferment, and tally within yourself the reasons for your dislike until your bias prevents you from remembering why you began to hate them in the first place, that is Water anger. It takes time to form, and perhaps just as much time to change.

But, in a more positive light, it also means that while Fire love is the fleeting infatuation of the young, Water love is what your grandparents earned from fifty years of sharing their lives with each other. It is a powerful, unshakable bond. We may use the same word in English to describe both these feelings of *love*, but the soul recognizes them as different as night and day — or as fire and water.

What runs through the deepest levels of your heart? What speaks to your soul? How easily do you hate, and how quickly and thoroughly do you love? What moves you to tears, and how often? How well do you relate to the pain of others? How well do you relate to their joy? How easily do you forgive? All of this is the domain of the Water totem.

The Light Above and the Dark Below

And so we come to the two final elemental totems, the two that aren't based in traditional alchemical humors at all. But at least to the practicing pagan, I hope the need to include Above and Below is implicit; "top" and "bottom" are unnamed but implied components of a ritual called a "circle" that is utilized and perceived-of as a *sphere*. And to everyone else, I hope to make the case that including "light" and "dark" fills an important archetypal gap in our structure.

The astute reader might have noticed that for each of the preceding totems, I took care to expound on both the "positive" and "negative" consequences of each personality in a practical sense. Each has its strengths and its weaknesses, and each can be used for both productive and unproductive endeavors in your life. Depending on your individual personality and understanding of yourself, you may like some of your totems more than others, and some may cause you more grief than others, but all are capable of both extremes at various times. But from a more abstract and metaphysical point, when you place positive or negative judgement on one aspect of yourself, the part that had that opinion in the first place becomes another aspect of yourself in its own right.

All of this is dancing around the fact that our unconscious mental templates all share — and utilize— the archetypes of *good* and *bad*. Now, I much prefer to avoid using "good/bad," especially in this context, as it carries with it such heavy moral implications. Positive/negative works little better, and regardless I don't want to imply that one has more practical value than the other — which is far from true. The binary "want/do not want" carries with it amusing undertones of Internet culture and might work, but is a bit cumbersome. For those of you who, like me, prefer to keep the Lord and Lady totems first and foremost a matter of sex/gender, one might be tempted to use the energy constants of *yin* and *yang,* but that would not be fully accurate— though also far from inaccurate, as there is some cross-over.[5]

However, from a simple linguistic perspective, the most efficient terms are *light* and *dark*. They keep the spirit of the positive/negative archetypes, but with less sense of moral judgement of the self that is not a part of the totemic path. Light and Dark are also as much elements of nature as the others, both with a metaphorical and a physical connection to these lives we live. Many people (including my other half) prefer *Above* and *Below* for their complete lack of moral baggage, but then they become directional only, and lose their connection to the physical world we inhabit. However, *Day* and *Night* could be fitting alternatives if you prefer.

When considered as elements of nature no different from the others, Light and Dark can be seen as both the most simple and the most abstract. On the one hand, it is such a pervasive paradigm that it colors nearly every life experience; on the other hand, its parameters are not only vague but far-reaching. They seem simple concepts and therefore closer to you (they have many similarities to the Lord and Lady totems, which are as close to your center as you can get without being your Primary). Yet the details actually separating Light from Dark can turn out to be be quite vague and intangible once you get down to it, therefore making them the most difficult to define and causing the Light and Dark totems to feel the farthest from you. In fact, these totems close the conceptional gap of explaining how there are aspects of the self that seem progressively "farther away" from the center and the

---

[5] Some additional parallels can be found in the terminology of other metaphysical disciplines, such as the fine (*sami*) and heavy (*hoocha*) energies of Andean magick, and the *rada* and *petro* division of spirits in contemporary Voodoo and other American ATR (African Traditional Religions).

essential self— but that are still nothing more than what *we are*, a single soul with many faces.

The **Light totem** (or Above/Day totem) must be defined along several parameters. It represents the ideal self, what we wish to be, hope to be, what we think we *ought to* be, how we'd want others to see us, and represents how we see ourselves projected into the future — where all of our fondest hopes for ourselves are kept. Conversely, the **Dark totem** (or Below/Night totem) is the opposite of this, and represents all that we wish we weren't, that we would discard if possible, what we are ashamed of or afraid of in ourselves, the parts we try to hide from others, and represents how we see ourselves in the past — where we were presumably more ignorant than we are today. They contain within them aspects of all of the previous totems, both for good and for bad, and what you like and don't like within each of them.

You will notice that these totems alone carry with them implications of time, future and past, the sense of change throughout life, but this can be deceptive. While you do grow and evolve throughout your life, our path of totemism holds that certain key aspects of your identity are permanent; you are always the same person, and you do not experience different totems in either the past or the future. Rather, these aspects of the Light and Dark totems represent your *perception* of past and future, and not your genuine experiences in past or future times, and this is an important distinction.

While we may recognize intellectually that both good and bad things happened before and will happen again, most people are fairly comfortable categorizing "the past" as the place for bad things, things that we have moved on from or grown away from in our lifelong quest to better ourselves— especially when even for the most pessimistic of us, hope continues to suggest that only good things should happen

86

in the future as we continue to work towards them. But it is equally true that we accept well the opposite paradigm: we easily romanticize the past, gild it into idealism, especially the era of our childhood— while all the while all of our anxieties and fears for a changing future, especially one that we know holds our own demise, can comfortably paint the future black. [6]

One of many reasons it can be valuable to include the *yin/yang* energies in discussion of these totems, and why it is so important that we not label these totems as solely good or solely bad, is that one of the primary lessons of *yin* and *yang* is that they cannot be separated from one another. The black shape of *yin* has a white dot within it, and white *yang* has black in its center. While your unconscious mind holds solidly to the archetypes of "good" and "bad," in practice gained through complex real-life experience, it becomes conceptually impossible to separate the two; most things in life are equal parts good and bad, worthy of ambivalence. By their nature, the Light and Dark totems are idealistic, imagining and coloring life in one way or another as opposed to accepting it as-is.

As characters, both the Light and the Dark totems are idealists— philosophers, poets, drunken bards, lazy academics, thinkers, dreamers, and not necessarily *doers*. They are the sort who have written books about places they have never been to, and who hold opinions on the lives of others whom they have never met. They are the armchair anthropologist, the slacktivist saving the world through Facebook, the small-town country preacher who judges the morality of the nation. They are the well-meaning hippie saving the world without a plan as well as

---

[6] As an aside, I do not find it a coincidence that nearly every religion has told a story of time with a perfect innocence in the beginning and a dark apocalypse at the end— we are simply projecting our own lives onto the universe.

the angry rebel who puts action above empathy and consequence. They are an invaluable source of advice but terrible at translating philosophy into action. And they are the most comfortable with lying, both to the outside world as well as to you, as a means of promoting an image or an ideology for a perceived greater good. They are also the most direct source to the deepest truths you carry within yourself and will hold no punches telling it like it is.

We perceive of one of these as a source of inspiration and strength, as a goal for this life; the other we see as shameful, dangerous, a source of weakness that impedes our progress. One of them we tend to like, and the other we don't. But it's not always so clear which is which. Here's the kicker: the one we put on a pedestal we may come to resent because his standards are too high, and the one we put in a hole in the ground we may secretly love to hate because he offers such satisfying escape from ourselves. Sometimes, in the most secret corner of ourselves, the self we *really* "wish we could be" is the Dark totem— we wish we could allow ourselves this freedom. *"Good" and "bad" are matters of perception, applicable only to the moment— and ultimately over-simplify our experiences to the point of inaccuracy.*

Now, all of this provides little practical help in separating the characters of the Light and Dark totems on day one, and I respect that. As we have all shared a similar cultural upbringing, I feel comfortable saying that for *most* people the Light totem is strongly connected to our individual religions, faith paths, and life philosophies, those we were raised with as well as those we've chosen as adults, and what those paths describe as ideal personhood. The Light totem is the saint, the martyr, the sage, the shepherd, providing us with a philosophy of patience, empathy, discipline, altruism, generosity, abstinence, or otherwise of responsibility to the rest of humanity or to sacred values over ourselves. Conversely, that leaves the Dark totem in charge of sin; it cares for the self over others, it wants instant gratification, base and primary pleasures, it disrespects the rules, and it tells us to go for what we want without worrying about what others might say.

From a more earthly angle, the Light totem is a successful person, a well-put together person, someone who makes their parents proud and lives up to every expectation and goal with grace and satisfaction. They are the mask you put on when you greet someone important with direct eye contact and a firm handshake. The Dark totem, then, is that uncle you wish you could "forget" to invite to Thanksgiving dinner, the one you feel you have to "explain" to new people before you introduce them because you are so afraid he'll say something to embarrass your friends, or you, or himself. They are the mask you put on to forget yourself and your troubles, to become someone else, the Halloween mask you wear to party all night and escape.

And if that last paragraph made perfect sense to you, and if it left you wondering what I was going on and on about confusing things with the entire rest of this chapter, I'll ask you this: Is there such thing as a selfless good deed? It's inarguable that if you get pleasure or satisfaction from the gesture it becomes at least a little selfish, and even the sage gains wisdom and good karma from his sacrifices. Let me ask another question: Is it possible to take care of others when you don't first take care of yourself? The mantra of the modern working mother, we have come to realize that we ultimately harm the very people we are trying to care for when we neglect the needs of their caregiver. Self discipline and abstinence are fine, and are indispensable tools along the path towards wisdom— but so too is indulgence. Kale and kombucha are great, but when you have a head-cold, a heartache, or a hangover, a bacon cheeseburger is medicine. Always, always, one is within the other. And more, one *without* the other is astoundingly unhealthy, unbalanced, and ultimately unproductive.

Do not trust your Light totem implicitly; do not despise your Dark totem. Both have an agenda, and both have wisdom to share, too. Both are worthy of your respect and your love, and ultimately both have your best interests at heart. After all, no one wants to be around that friend who can't stop talking about being vegan. And it just wouldn't be Thanksgiving without your crazy rude uncle, because let's face it: his complete lack of shame makes him absolutely hilarious.

Who are you, and what do you want? Is who you are now who you want to be? How do you separate what you want from what you need? And how does that relate to what you ought to be? All of this is the domain of the Light and Dark totems.

All Together Now: The Road Trip

The characters have been cast and the plot of your life is unfolding as you speak. Your nine totems are each unique voices within yourself, and each of them are offering direction. Like a new manager in an office conference room, how do you delegate tasks and assign jobs amongst such a diverse team? Like a disgruntled school-bus driver, how do you ever begin to establish order and rank among so many loud and opinionated voices?

When explaining the real-world functionality of the nine totems, my favorite metaphor to use is that of a car-full of people on a road trip. Ultimately, all of them are in relative agreement that it's time for a journey, but each also has their own opinion not only on where they should go, but also on how to get there, how to drive, and how often to stop for snacks— yet clearly there is only one steering wheel. In daily life, the voices of your totems within yourself behave much the same way, and you have to decide whether to act from the influences of one over another.

Ideally (and we will get into non-ideal situations later), your Primary totem should drive. He or she is the most developed personality, making him or her very much like the "adult" in the car; we are designed at the level of our unconscious templates to default to leaving the Primary in charge. However, both the Lady and Lord totems are also responsible adults in their own rights in this scenario. Perhaps they all work well together: they trade-off at different points so the other can rest, or one holds the map and navigates for another, or one holds the bag of chips so the driver can keep one hand on the wheel. Or, perhaps the Lord or the Lady don't trust the Primary so much and are persistent backseat drivers, second-guessing the Primary every time he or she makes a turn. But either way, they are available to drive if the need arises, almost like back-up Primaries, and that is precisely why they are there in the first place. After all, anyone who drives for too long will get stressed and need to rest, regardless of how good a driver they are.

The elemental totems, however, are better suited to remain passengers— most of the time. Their skills are more specific: perhaps one of them sees better at night, or has more experience with winding mountain roads, etc. There are certain situations in which they are exactly the best driver to choose—but when that situation has passed they should give back the driver's seat. Elemental totems are ideally meant to take over for specific situations suited to their areas of expertise, but as their personalities are far more limited, they do not have the skill-sets to be in charge long-term, and important decisions made by the elemental totems can be limited, not well thought-out, or seemingly immature in nature, a little like they were made by well-meaning teenagers.

The Dark and Light totems are the least suited to be driving, and the times in your life when you allow them to take the wheel should be limited. They will be confident in where they're going, and while one might be telling you to get to South Dakota to protest the pipeline and the other is telling you it's time to get drunk and get laid, both will care very little about what route you take— or find it important to plan a realistic route at all, let alone plan for what they'll do once they get there. All of that flighty lack of planning will likely drive you off the road or even get you lost. However, when the *Primary* gets lost, turned around by every road sign and distraction of every-day life, the Dark and Light totems are there in the very back seat to remind us of where we are all trying to go in the first place.

PART THREE
Finding the Totems

Chapter One:
Points to Consider

As I already mentioned, our path of totemism is not a system of **geomancy**. It is not a method by which one interprets omens, messages, or other metaphysical meaning from every wild animal sighting. That is to say, this book is not a dictionary of "animal meanings" that tells you seeing a bear means this or seeing a squirrel means that. That is a completely separate area of metaphysical work.

However, that certainly does not mean there is no meaning to be found in having one animal as a totem compared to another. Not everyone's inner Fire tendencies are the same, this is expressed by different people having different animals as their Fire totems, and the ways in which each of those animals are different from each other will express the differences in their human bearer's characters. The totem is not just a talking head, after all, but an entity with a character and personality.

At this point, you are ready to begin the process of discovering your personal totem animals. I acknowledge that was a lot to go through to get to this point, but I promise you will have a lot more productive venture with all of this preliminary knowledge underneath you.

However a few important points need to be made before we can begin. First, it is essential to keep in mind throughout this entire process that your nine totem animals are already set within you. The process is a matter of discovering and uncovering them, and there is no element of choice involved; your unconscious mind is already aligned with the animals that are the best metaphors, energies, or kindred spirits for itself — whether you are aware of it or not. *You already are who you are.* Further, the process of unraveling the exact parameters of how you define each totem (that is, how you personally understand the conceptual boundaries of the elemental archetypes, the gender/sex binary, the dualistic creative energies, and the contrary self) are also already set and decided within you. Some of you may have read through my personal descriptions of these ideas and had momentary insight as to how I might be right or way off-base; such insight may be an epiphany into your own existing (though perhaps yet unknown) understanding of these concepts.

Another caveat that needs addressing is the subject of "fad totems." This is something that most authors of totem books will bring up (though they may call them different things), and on this point we all are strongly in agreement: *do not confuse a desire to have a certain "cool" totem as a genuine connection to that animal.* Doubly-so if your own sense of ego is insisting you need the largest and most impressive animals that you feel carry some kind of clout.[7] We are not all Wolf people, or Eagle people, or Bison people —and that's ok! All animals have their wisdom to share and their own power. There is not only no shame in having a smaller or less conventional totem animal, it is for the best; we would be absurdly boring— and incapable!— as a species if we were all relatively the same inside. And while they may seem impressive, Wolf, Eagle, and Bison definitely have their weaknesses, and other less-cool animals will succeed where these rock-stars fail.

And lastly, you will not necessarily discover your totems in any specific order. That is, the first animal you uncover may *not* necessarily be your Primary, the second the Lord or Lady, etc. They can come to you in any order, and the second half of the discovery of each animal is determining its position within your nine (just to make things even more complicated, unfortunately!)

---

[7] This also applies to the cutest animal, or the toughest or scariest animal, or to an animal experiencing its fifteen minutes of Internet fame like Owls or Sloths.

Chapter Two:
Animal Connections

There are a considerable number of ways you can come to know your totems. In some cases, the totem will make itself known to you in a sudden epiphany; in others cases you may actively seek it, and provided that you are open and patient, you will get your answer. In either case, you will need to trust your instincts — when the right animal comes to you, you will know it is right in a way beyond description.

As I stated before, many people already have a fair idea of what one or some of their totems are or might be. A strong inclination, or a strong affinity for or connection to an animal, may very well be hinting at a totem. (A strong attraction to a specific animal doesn't *automatically* make it your totem, Primary or otherwise, but it might be.) Many people have found that their favorite animal or animals as a child turn out to be one of their totems, especially the center three. As I've said, they are with us throughout our entire lives. Conversely, an unreasonable fear of an animal (that is, a fear not rooted in an actual traumatic experience), and especially a fear that has been with you since the nightmares of your childhood, might be pointing you towards your Dark totem (or your Primary, for that matter, depending on your relationship to your true self).

Suddenly developing an interest in an animal you never had interest in before can also be a totem asserting itself. My Lady Elephant totem revealed herself to me in this way. Not long after I had first moved in with my other half, one day I simply found myself absolutely fascinated by elephants— when I never had thought much about them before. I couldn't explain why they were suddenly so inexplicably awesome, but they were, and I couldn't get enough of them. For me, the emergence of my Lady totem was a result of me taking on the role of "the lady of the house" for the first time, when up until then I had only been daughter, roommate, or tenant and had never needed that side of myself before.

As I mentioned in the second chapter of Part One, an affinity for an ancient deity that carries an animal energy, a meaningful wild encounter, or a relationship with a special living animal may also be pointing you towards a totem. Keep in mind that in each of these cases, your true totem may actually be a similar or related animal (what we call "of the same *kind*," an idea we will soon discuss) and not the exact species involved in this interaction. After all, no matter where you live or where you travel, your average person will only have access to a limited selection of what Mother Nature has to offer— and your totems can come from all over the world. Be aware of what animals live where you do, and know that your totem may be speaking to you through its closet available counterpart. And though we like to think we know most of the animals out there, you'd be surprised at how many species exist that you've never heard of, so keep an open mind.

For example, everyone has access to dogs, and we'd assume a strong affinity for dogs must be a connection to Wolf or Coyote, or less commonly to Dingo or Jackal— the basic types of canines we're familiar with. But if you look-up "canines" you will discover there are dozens of distinct canids, including some that are practically unheard of in the West like the African Wild Dog, the Dhole, and multiple quite distinct species of both Wolves and Jackals like the Tibetan "Wooly" Wolf or the African Golden Wolf. Then there is the sister genus of *Vulpes,* the Foxes, adding another dozen species to consider.

Some people have also had experiences where someone knowledgeable (or who is at least supposedly knowledgeable!) has told them their totem, either through some kind of "totem reading" or by intuition alone. Whether this is the archetypal wise old Cherokee woman or just another neo-pagan with a deck of animal oracle cards, their input should be taken with the proverbial grain of salt. It is true that often others who are very experienced with these matters can read the signs of the animals in you, or perhaps just see clearly what you yourself cannot. *However*, please remember that ultimately, your totem animals are *you*. No one knows more about your essential self than you do, so you always have "power of veto" over someone else's impressions. If you believe the person to be wise, consider their suggestions, especially if you feel some ambiguity on the subject; but if their reading doesn't intuitively feel right, you should politely move on. Please also keep in mind that as you have nine totems to choose from (and you could have temporary spirit guides around you as well), the impression of the animal that the old woman saw in your aura doesn't *necessarily* have to be your Primary totem. (My other half consequently does totem oracle readings, and has amassed a considerable amount of practice and experience doing so, and yet this is the exact advice he still gives to anyone getting a reading.)

It is also possible to be visited by the totem in a dream, a sudden vision, or during any kind of spiritual ritual or exercise such as meditation or prayer. Now, animals are regular visitors to the landscape of the spirit as perceived of by the mind, and encountering animals in the spirit world can happen regularly. Use your common sense and remember that just like with the real world, not every encounter has profound meaning or is an automatic indication of a totemic relationship. If you are unsure, return to this sacred/altered state of being and ask to be given more information about the encounter and if it has any meaning for you. Speaking the words of the question within your own mind is often enough to unlock the answers you're seeking.

In a similar vein, I feel that entering into a quiet state of mind or meditative state and requesting that your totems show themselves is also a valid technique. I will point out here that my other half feels there is more value in waiting for the totems to reveal themselves on their own time, and that they will show up exactly when they are needed— and no sooner. I see value in both approaches.

On the one hand, there is good sense in acquiescing to the wisdom of your higher and essential self, and patience in place of instant gratification is a valuable skill for anyone to learn in the Internet age. Insisting that your totems show themselves *this instant* when they aren't ready to is the best way to set yourself up to get an incorrect answer— to mistake a different animal spirit for a totem, for example, or to mistake a totem from one position with another. And there is wisdom in asking yourself if you are truly *ready* to know your totems in the first place, to know your true self. If you are not ready to meet your soul face-to-face and you force it anyway, then the bad time that ensues is only your own doing.

But on the other hand, they are *your* totems, they are a part of you, and if you want to openly seek them and request audience with them I see no harm in being assertive. I will also point out that you don't necessarily have to request that all nine show up at once, and a fair middle ground might be to assertively ask that just one totem show itself, and then whichever is the most ready can comply, gracefully respecting others that may wish to make a more appropriate entrance at a later time. You may well have your best chance for success seeking your totems one at a time, with a unique approach for each one.

Overall, making the decision that you are ready to know your totems is often enough to make you receptive to meeting them — though it may or may not happen quickly. Neo-pagan culture is usually adamant that "putting intention out there" is the first and most necessary step of any endeavor, especially a metaphysical one. While I don't always share that sentiment (I'm usually more in the camp of action over wishful thinking) I do believe it is applicable in this case. Project the intention that you want to know your totems, open your heart and your mind to the possibility, and be ready to listen to what speaks to you.

But in any case, just because you ask doesn't mean the totems will comply. And just because you *didn't ask* doesn't mean they won't show up, regardless. If you would be interested in some assertive approaches, please feel free to make use of the rituals that will be provided in the Ritual Appendices at the end of the book.

Chapter Three:
Animal Meanings— Knowledge is Power

When an animal has made itself known to you and you are fairly sure it is a totem, the next step is to get on the computer and research that animal. The most important insight to be gained from the totem comes from the animal itself— that is, it's biological information. You will learn more about totemism from studying your totem animal's habits, habitats, diet, social structure, mating habits, and their relationship to nature, than you will from any metaphysical resource or geomancy text. Homework through research is a key component of the path of totemism, expectations of grandiose and esoteric midnight rituals not withstanding.

For example, a man with a strong stallion as his Fire totem will learn about his passionate side by studying horses, and will find that his own impulses are already in-sync with the behaviors of a reactive, competitive, libidinous stallion. But he may still have yet to learn that a horse is also innocently curious and playful, and that as both a prey animal and an animal with competitive ranking between males, horse also brings a permanent sense of caution that can become fear of loss or anxiety in a man — even overreaction in the face of a perceived threat.

While scientific knowledge is king, it is also valuable to understand the mythology surrounding your animal, or how it was or is understood by other cultures (or your own), as that has almost certainly affected your preconceptions of that animal. However, it is vital that you recognize the concept of **cultural bias**, which means that such observations of the animal may be clouded by the specific experiences of the people making them. Mythological interpretations of an animal can be insightful, but they are secondary in importance to scientific, un-biased observations of the true nature and behaviors of the animal.

For example, there is an obvious disparity between the way Wolf is portrayed in European mythology and folklore compared to Native American myths. To the First Americans, Wolf is often seen as a powerful hunter, leader, and strong teacher or guide; in contrast, fairy tales of European origin set Wolves as the "big bad wolf" who eats lost children and blows down houses. But even indigenous Americans that lived in complex, urban city-states such as the Mississippian cultures domesticated no large food animals and remained hunting cultures; Wolves were seen as fellow hunters to be admired and emulated, who at worst were worthy competition for the same game. But to agrarian Europeans who raised their meat on the farm, the Wolf no longer represented admirable human traits or skills and became nothing more than a danger to livestock and small children.

Both mythologies represent an incomplete, though not necessarily untrue, view of the Wolf, passed through the lens of experience. Especially when we're dealing with contemporary interpretations of Native American myth, these stories tend to white-wash Wolf (killer pun absolutely intended) as a noble and helpful teacher to humanity, forgetting how harsh and violent Wolf's lessons can be— and on rare occasion that lesson has been that humans are edible. In contrast, any culture that has separated itself from humanity's original role in nature as a predator will quickly forget the value in any hunter, even cultures that still lived very close to the land in the way ancient Europeans did, and they would see nothing more than a one-dimensional villain in a very complex and intelligent creature. One only needs to look to the legends of the werewolf to understand how undesirable a wolfish character really was.

Chapter Four:
Animal Meanings — A *Kind* of Animal

Now, it is exceptionally common for a person to initially receive their first impressions of a totem animal in what I will call a *kind*. Animals of the same **kind** mean animals that common perception and common-sense reasoning would group together by shared characteristics, behaviors, and/or ecological role that may or may not include a close genetic relationship as science defines it. Now, we use *kind* in place of the more specific and scientific taxonomic *genus* or even larger *sub family* for an important reason: our perceptions of which animals are "of the same kind" might be a little different from how science classifies things. The North American Red Fox and the Gray Fox are a great example — both are not only different *species* but different *genera* as well, and yet are both comfortably thought of as "foxes."

It is important to remember that the niche an animal inhabits in its ecosystem often exerts stronger forces on its evolution than even its DNA, so animals that live in very similar environments and eat similar foods are likely to evolve to physically resemble one another— or to not evolve so far apart, if they started out as the same animal. But more, we will notice a similarity of "energy," a more difficult to describe but understood "sameness" between them that would encourage us to consider them the same *kind*. There are "parrots" from South and Central America, from Africa, and from Australia. They are widely different, and yet we recognize the sameness between them. A

European explorer who had perhaps only ever seen an African Gray nevertheless looked at a Blue-fronted Amazon for the very first time and said, "That's a parrot," even though the two birds have as many differences in appearance as they do similarities.

Now, this concept of *kind* does not have concrete parameters, for obvious reasons, and it's an idea that is comfortably simple at first glance but begins to unravel the longer we look at it, so I caution you not to over-think it. For one thing, not everyone is going to agree on which characteristics are required to be shared to place animals in the same *kind*, and different people are going to see things different ways— especially for their own totems. Rather than a hard-line, this is a more generalized concept used for general reference, and not a place where I want someone to get frustrated and tripped-up in the details. Just ask yourself, "Are these the same kind of animal?" and you are going to answer, "Yes," "No," or "Sort of." And you can work-out the sort-ofs by more research on the animals in question. It's not meant to be more complicated than that.

So, for an example of how we use the concept of *kind* in our tradition, I will give some examples. As an aspect of your own totemic research, you can build on for your own from here.

An extremely large *kind* of animal my other half and I reference is "deer." However, most all animals in the large taxonomic *family Cervidae* would be considered "deer" by common reasoning, and that *family* is divided into three distinct *sub-families,* with each further divided into many dozens of distinct *genera* and finally even more individual *species*— all added together with similar species of water-deer from Asia that we also call "deer" even as they are not even in the taxonomical *family Cervidae* at all. This gives us many hundreds if not *thousands* of distinct possibilities for your "deer" totem — while your average American might only be able to name five to ten species of deer.

However, someone with a closer relationship to this *kind* may decide instead to name "elk" as the "kind of animal" they're talking about, to mean the ten-or-so types of larger deer with forked branching antlers, distinct from "moose" and "reindeer" whose antlers are palmate, from smaller deer, or from the little water-deer of Asia that are certainly distinct in many ways. But on the other hand, someone with little interest in this *kind* at all (such as a person with a large predator totem) may absently lump all deer together with antelopes and wild goats into a single huge *kind* of animal that has hooves, lives in herds, has head-weapons, and is tasty to eat.

Most *kinds* of animals we talk about are not quite as large as deer. For example, even if we consider all the species someone may never have heard of, there are still fewer than twenty-five or so known species of the canine kind to go through, and the "canine" or "wolfish" *kind* we speak of is fairly easy to spot. Earlier I suggested that most people might also consider all vulpins, foxes, to be of the same *kind* (they're also "canine like"). And we sometimes make the argument that aquatic mammals that live and hunt in complex social groups such as orca, dolphins, and perhaps even sea lions could be lumped into the wolfish *kind* as well, considering they live very similar lives to pack canines, just in the sea.

These are all judgement calls; *you are looking at degrees of similarity and difference between the animals, and the number and quality of those degrees of separation makes the case that the animals are a little more or a little less of the same* kind. My husband's Wolf totem lets him look at an Orca and see enough similarities that he considers it as the same *kind*, but someone with an Orca totem may feel that

Wolf's lack of knowledge of the sea categorizes him only as "sort of" the same *kind*, at best.

Some other *kinds*, as we define them and reference in this book, include things like raptors (hunting birds), intelligent birds (putting together Parrots and Corvids by shared qualities), song birds, panthers/large cats, equines/Horses, and the ungulates/large hoofed herding animals such as Bison, Aurochs, and Wildebeest.

So why is *kind* such an important concept in the first place? Well, it's because nearly all of us come into totemism without a wildlife biologist's extensive catalogue of animal knowledge, and so when we see an animal— in the physical world or the spiritual— we are most likely going to first identify it by what "kind" we think it is. I don't think most of us could tell the difference between a Red-Tailed Hawk, a Goshawk, and Harris's Hawk at first glance; most of us would be lucky to know it's a hawk rather than a falcon or some other type of hunting bird. *You're more than likely going to identify a totem animal's* kind *first, and only afterward work out its individual species.* I bring up again the idea that most of us aren't even aware of how many species there actually are, and are unaware of how much we don't know. We want to make certain that we don't see a "deer" in a dream, assume it's an American White Tail because that's the only one we can name, and then miss out on the fact that it was actually an European Red Deer— a different animal from a different part of the world that has different lessons to teach you.

It is clearly important to distinguish differences between individual animals of a *kind*. However, it is equally essential we acknowledge their similarities. This will come into play a little more in the Advanced Introspection section (Part Six), once you have a little more experience working with totems. But even as your totem will be one specific species of animal, there will be knowledge to be found in understanding (and sometimes utilizing) the magick of others of its *kind*, both for yourself and when you are dealing with other people. It is important to understand that you are speaking to a Red Deer instead of a White Tail, because what they have to say will be different and it is important to honor the animal by accurately acknowledging it. But because they are so alike, much of what they have to say will also be very similar. Even if your totem is a White Tail, sometimes there may be value in speaking to a Red Deer because he will give a slightly different perspective on that aspect of your sacred self. And often if you are trying to make an educated guess about another person's totems, you may only be able to get as close as its *kind*— but depending on the situation, that may well be all you need.

Other books and teachers of totemism will sometimes propose the idea that all animals within what I call a *kind* should all be thought of as a single totem; that is, they would say you have "Deer" as your totem, not "a deer", and while you might know the individual species ("Reindeer" or "White-tailed Deer"), they would still say the entire species is your totem, averaged together into a singular entity representing them all. This idea can be attractive because it means you don't have to do any homework, but it has the quite unfortunate side-effect of glossing-over a lot of very real differences between different species, including most importantly the topics detailed in the list of questions below: differences in environment, social structure, size, and even diet, which will all reflect important aspects of how you think and act, and of who you are— which is the whole point of totemism.

Further, as our path of totemism holds that your totems are the faces of your individual and unique personality, it is only reasonable then that each of your totems is also an *individual* animal spirit, a unique entity and personality in its own right. This aspect of the totem as an individual is most apparent in the three center totems, where at the very least they must be a certain sex and therefore cannot be the entire species. Now, that is NOT to say that you will not have a deep connection to the entire species, and you absolutely will. But consider that two people with the same Primary totem— say, Raven— will still have distinct personalities, will be different people even as they may think very similarly. This is represented by them each having uniquely different Ravens as their totems. And if your totem is an individual, just like with a living animal, he or she must be a member of one specific species. I understand this is very different from the way other paths of totemism are taught (specifically, the modern versions of some Native American paths) but as I have said, our method is not seeking to recreate or imitate any culture's traditions.

Chapter Five:
Animal Meanings — Identifying the Individual

So once you have a sense of what *kind* of animal you are dealing with, how do you determine the exact species of your totem animal? Largely it is a matter of discerning its habitat (or environment) in combination with the specifics of its appearance, and this can usually only be done through research— yes, dry old academic research. If you had a dream about Turtle, try to remember details of what it looked like, and research Turtles; look at photos of Turtles (and Tortoises!) online to find one that matches what you remember, or for one that feels right intuitively; think about your dream and try to remember what environment the Turtle (or Tortoise!) was in, as that can help you differentiate your totem from others of its *kind* that live in different habitats.

Now, that is not to say that this information will be easy to find, or that it is even necessary for you to begin working with, talking to, and learning from your totem — or for that matter, that you will ever know for absolutely certain; my Earth totem is a snake that I'm fairly sure is a type of python, but she doesn't seem to think it's important for me to know and I've yet to work it out on my own, so maybe the specifics don't matter in this case. But on the other hand, when I first met my Primary totem I did what most people would have done and called him a "black panther"— not realizing there is no such animal. He was very adamant that I know a "panther" is not a species. Rather, today I consider "panthers" to be a *kind* of animal. All large felines in the genus *Panthera* can rightly be called "panthers," including leopards, snow leopards, jaguars, lions, and tigers, and commonly the term is also (inaccurately) applied to cougars as they are not of that *genus* (though I personally consider them of the panther *kind*). All of clan *Panthera* live in different environments, hunt a little differently, mate a little differently, live a little differently—and nearly all of them can occasionally produce black offspring. Especially initially, it was very important for me to know he is a Jaguar and not just a "panther." But over time, it has become equally important for me to know that all of the panther *kind* represent the same base skill-set applied to many varying environmental circumstances, as though they represent different variations on the same template.

The most thorough way we have devised for our tradition to identify the precise species of an animal is to research the following information for each animal in question. However, this information will also be invaluable to have about your totem animals even if you already know exactly what species they are. Research the answers to these questions for every spiritual animal encounter you have: the lessons they have to impart will be found through application of this knowledge. This list of questions will also be available in the Appendices for easy reference.

Five Identifying Questions for Totemic Knowledge:

1) What environment does the animal live in? (The desert? Jungle? Or widely spread?) And does that environment carry a strong elemental connection? (The sea, the sky, or the earth? The frozen ice or dry sands? Strictly nocturnal or diurnal?) And does the animal have to make any adaptations to any seasonal variations or cycles? (Change in physical appearance like coloration or coat thickness?

Hibernation, migration, or change in diet?) What is the nature of that seasonal change? (Cycles of cold/warm? Or wet/dry?)

2) Is it a solitary animal, or does it live in a group? If a group, how is that group organized, and are there different ranks or roles for individuals? How permanent is the group? Most importantly, what rank does your individual totem hold within that group? What about pair-bonding between mates; does it pair within a larger group or in place of it? How much of what the animal needs to know is learned from others of their species, compared to relying only on instinct?

3) How different are the males from the females? Are there strong differences in appearance? Do they behave differently, have different roles, or do they live basically identical lives? Is there much competition between males for status and access to females, or do the males concentrate their efforts on impressing the females directly? Do they form some kind of bond with their mates, and is that bond just for the season or for longer? Who raises the young— directly, or indirectly?

4) Is this a large animal, a medium-sized animal, or a small animal? How likely is it that it could physically over-power another animal? That it could be over-powered? How does its size translate to its food and shelter needs?

5) Is the animal a predator, a prey animal, or both? Keep in mind that most all small animals, regardless of what they eat, can be prey to larger predators on occasion. What about scavenging? Keep in mind that most all predatory animals will scavenge if the situation warrants it.

Once you have addressed each of these questions for each totem animal you discover or spirit guide you deal with, it will be valuable for you to revisit the following section to help you better understand what these animal traits mean for you and your personality:

Environment

I chose to address environment first because determining specifically where your animal lives is usually an aspect of discovering which species your totem is in the first place, and that is generally one of the first tasks a person must address upon understanding a totemic connection.

Generally speaking, an animal's environment speaks to its physical needs and its adaptability. An animal of the jungle or the tundra is more limited in what it can adapt to, and that translates into a human personality trait that requires more specific circumstances to feel healthy and satisfied than an animal able to live nearly anywhere. Animals of very hot or cold areas may be less able to deal with periods of inactivity and/or increased or stressful activity compared to animals who can cope with a greater range of seasonal temperature. Animals who eat only limited types of foods may require very specific stimulation to keep them happy, compared to animals who are quite able to eat anything that comes into their mouths. Humans with totems with very specific diets may be picky eaters — even delving into orthorexia— compared to those with totems who scavenge, who (god help us) see an inedible meal not as a disappointment but as a challenge.

Now, we can begin to see the interconnectivity of all the totems — as aspects of a single human personality — become very evident when we contend with animals who live in an environment associated strongly with one element but who are seated as the totem of another. For example, a person who has a water-dwelling animal (with Water connected to emotions, remember) seated as the Earth totem (whose concerns are the body) they would

116

likely be unable to separate emotional needs from physical security. Fulfilling those emotional needs becomes as important to their survival as food and shelter. Bird totems usually carry Air energy (which is of the intellect), so a person with a bird seated as any totem other than Air will find that they tend to "intellectualize" that other part of themselves; a bird in Earth might suggest the person cannot ever feel comfortable with academic idleness; a person with a bird in Light might feel the ideal person is the scholar, and that learning is its own end; a bird in Dark might mean that person is unable to feel comfortable around individuals outside of their echo-chamber of shared ideology.

Further, the ways in which those animals respond to *seasons* of environmental change can be telling as to how a human who bears them as a totem can do the same, both metaphorically and literally. It can be difficult for us to remember in our modern world, but humans as well used to live a seasonal lifestyle— hunting in the early winter, planting in the spring, harvesting and preserving in the fall, and crafting and snuggling close in the winter. These cycles — or rather, a failure to acknowledge our instinct to change to adapt to these cycles — can have a profound affect on how well a person copes with long humid summer days, winter mornings when the sun hasn't even risen when you have to leave for work, or for that matter, terrible spring allergies. Hopefully, you will have totems from a variety of ecosystems, giving you a variety of skills to draw from to deal with the constant presence of environmental change that is life on this planet.[8]

---

[8] This concept of environmental adaptation may also lay the groundwork for how you would cope with physically moving house from one ecosystem to another, or even with just visiting a new ecosystem for a prolonged period of time.

Now, I must make a confession: it took my other half and me a lot longer than it should have to realize this sort of adaptational information could be an important factor for totem animals. But there is an equally important reason for that: neither Wolves nor Jaguars alter their behavior all that much throughout the year, and so it simply didn't occur to either of us to think of it in the first place. There are times when the coat gets thicker, and prey more lean or difficult to catch, but for the most part, not a lot changes. But our other totems (or at least mine) had a lot to say on the matter, once I thought to ask them, for the best way to live with the seasons and not fight against them.

If we go back to our example of Foxes, we can see how at first glance it may not seem so important to differentiate between one type of Fox and another. But while there may be similarities, there are some critical differences between the lifestyles of an Arctic Fox and a Red Fox, considering that the Red lives on two continents, everywhere from the cold highlands of Scotland to the steaming Louisiana wetlands, and the Arctic Fox is restricted to the northlands of Canada only. And when we consider the broad habitat of the Gray Fox (that isn't even a true "fox," at all, remember) we get a sense of the importance of *kind.* The Arctic Fox and the Red Fox might be more genetically similar, but the Red and the Gray live in, and deal with, more of the same situations, making them at least in some ways more similar to each other than to the Arctic. In a broader sense, the role an animal plays in its ecosystem, specifically in regard to where it lives and what it eats, is often more important to the totemist than genetic relationships on the evolutionary tree, an important relationship we summarize by the concept of *kind*. [9]

Social Structure

Whether your totem animal is a solitary creature or one that lives in a group is of even more importance to your character, for reasons more straight-forward than environmental. Humans are social animals with strong independent streaks, and so we relate to the pack and the herd as well as the solo flyer at various times and in various circumstances.

More so than anything else, your totem's social structure will reflect how you relate to other people, and all types of animal social structures lend both strengths and weaknesses to a human character. A person whom we might call "well-rounded" will likely have a good balance of solitary and social animals in their spread of nine totems, giving their human bearer the ability to adapt to being alone or working with a group depending on need. However, you will usually find that the social-status of your Primary totem has the largest impact on whether you are a shy loner, a comfortable follower, an obligate leader, or socially flexible.

------

[9] For another example we can return to the Cougar, who might be genetically more closely related to the Jaguarundi, (a medium-sized and unusual looking cat) as well as to a number of smaller cats of the Amazon rainforests, than it is to the other large cats of the world. But it is widely adaptable with a broad range, will eat any animal it can catch and it can catch all but the largest animals, yet it prefers to watch first and avoid a fight despite the security of its large size— to name just a few of a wide area of similarities to the true panthers of the world. To the totemist (as well as myself) the Cougar fits better playing for team *Panthera* than as "the largest of the small cats" as she is sometimes known.

As one might expect, a solitary animal provides the foundation to be happy and comfortable alone, but it also may cause the person to be quite uncomfortable or unhappy around too many other people. The solitary animal's largest area of weakness can often be when it is required to take-on a leadership role. My Jaguar is a fine example. Mothers will raise their cubs, males and females come together for mating, and some evidence suggests that so long as prey is plentiful, individual adults can form "friendships" with one another and spend time together. But each adult Jaguar maintains his or her own hunting territory; they are creatures who occasionally take time to be social in their otherwise solitary lives. Throughout my life my totem has had very little of value to say on how to give compelling speeches to motivate others, let alone how to manage people in an office. A solitary animal of large size might be tempted to try and intimidate others into listening, but rarely if ever is that successful.

Animals who form pair bonds, such as most birds of prey, are fairly similar in character to solitary animals, with the exception that they require a single special person in their lives to the extent of all else. Similarly, animals who congregate in groups for safety but who otherwise observe no strong ranking or order within that group— such as some flocks, schools, clowders, etc— are also similar to solitary animals, even as they may have a need to be around others; they are the sort who keep a few acquaintances but fewer close friends, or who may consider going to a public venue like a restaurant or the movies to be all the "socializing" they need.

In a more abstract sense, a solitary animal as a totem (especially an elemental totem) may reflect that aspect of the person's character being less interconnected to the rest of their personality, and it may be less likely to "play nicely" with the other totems in the name of balance— especially considering the totem on the opposite side of the sphere (see Part Four, Chapters Three and Four). A schooling animal may represent a side of yourself who understands the value in going along with the group, but who may have difficulty asserting itself when necessary. [10] Finally, a pairing animal may need, and then be comfortable with, just a single important activity, concept, or idea; the sort who might be fine with anything so long as he has football in his life, for example.

Animals who live in groups with more complex social structures, on the other hand, bring a completely different game to the field. Their strength is understanding the group dynamic of humans and recognizing how to navigate it to their bearer's advantage — or at least they try to, depending on which animal we're talking about. It can get interesting when a pack or herd animal tries to apply its knowledge of how a group "should" function to a human interaction that follows slightly different rules. Wolf, for example, is quite used to the idea that there is always a leader in a pack, and he may even depend on that structure of leadership to feel stable in life. But Wolf packs are always led by the most fit and experienced male and female wolves of the group, often the parents of the other pack members. So when a human group is led by someone who lacks the basic qualities of a fit leader (an experience with middle-management most everyone can relate to) it is counter to Wolf's sensibilities. In a pack, it is natural for a more fit individual to step in and take over from an unfit

---

[10] As an example, I have a pairing animal for Air (Magpie) and an Ermine for Water, a weasel that is usually solitary but that sometimes hunts together in what can only be called "swarms." These types of social structure make the two totems not terribly compatible for a harmonious working relationship, leaving my Air and Water energies often at odds. It will leave me convinced I can be emotional or rational, but never both at once, and rationality often bullies emotionalism until it is repressed— which then in turn becomes overwhelmed and explodes into quite unexpected fury.

leader, perhaps leading Wolf people to instinctually over-step their bounds and try to "take over" projects from others they feel aren't doing them correctly.

On the other hand, the biggest weakness of the social animal is its dependence on that group. Consider what I just mentioned about Wolf; all herd animals, as well, make the natural assumption that there *must* be a social structure, a hierarchy, and when one is absent it is their instinct to create one — even when one may not be necessary or even wanted by other people. They may not do well in egalitarian work groups, for example, unless they or someone else takes them over. And they may have difficulty understanding and interacting with loners or with being alone in general. That person on the subway who insists on striking-up a conversation with someone reading a book or listening to music with earbuds — he or she may very likely be unaware of the influence of a strong social animal totem within them, and may have simply never considered that someone would actually *want* to be left alone.

Things can get ugly when the natural "social competition" that occurs between group animals that is ultimately part of the bonding process (the play-fighting and competitive butting of heads and so forth) is exerted onto a solitary animal who may interpret any such jab as an attack rather than a game. If you have ever been around a school or office dynamic in which one person feels "bullied" by what others might just consider "playful banter," or where someone has difficulty telling the difference between a joke and passive-aggression and the "popular girls clique" takes full advantage of their social ignorance, you may be dealing with this totem dynamic.

There is a strong pattern I have noticed about the Primary totems to be found among members of the neo-pagan community: there is an overabundance of solitary animals, many of them predators. This has led to more than one person within the pagan community wondering at this apparent imbalance in distribution, and when I move to explain this dynamic the way I understand it, it leads to a lot of undeserved smugness, which I hope now to dispel. Yes, the way I understand totems leads me to believe that all the people out there with "hoofed" totems, the Bison, the Deer, and all of the Antelope, Aurochs, and Big-Horned Sheep— these are the people who feel more comfortable staying with the religion of their childhood, usually Christianity, and do not convert to paganism. "Sheeple" jokes might be inevitable, but are misplaced. Rather, I believe the reason is far from ideological, and therefore any implications that it is an intellectual issue are quite misguided. I simply observe the priorities of herding animals and infer that for people with these totems, spiritual fulfillment comes from the intense feeling of "belonging" that comes from church, especially when one has a history there, family and life-long friends; that is worth more to the hoofed herd totem animal than whether or not they agree with every single teaching of that church. Belonging can even supersede asserting individuality, leaving many people with totems who are quite comfortable to never be seen or named because belonging to a strong community is more important to them.

Meanwhile, anyone who has tried to organize pagans into a collective group effort has observed that it's almost literally a matter of "herding cats." We attract a lot of people whose instincts predispose them to resist any attempts to control them, and they are attracted to the lack of structure that our open-ended theology and lack of orthodoxy provides. Most predators scent-mark territory, and there is a noticeable tendency to prefer being "right" over respecting other's feelings or preserving group harmony. There is no difference in intellect between the two groups; they simply have different priorities and need different things from their religions. And so paganism corrals together all the Hawks and the Tigers and the Weasels as well as the Raccoons and the Snakes and tries to fit them together into a single umbrella identity wherein one gets eight opinions upon asking a question of six people, leaving the few Bison or Wolf pagans in charge of organizing the inherently unorganizable. A solitary animal is predisposed by nature to leave its mother once it is grown, and a person with a solitary totem is predisposed to resist someone telling him or her "what to do" once they are past childhood— leaving them in a James Dean-like constant state of aimless rebellion. I have complete confidence that the children of pagans who have solitary animal Primary totems will in turn rebel against paganism once they are grown.

Sex

Over the years, my husband and I have debated over what is the best way to help other people discover their totems. Inevitably, the suggestion arises that we should compose a list of questions a person could answer that could point them towards a general category of animal, if not a specific kind (large herd animal, small predator, non-predatory bird, etc). However, this approach leaves the totem seeker in grave risk of over-thinking the process, leaving more room for confusion than answers— especially considering we would have no way of knowing which answers came from which of their nine totems. It is far more effective to leave the discovery process organic, and to leave the connection between animal traits and corresponding aspects of human personalities for after the animal is already revealed.

Still, there are a few of these types of questions that can reveal a great deal about a person's center three totems, if not the Primary itself, before they have even begun to look, and one of the big ones has to do with sex. Answer the following question: *Do you believe men and women are basically the same, or do you believe there is some fundamental difference between the sexes?*

If a person just answers based on how they feel, and without stopping to over-analyze their opinion or worry about what is the "correct" thing to say socially, this will tell us pretty clearly whether or not their Primary totem (or the Lord or Lady, if that totem is speaking over the Primary) is an animal with inherent physical and social differences between the sexes. This says nothing about whether the person feels one sex (or gender) is inherently "better" than the other; the question simply asked whether they were "different." Conversely, there will always be inarguable physiological "differences," and it so leaves the person to define "different" along their own parameters.

The reader might infer that I myself have put a considerable amount of mental energy towards understanding this human concept of "gender," considering how much I felt it necessary to expound on the idea in earlier sections. Honestly, in the past I have encountered people who needed nothing more than a few simple sentences to understand what I took pages to work through, and this astounds me:

"Your Primary totem is the opposite sex from you because he/she is your opposite, and the Lord and Lady totems are your masculine and feminine sides." *Done.*

To my understanding, the reason for this is that my Primary totem is Jaguar and Jaguars inherently have little to no difference between the sexes. Males are a little larger than the females and are more likely to fight one another, but other than that they live basically the same lives, defend their own individual territories, and hunt the same way and with the same degree of skill. I recognize that in humans different sex hormones can have different effects on human brains, and I understand that personal experiences based on societal expectations for males and females create slightly different lives. But in general, I have never seen any real connection between genitalia and personality, behavior, or ability, and I find the idea of concretely defined gender roles absurd. But, that is because Jaguar doesn't see that connection either.

It has taken me most of my adult life thus far to make my peace with the idea that "different" doesn't necessarily imply "unequal" — (even as it still does to some people). I have known many people who have full respect for both men and women who *also* believe there is a fundamental difference in the way that men and women *think* and *behave* that is not a byproduct of culture. That kind of thinking is all Greek to the Jaguar, but it probably makes perfect sense to all the Stags and Does out there, the Lions and Lionesses, and to all the vast array of song birds.

As I have stated before, the concept of gender is unique to humans, as is the idea that each sex has a specific role they are expected to fill in society; because gender definitions vary so widely across cultures, adhering to them carries an element of decision, as it is not a direct result of biological sex. But there are a considerable number of animals for whom the males and females lead very different lives, and may even have significant physical differences, and when we are dealing with a totem within a human mind this can all spill over into an understanding of sex that produces this view of human gender as an inarguable necessity. For all I know, sex hormones and other factors might have a much larger influence on behavior than I'm seeing; perhaps the people who see a more pronounced "difference" are more correct than I give them credit for and my own totem is preventing me from seeing it. Ultimately, though, in terms of totems, the objective reality really doesn't matter; we are in the realm of perception, the inner unconscious template of the mind, and whichever way a person understands it is going to be reflected in their totems and their behavior.

Along that same line, the sex of each of your totem animals may matter a great deal— or they may not matter at all. It just depends on the animal. A Lion is a leader whose authority comes from his size, various expressions of dominance over the other members of the pride, and his ability to fight off rivals, and while theoretically he can hunt, most of the time he uses his strength to fight off other lions and expects to be fed by those he leads. A Lioness, meanwhile, is involved with none of these things. The dominant Lioness has to maintain a tight relationship with her female kin to form an effective hunting team, giving a very different perspective to leadership. She spends her life perfecting her hunting skills, because skill is more important than bulk when it comes to over-powering another. She is comfortable giving her kill to the male for the protective role he fulfills, but her stronger social bonds are with the other lionesses, and if the male is defeated she will often welcome a stronger male in his place. Despite being the same species, they have very different influences on human characters when seated as totems.

And here is where the concepts of social organization and sex intersect in the animal world. Not all animals who form social groups have great differences between the males and females, but animals with strong sex-differentiated behaviors almost always form social groups— even song-birds, though their group dynamic is more fluid. But even with our tiny feathered friends, the concepts of social status and mating are often inseparable. So too, then, are they linked within the minds of humans. Animals who compete with one another not just for the opportunity to mate, but to "keep" that mate as part of their social group or pairing, can translate a great deal of anxiety, even jealousy, into a person regarding everything related to status and relationships. Yes, it is true that sometimes solitary hunters, browsers, or grazers have to fight to defend their individual territories, or to assert themselves when it is time for a mate. But for social and sex-differentiated animals, that struggle is an unending daily activity; a male Fox might fight another male for the right to the vixen, but after the deed is done they all go their separate ways, whereas a bull Walrus risks losing one of his cows every time another fit male goes by. In a human character, this leaves us with someone who will never be comfortable with a significant other who winks at the waiter or who gets a text from a coworker of the opposite sex, and it will have little to do with how much they trust in their relationship.

Further, animals in this category, as well as many solitary creatures, have very different instinctual strategies as to how to raise their young, and this too can spill-over in a human mind into ideas of who "should" do what when it comes to raising children and taking care of a house. Some animals, like Raptors and Parrots, share equally the duty of sitting on the nest and feeding the chick— perhaps the ideal model for a modern working family. For other pairing animals, the male's role is to keep the territory safe from other males and from predators while the female raises the cub, such as with Crocodiles and Tigers, leading more towards a couple who considers it a fair balance for one to work outside the home and the other work within it. For other animals, the female is the primary caregiver but she is assisted by others in her social group, such as the help given by other females in herding animals, or the help given to the alpha female Wolf by both males and females in the pack with lower rank— perhaps all leading to an individual person who finds it an impossible idea to raise their children away from their own parents and extended family, away from their church or the town they grew-up in, or perhaps they just naturally expect "the village" to lend a hand— their friends, coven, or chosen family.

Size and Predator/Prey

Like with social structure, the connection between a totem animal's size and whether they are a predator or prey animal— and the effect of both on its human bearer's character— should be pretty straightforward. In the lives of real animals, generally speaking the larger an animal is, the safer it is from predators— and that translates into confidence in a human mind, or possibly into compensation. The concepts of size and predation status are so interrelated in the animal world it is more efficient to discuss them together.

For our purposes, we think of large animals as those who are large enough that adults are usually invulnerable to predation, with perhaps only the very young or the very old put at risk. They are also animals who are large enough that others cannot usually chase them off their food or out of their territory. "Largeness," in this case, is relative only to environment. For example, a Dingo might not be considered a large animal compared to others we can name, but it is the largest predator on the Australian Outback, so it will behave as a large animal. Yet even as a Coyote and a Dingo are pretty similar in actual size and weight, on the North American continent there are Cougars, Wolves, and Grizzly Bears to contend with among others, making Coyote a medium-sized animal in his environment.

A large-sized animal generally brings confidence to the table, but it is very easy for that to lazily bleed into over-confidence, so take heed. Especially when we are dealing with large predators, their largest area of weakness is that they don't expect to be attacked. Unless they know they have committed an offense and are expecting revenge, large predator totems assume they will always be the hunter (scavenger at the very worst) and not the hunted. A man with a Cougar totem may have literally not seen it coming when a guy with a Reindeer totem went after his job promotion— even as it was plain to everyone else in the office. But constantly jostling for status is part of daily life for any deer, and so Reindeer guy in turn might not understand why Cougar guy was so personally insulted by what to him was "just a part of doing business."

Further on that note, there is a bit of a gray area for many large herbivores, whom we can still think of as large animals but who do fall to predators— and who definitely behave as prey. People with Horse totems or Bison will play a strong offense as the best defense, and can be at risk of underestimating their own strength; a Horse person might smell the stink of a predator on a new acquaintance and react defensively, even aggressively— failing to realize that a Snake or a Ferret is easily trampled by a thousand-pound Horse and was never a threat. They are the sort of person who walks into a new social situation — a new office, a new coven, or their new boyfriend's circle of friends—just naturally expecting to be drawn into an existing and ongoing struggle for social status; they "come out swinging," and may be quite unaware that their attempt to "keep up" is experienced by the others as too assertive, as bullying or teasing, or as unprovoked aggression.

Meanwhile, large and medium-sized predators are more likely to hang-back, perhaps hide, assess a situation and avoid the potential injury of a fight— unless there is something they want that is at stake, or unless they are under direct attack, or if they consider it worthwhile to exert their size and take something from another, whether that be food, territory, or mates. A predator's concerns are largely about whether it is worth the effort to go after something and if they can keep that acquisition away from other predators; competition and status have much less to do with it. Rarely, if ever, will they strike first— unless they're after something specific. Even as the "Big Bad Wolf" makes a handy villain in children's fairy tales, larger predatory totems make for far more *predictable*— and therefore trustworthy— individual people, at least in my opinion.

Small animals, meanwhile, always have to be aware of what's around them. Even small predators like Weasels and Snakes can be and are eaten by other predators, so in a sense every small animal thinks as potential prey. Where largeness may bring issues around overconfidence, smallness in a totem may bring issues with overcautiousness, or even fearfulness. Everyone should agree caution is a pretty vital trait for a human being (a person with a Mule Deer Primary totem might be well advised to listen to the Rat or Wren totems they carry elsewhere in their nine, if she/he reminds them that sometimes its okay to live to fight another day). However, too much caution can become debilitating in a human being.

Small animals tend to be split into two camps: those that prefer to hide and those that will sometimes stand their ground — usually in a very violent way that even the largest animal has to respect. The "stand your ground" type are the animals we're very comfortable labeling as the most vicious— your weasels and 'possums, some types of snakes and small cats, and some types of spiders and other insects. It's important to remember that these animals feel they *have* to bring such a big game to the field to get others to respect "the little guy," but most people may not realize how exhausting such a response can be for that animal. That is, the Aurochs person might head-butt someone for the sheer fun of it and hardly be winded by the exertion, but the Ferret person only cranks their viciousness up to eleven when they feel they're in a life-or-death struggle, and the experience is both psychologically and physically stressful and exhausting. As a child who grew up in the deserts of the American southwest, I was often told, "rattlesnakes don't *want* to bite you, they only do it if you leave them no choice," and this generally holds true for most all small animals who will fight-back. Except in situations in which life has taught a person to always be on the defensive, generally speaking if you find yourself on the receiving end of an attack from a small animal totem, you've done something to deserve it.

However, the majority of small animals (including those that can fight back) usually prefer instead to run and/or hide in the face of danger. In a human, this may be perceived as cowardice, but that is a misrepresentation; it's really strategic maneuvering. While such a totem possibly can lead a person towards being overly shy or timid, in general a person with a small animal totem simply sees more value in maintaining their safety and conserving their energy over any value in indulging in a fight— even if it means losing out on something. The sentiment, "surrender now to fight another day" is apt for all small totems. It can be true they might make a person overtly shy, anxious, unassertive, or even fearful, and that person's Dark totem might reflect that fear of fear itself. But very small animals have a strength that few others have: the ability to virtually disappear, whether that be into a hole in the ground, into the air, or up a tree. Because of this, the true power of the totem is solid confidence in your ability to survive.

Let's say that guy in the office who had his promotion stolen from under him by Reindeer guy instead had a Rabbit totem. If so, he might have a very different perspective on the situation than Cougar, allowing him to more easily cut his losses and get on with his life; he might even be grateful that the hot-headed Reindeer guy has moved on out of the office so he can get back to his original job he was perfectly comfortable with anyway — especially with so many hot interns around the place, all things considered with our friend Rabbit.

For an example of a small totem, a good friend of mine has a Deer-Mouse totem, and she is by no means meek, timid, or vulnerable in the face of people with larger animal totems. Rather, Mouse's ability to zip away and disappear into the smallest of crevices gives her the perspective that there are few situations she can't get herself out of if she chooses, giving her a perfectly confident and sociable personality. She can be reclusive (the joke was once made, "the two times a year you actually see her, you'll really enjoy it"), but that is by preference, not as a result of any social anxiety, and she is self-sufficient and capable in a way many are not, especially when it comes to maintaining a comfortable home on minimal resources. One might think that two people with Primary totems such as ours would be naturally at odds, hunter and hunted, but in fact we get along very well precisely because we see each other neither as a threat nor as prey. From an animal perspective, Mouse is too small for Jaguar to truly consider it a food and Jaguar is too big to breech the safety of a mouse-hole. There is no perception of danger, challenge, or temptation in either direction, leading to the human perspective of two women of about equal ability and power with no conflict between them— despite having two vastly different Primary totems. In short, a small totem does not make a small person.

And so that leaves us with those in the middle, the medium-sized animals. In general, animals in this category get both the benefits and the detriments of both worlds, and whether they behave more like a large animal or a small depends entirely on the situation and who they're up against. (It should be noted that small animals who are predators or omnivores have traits in common with this group, as they at least feel "larger" than whatever prey they take.) Someone with a Pronghorn totem doesn't have to be as cautious around Fox or Hawk as someone like Hare does, but he still has to be cautious around Wolf. And while in general his fleetness of foot and sharp horns give him a good chance of teaching a Cougar or overly advantageous Bobcat a valuable lesson, he can also fall to both, and a

Pronghorn can be bullied off its territory by wild Horses if good feeding ground is scarce.

When applied to human character, both predatory and prey totem animals of medium size give a person social and intellectual flexibility to deal with a wide variety of circumstances; they know they are capable of eating or of being eaten by another, that they are equally capable of being the aggressor or of backing down, of playing someone or of being played. Sometimes, in a human character this can lead to feelings of alienation, of uncertainly of one's place or role in larger society. It can cause social anxiety if a person hasn't made their peace with the fact that for them *every social situation will be a unique dynamic* requiring a unique approach, that there is no "one right way" to talk to people. But once the true power of this totem is known and accepted, such people can be very successful in life— even as those very qualities of capable flexibility may make them seem untrustworthy to others. Many animals that common folklore labels as the most "clever" (American English again), "troublesome", or even "mischievous" are part of this category: larger Foxes, Raccoons, Crows and other corvids, most Parrots, Badgers, and of course the poster-child for medium-sized mischief, Coyote. But they are inarguably also viewed as among the most intelligent in the animal kingdom.

PART FOUR
Every-day Use

Chapter One:
Animal Speak

Not long after I had first moved in with my other half, one day I found myself with a strong desire to find some personal space and conduct a shamanic journey (no small feat in our first small apartment). While he waited patiently in the kitchen, in true cat-like fashion I found a tight corner behind the couch and entered into this more active and advanced form of meditation with the intent of interaction with the non-ordinary reality or spiritual realm — a **shamanic journey**. I still remember vividly what I saw: it was a bleak and desolate winter scene, and a small pack of thin and desperate Wolves were shivering around the remains of a half-bare and frozen carcass. I suspected that one of the Wolves was my other half's Primary Wolf totem, though I didn't recognize her in her emaciated state, and she was quite insistent that I eat from the carcass, encouraging me with low and vaguely threatening growls. I very much did not want to, and I could sense that the other Wolves were just as disgusted by the state of the meat, but the female in authority was adamant. The entire scene ached with desperation and sadness— with an undefined undertone of violence.

Clearly, it is important to discuss how to truly commune with totems in a productive way. Totems can help you gain further insight or understanding into yourself, as well as give advice or wisdom, through deeper reflection making use of meditation, shamanic journeying, or dream analysis. However, as was my experience with my husband's Wolf totem, you may find it difficult to understand what the totem is trying to communicate. It is usually the case that entities of spirit prefer to communicate in metaphors and symbols that are not easy to interpret at first glance.

When I awoke from my shamanic journey and rejoined the waking world in my apartment, I wasn't sure what to make of what I had seen. I had some concerns over the meaning in such a negative vision, especially since it involved my other half's totem treating me in such a harsh way. But it was important that I brought up my concerns with him, because he interpreted the scene in a completely different way from how I had first seen it. Perhaps some of my readers will have some sense of what it means for a Wolf pack to share a winter kill, but at the time I did not. What had first seemed to me to be a scene of desperate violence was to him a perfectly clear message of inclusion, as a lead Wolf would never have insisted that I eat if she did not consider me a member of her pack. I remember him being quite pleased to hear what I had been shown by his totem, and I suspect it was all the more satisfying to him because I clearly did not understand the symbolism — and therefore it had to be genuine.

Totems, as entities or archetypes or however you wish to best understand them, can communicate with you in a wide variety of ways. I have also found that each person's totems seem to vary in how they prefer to speak to their bearer, carrying a preference that is itself an aspect of their personality. For some people, the totems speak with words, sometimes clearly enunciating them like cartoon characters, other times projecting them telepathically without movement of the mouth. For others, the totem may serve as a facilitator or guide to show the bearer the message, and there is a sense that the totem "takes" the person to witness a scene or environment— rather like they are showing you a short film of what they want you to know. Sometimes the totem will be an active player in that scene, while at others they may seem a spectator, and you as well can be either in varying circumstances.

Most often, however, the totem will communicate with you using the same combination of body language, posture, facial expression, actions, and vocalizations it would use to communicate with others of its kind. When we combine an animal's natural method of communication with their species' paradigm (or unique understanding of the world) we get what is defined in the discipline of totemism as **Animal Speak**. (Though it should not be confused with the well-known totem book by Ted Andrews of the same name!) Animal speak is the unique *animal* way a totem will likely communicate with you, and can be interpreted only through comprehension of how that animal lives, thinks, and understands the world. When you sit down to research your totem animals, keep in mind the need to understand how it might communicate with you, how its animal speak would look and sound. Even as there are some areas of overlap, there is no single language of animal speak common to all animals. A Wolf's powerful symbol of a winter kill has little significance to a jungle hunter like Jaguar, and a gesture of maternal insistence that I eat to survive might be lost on an animal used to fending for itself — or be mistaken for aggression.

Of course, on the converse side of this metaphysical conversation is how you will speak to your totems. Here, it is not important that you use any special form of animal speak— speaking with words, either aloud or in your mind, is just fine. There is a more advanced form of totemic exercise usually known as **shapeshifting** in which the person seeks to unify their spirit and their totem's into a single entity, and one method of initiating such a shift involves imitating the animal speak — the posturing, movement, and vocalizations — of the totem while in a trance state. However, no such action is required to form a deep and productive relationship with your totems. (And as this is considered a somewhat advanced technique and this is intended as an introductory book, a ritual on shapeshifting will not be included here.)

Now, on the other hand, it is important to be aware of *how* you speak to your totem. Be polite, be respectful, and while it is fine to be assertive, don't be demanding. Remember, ultimately your totems are *you*, your essential self— so treat your soul with respect and dignity. They do not have power over you, only influence, so do not grovel before them as though they were gods; neither are they servants of you, though they will respect and accommodate you, so do not make demands of them. Often you may bring a concern to them and receive a response different from the one you wanted, or that you are unable in the moment to interpret or understand.

You may often become frustrated with them, but that is an important aspect of learning to accept your entire essential self as you truly are; your totems can only give the answers they have. So remember that negative self-talk makes things worse, not better. Respect them as you would want others to respect you.

Chapter Two:
Building a Bond

Once one of your totems has chosen to reveal itself to you, it is important to acknowledge and to honor that aspect of your sacred self in some way. As is the case with most aspects of our tradition, there exist a wide variety of ways in which you may appropriately accomplish this. I will suggest several options, and you may proceed as you see fit.

A straightforward yet valuable method is an affirmation, a formal declaration of your recognition of a face of your essential self, and of the fact that your totems are the true you and you love and respect them as such. Such an affirmation is provided as an aspect of the Totem Wheel exercise in the Rituals section, and I would advise you utilize this exercise even if you do not fully use the Totem Wheel method to seek and find your totems.

Similarly, you may wish to approach honoring and acknowledging your newly discovered totems in a more directly spiritual way than my affirmations. Depending on your religious path, you might consider holding a ritual to honor the animal according to that path, such as a Druidic feast, a Wiccan circle, a drumming circle, or a prayer said according to your own proclivity.

Another straightforward way to honor your totems is to visually represent them. Many people choose to create alters to hold images of their totems, such as small figurines or perhaps framed photos, along with other objects that might speak to them spiritually or be part of their larger religious practice (for example: sacred books or sage for smudging). Pagans will often create such altars formally, and dedicate space on a small table, shelf, or perhaps mantlepiece to the adoration of the gods or spirits they honor and revere. Depending on your spiritual path, informal altars are perfectly fine (or when space is set aside without special ritual). However, you will find that it is exceptionally helpful to have set aside a special, specific place in your home where you can go to think about, and visit with, your totems. After all, humans are visual animals, and actually seeing an image of your totem is often more helpful than envisioning it in your mind. You may also consider putting images of your various totems in different places around your home where the characteristics of that totem will be in-sync with the nature of the activities you perform there (an image of your Air totem might do well above your desk or in your studio, for example).

For most of your totems, this may not be a difficult effort, especially considering that your totems have a good chance of already being your favorite animals anyway, and you may eventually end up with images of them all around your home. Consequently, you should see my house. Even those who know nothing of our spiritual path will walk through our front door and be immediately greeted by Wolf from paintings and figures around the room. Someone who stays a little longer notices Jaguar— whose presence is represented but not as obvious, as he prefers it. And anyone who enters my kitchen comments on my sizable collection of Elephant (and Mammoth) figures in my kitchen window.

Alternately, you might consider a pilgrimage. You could visit the animal in the wild or in a zoo and acknowledge him face-to-face. Or you could plan a hike or a camping trip to a place where your totem lives, or could live, or at least would enjoy, and spend some time appreciating an environment that could be "hers." You could do so in a place where the animal might be, and wait patiently for a sighting— or who knows, just because you don't see the animal doesn't mean the animal won't see you.

Another route is fellowship. Seek out others who have the same totem, or at least a love and appreciation for the animal, and spend a bit of time hearing their observations and their insights into the nature of the beast. Remember, you do not have to take everything that is said as totemic canon, just respect the individual providing it. Remember the concept of cultural bias we talked about in regard to the mythology of a culture, and appreciate that an individual's opinion represents the cultural experiences of one, filtered through the lens of their own experiences. Holding fellowship with the animal itself, or a closely related *kind*, is also an option, if you live near to where the animal lives in large numbers, or perhaps through some kind of volunteer situation with a rescue or refuge.

Consequently, I have found that another great way to honor your totems is through education and conservation work. Though of course common animals can be totems, unfortunately more often than not at least a few of your nine are going to be threatened or endangered. Donating money or time to organizations working to protect your totem animals is a powerful way to honor and acknowledge their existence— and further your own learning in the process. Personally, I have found that such organizations often sell items bearing images of the animal with the proceeds going to conservation, creating a win-win situation when you are looking for appropriate images or representations of your totem to use in your home. And if you cannot or do not wish to donate to outside organizations, it also honors the totem to contribute to bettering public knowledge of the animals, and speaking to others about their true nature and behavior can help correct faulty public perceptions that can be detrimental to their ultimate survival. A person with a Shark, Cougar, or Wolf totem might often remind others that disgruntled Cows and rutting Bucks kill *considerably* more people than those more "dangerous" animals, for example.

Even if your totems aren't endangered animals, your opportunities to see them in the wild may still be slim to nil, and you may never have an opportunity to see them in person outside of a zoo or rehabilitation center of some kind. Not everyone has the benefit of being able to observe their totems in every Gray Squirrel and Cardinal that frequent the backyard, after all. My other half and I have seen Wolves in the wild only once, at Yellowstone Park. But even though I have been to the Amazon rainforest I have never seen a wild Jaguar and likely never will (even as he probably saw me!), so realistically my only chances to see them are at zoos and big-cat rescues. Though not all for-profit zoos have an animal's best interest at heart, a reputable rehabilitation center or rescue may be your best opportunity to see and interact with your totems in person, so supporting their continued existence is a powerful way to show your respect to the animal.

Often the question will arise on the of use of real skins, bones, or other body parts of animals in totemic ritual — is it necessary to utilize a real piece of your animal to understand its true power? Ultimately, I think you should obey the law and honor your own sense of ethics and common sense, but if possession doesn't violate them, I will then say that is up to the individual. On the one hand, yes, there is a special magic in being able to touch and hold and have a pelt or a claw or a skull of your totem, and it is often thought of as the "traditional" way to connect to a totem animal (whatever "traditional" is supposed to mean). But on the other hand, it is not always ethical — or legal — to hunt certain types of animals or possess their parts, depending on their conservation status or usefulness for other things such as for food. Personally, while I believe humans have the natural right to utilize animal parts in this way for magick, I do not believe that right ever supersedes the rights of the animals if it impacts the species' survival. Please use common sense, do your research, and obey whatever your own sense of ethics tells you. If your totem animal is a Reindeer or a White-Tailed Deer, these animals are in no way endangered and are commonly hunted for food; Coyotes and Foxes are trapped regularly in many States to cull pest populations. By all means, use their antlers or hides or bones in your rituals or on your altars if you choose to. But as much as I would like to have the skull or the hide of a Jaguar, it is neither ethical nor legal for me to have them, and I will never encouraging poaching that could harm their populations.

However, if you are creative, there are ways to still have a physical piece of your living totem animals without harming them— or at least a close impression of a living animal. For example, we once visited a Wolf sanctuary that sold little vials of naturally shed wolf fur as souvenirs. The sale of any Elephant bones or ivory is strictly prohibited by international law, but the preserved bones and teeth of Mammoths and Mastodons are considered "rocks and minerals" and are usually legal to buy and possess, and are more commonly available than you'd imagine. If you volunteer your time with a predatory bird rescue, they may look the other way if you take home a naturally shed feather or two (though please keep in mind, possession of such feathers is a felony in the US). Yellowstone Park sells casts made from the tracks of wild Wolves within the park, and several big-cat rescues around the country do the same. High-quality resin casts and replicas of teeth, claws, and skulls of a variety of animals (made for use by taxidermists) are also available online. I've even seen zoos sell paintings made by Penguins walking through paint.

Be creative. And on that note, there's also a wealth of unique and beautiful animal artwork in the world made by humans — and supporting an independent artist doesn't exactly hurt your karma, either.

Chapter Three:
Everything in Balance — In Theory

Previously, in the section explaining why you carry nine totems, I touched a bit on the importance of balance, of the interaction between totems, specifically when you are dealing with the push-and-pull struggle between totems on opposing sides of your center. I will return to this idea now in greater detail. We will discuss normal totemic interactions within a balanced person, the every-day flow that simply defines how well one manages life; and we will discuss more problematic instances of totemic imbalance, where a person has difficulty with one or more totems asserting control inappropriately. I will discuss everything first theoretically; in the chapter after that I will review these ideas through some practical examples.

To begin, within our path of totemism, **balance** refers to a state in which you are able to function well in your own life, comfortable with the influences of all of your totems (and corresponding aspects of yourself), where no one totem has an unfair or unhealthy influence over another. Our definition of balance is not necessarily some perfect state of spiritual awareness or zen or nirvana as it may sound at first take, or as is sometimes implied in larger neo-pagan culture; instead, it refers to a more earthly *functionality* within yourself without much of any internal conflict or uncertainty. Your current state of balance is a barometer of how decisive or indecisive you may be, how focused, confused, conflicted, or lost you feel at any given moment, or in short, how much you "have it together."

A perfectly normal person, whom we would consider balanced, will still experience a shift from the influence of one totem to another as they move throughout their day, face challenges, solve problems, and make decisions; the difference between balance and imbalance is a matter of magnitude and degree. *Feeling a push or a pull from a totem simply represents a normal and reasonable shift between the dominance of one aspect of your character to another.* A totemic shift will happen as a result of your reactions to your experiences and your ability to respond appropriately to the events of your life. We call these **defensive shifts**. In fact, you may find that you enjoy, or even feel empowered by, shifting from the influence of one totem to another, depending on the situation you're in. That's all perfectly fine.

When we are talking about **imbalance**, or areas in which the relationships between totems may contribute to imbalance, we are talking about *chronic* and/or *overwhelming* situations, where one totem is dominating or speaking over another and affecting how well you are able to function. This is a situation in which one aspect of your personality dominates the situation to your detriment, or otherwise against your higher Will. This is an important distinction, and what you decide is "normal, functional, and balanced" vs "non-functional and imbalanced" for you as an individual is part of the path of totemism.

While it may seem at first that recognition of the uniqueness of your totems is paramount, there is actually as much to be learned of the essential self, if not more, in observing how they interact with one another within you. In a larger, over-arching sense, how well your totems "play together" is a fair estimate of how balanced you are internally. Once you become aware of how "together" (or not) you are and understand just which totemic interactions are responsible for it, the next step will be working with them to understand how to find that place of functional harmony that will serve you better in your every-day life.

So how do we understand this interaction? Areas of conflict or harmony between totems will play-out according to how they all relate to the Five Identifying Questions and so relate to one another. As a reminder, they are:

Five Identifying Questions

1) Environment— relates to physical needs and creature-comforts

2) Social Structure — relates to functionality within various forms of social groups

3) Sex and Mating Strategy — relates to views on romantic relationships and gender roles

4) Size— relates to perceptions of vulnerability and advantages when facing other animals/people

5) Status as Predator, Prey, and/or Scavenger — relates to perceptions of vulnerability and advantages when facing other animals/people as well as food/diet needs.

A larger animal, predatory animal, or otherwise more confident or crafty animal may exert more dominance over a smaller or meeker animal, and in turn a smaller animal may be able to redirect the focus of a larger animal or otherwise avoid or out-maneuver it. An animal who lives with one style of social structure may try to direct or control its corresponding animal according to the rules of that structure— and find themselves at odds with an animal who won't (or can't) properly comply. Animals that are each predator and prey, especially if they are of a size relationship that one might realistically hunt the other in real life, can produce a very lively and competitive relationship, reflecting aspects of yourself that are very active and constantly adapting and changing. An animal who lives in an environment strongly associated with an element (such as in the water, the sky, the night) will assert that elemental influence in a way that it cannot be separated from the characteristics of the totem position it holds.

The interactions you are most often going to be dealing with are between totems on opposing sides of your center: usually Air against Water, Earth against Fire, and Light against Dark, (or however you arranged the elementals so they feel balanced to you); these relationships represent aspects of human character we're pretty comfortable seeing as conceptually opposite from each other (intellect vs emotion, impulse vs preservation, and idealism vs hedonism). Many people will also experience the Lord and Lady giving opposing information and influence to one another, while others may experience both of them as contrary forces to the Primary, pulling it to either side.

Resolution of totemic conflicts or of strong totemic assertions can take many forms. The most direct way to counter the strong influence of a totem is to consciously appeal to and draw upon the energy of its counterpart, of the totem across from it in the structure of nine (Fig 1C). You can try to confront the overly-influential totem directly, either to resolve the issue through understanding or through suppression, but I would advise that you still consider the influences of the totem seated opposite it, as not only has it almost certainly influenced the situation, it will all but certainly hold the key to pulling yourself back to a place of balance between the two. Remember the allegory of driving the bus. It's not enough to tell the totem who's hogging the wheel that he should drive differently; you need its corresponding totem to take the driver's seat and get the bus back in the correct lane. The comparison to points on an axis is another example to remember: if your value is moving in one direction along a line, moving it back toward the original point of value requires moving in the opposite direction.

Now, there is another side to utilizing the balance point between totems on opposite sides of your nine, and that is when you *choose* to pull yourself out of balance temporarily and purposefully shift toward the strong influence of a totem. We call this an **offensive shift**. While most of the shifts you experience will be unconscious reactions to the events of your life, an instinctual defensive action of your mind, a true master of the essential self must learn how to consciously and actively shift *into* the energy of a totem to take advantage of its power. However, in order to do this effectively, you need to be able to do it confidently, certain that you can back-away to the center point once you are finished. Doing so on purpose requires that you first master defensive and unconscious shifts, and be able to find your way to your place of every day balance at Will.

Chapter Four:
Everything in Balance — In Practice

That is a lot of information to take-in from a theoretical perspective, so let's explore it through some examples. Let's create a person, we'll call her Amber, and explore how she would experience balance, defensive shifts, imbalance, and offensive shifts. For simplicity's sake, we'll just deal with the totems of Earth, Air, Fire, and Water. Amber will have a Scarlet Macaw in Fire, an Aldabra Tortoise in Earth, a Brown Bear in Water, and a Mountain Goat in Air. To begin, we must take a look at the totems' basic animal characteristics.

Macaws, like all parrots, are exceptionally intelligent animals with as much curiosity as the proverbial cat. Birds carry an Air association, so if this were an Air totem, it would simply reflect a very active, lively intelligence. But seated as Fire, this means Amber's character is unable to separate her intellectual side and her passionate side, linking ideas and obsessions into a constant stream of motivated creativity. Parrots are foragers and prey animals, meaning they are constantly maneuvering, exploring, experimenting— leading to a human character that requires stimulation like a body requires food. But parrots also carry a deeply-engrained need for routine behaviors and habitual actions, as well as a need for a long-term mate and partner — that is, for order. For Amber, this means it's not only important that she never stop learning new things, but that sticking to a schedule and being disciplined in that schooling, creative venture, and other intellectual pursuits, is an absolute necessity.

Meanwhile, even as we may at first connect the general tortoise type to water, a bit of research will show that the Aldabra Tortoise lives exclusively on land, giving it a solid Earth elemental connection with no overlap of multiple elemental energies (as there was previously with Fire) affecting Amber's Earth energy and therefore sense of physical security. Aldabras are usually slow and unhurried animals, spending most of their time grazing— though the massive amount of vegetation they consume alters the very ecosystem they live in. When combined with their enormous size (which gives adults security from predators) and their renowned longevity, it would provide Amber with the stability of the proverbial rock— and the stubbornness to go with it. If you have ever had the pleasure of seeing an Aldabra Tortoise in person, the zookeeper will no doubt have explained that the animals *only* move when *they* want to, and cannot be otherwise encouraged. But when *they* want something, nothing will stand in their way— they will knock-down fences and walls to get to grass they want, and the males will actually run when they see a female. Amber is likely inflexible when it comes to her clothing and decorating choices; her diet, exercise preferences, and weight; and her attachment to any choices she's made for physical aspects of her life. And when she does decide to make a change— she's having it, full stop.

Amber's Brown Bear in Water carries an Earth association, and they are a usually-peaceful omnivore who can also be an exceptional hunter. Their huge size and independent nature usually cause them to not care about what any other animal does or says and giving a person who carries it in Water the emotional strength to be absolutely unbothered by others' opinions 99.9% of the time. Bear is also slow to anger— but is absolutely formidable when moved to fight. However, when it's wounded, or tired, or just feeling the onset of the "little death" of winter, Bear's instinct is to withdraw into its cave and hibernate until it feels safe again. Seated in Water, Amber's Bear instinct would be to deal with strong emotions or emotional trials by ignoring it, by explosive expression, or by withdrawing emotionally or physically shutting-down and withdrawing from society— instead of facing her problems and calmly working through her feelings.

In Air, Amber's Mountain Goat is the only animal whose sex makes a difference in its influence. As a male, we can assume that it is either a herd leader or that it wants to be, and as such it is his instinct to control the actions of others and control space — to keep other males and potential predators out of his territory, and to keep his females and their young safely in it. Generally speaking, most female herd animals are predisposed to follow the guidance of their leader (whether that be a dominant male or the herd matriarch or both), so more likely than not any conflict for the Mountain Goat will be against rival males or threatening predators — that is, against enemies.[11] Mountain Goat has two main defenses: attacking with its sizable horns and its instinct to live in the higher and difficult to reach mountainous areas. When cornered, Mountain Goat is either going to retreat to higher ground or to try to attack with a sound head-butt.

Now, a lot of how Amber responds to life will also be affected by her Light, Dark, Lord, Lady, and Primary totems. But for the sake of simplicity to explain balance, we're going to pretend she only has to deal with the elemental four. So let's walk her through some situations to illustrate how balance works:

------

[11] On another note, I have no doubt that Amber would greatly enjoy intellectual sparring, debates, and heated arguments almost like a sport.

Amber has ordered a coffee and the barista has gotten her order wrong. The cafe is very busy and loud, and getting someone's attention to fix her order will mean speaking-up and asserting herself above the chaos.

Now, as someone with larger-sized totem animals with strong Earth connections, Amber is not going to be the type to be intimidated or consider her needs to be less important than others', so she will not back-down and accept the incorrect order, but she is also less likely to get angry or offended, due to the stabilizing effect of so much Earth energy. However, getting someone's attention will mean interrupting the barista and pushing herself in front of other waiting customers. It requires assertiveness, a sense of self-importance, and bravery; the influence of the Fire totem.

If we assume Amber is a generally balanced person, she will shift into the influence of her Fire totem naturally and unconsciously. Recall that her Fire totem is the Macaw, who will add intellectual Air to her Fire and back-up her assertive request by showing what she originally ordered on her receipt and over-explaining the situation. Macaw may very well have difficulty controlling his volume when speaking-up, but in this situation a loud voice is an advantage over the cappuccino machine. Amber is given an apology and assured the order will be corrected, and her Fire totem will step aside at the behest of the influence of her Aldabra Tortoise in Earth, who is more than content to wait patiently while the order is remade. We would call this a perfectly reasonable defensive shift.

But life is not always that easy. Let's put Amber into the same situation but give her Earth totem an unreasonable advantage: we'll say she's physically tired and her blood sugar is low. Now, instead of acquiescing to Macaw's instinct to speak-up, the Aldabra Tortoise refuses to be moved. Instead of pushing to the front to get the barista's attention, Amber waits in line again behind six other people and just decides she doesn't care if it takes extra time— her Earth totem giving her what we might call *too much* patience. However, we would probably still consider this a healthy and reasonable defensive shift, provided the Aldabra gives up control after the sugar and the caffeine kick-in, and assuming he doesn't do this kind of thing so often it impacts her life.

So, what if that thing I just said were true? What if Amber's Aldabra Tortoise is especially large (making it of great age), and her Macaw is especially flighty, making Earth assert control so often that Amber has trouble getting things done at anything other than a tortoise's pace. She faces situations in which she should react by lighting a Fire under herself— she should be speaking-up, getting excited, getting angry, getting aroused— and instead her Earth concedes that there is no use in getting bothered, because they'll get there eventually anyway without all that needless hurrying. Amber is aware that this happens and would like to change it; she knows she is standing in her own way a lot of the time. She would like to speak-up for herself, to care enough to put herself first, but a strong part of her just can't be bothered. We could call this situation imbalanced.

Resolution of this imbalance would be a matter of Amber appealing to the Macaw whenever she feels the too-strong influence of the Aldabra Tortoise, or otherwise in situations in which she would like the motivation to move and to feel energized. She would need to master an offensive shift toward Fire. This requires that Amber have some level of self-awareness, to have spent some time in self-reflection to know and identify which aspects of herself have influence on her thoughts and behaviors. But once identified, appealing to the excitable, intelligent, playful Macaw will give her exactly the influence she needs to overcome the patient, plodding Aldabra— and possibly ignite that part of him that plows down walls and runs towards a pretty female. Remember the metaphor of the road-trip. Like all of the elemental totems, Earth lacks the skills to be driving long-term, and if he's grabbing the wheel all the time and won't listen to Fire when it's time to give it up, that is a problem. For the Earth totem to take the wheel as a response to a physical need is not only acceptable, it's perfectly normal, and he may wisely pull the car hard to the *right* to the side-bar for a moment to deal with that need. But getting it together after that initial response requires that Amber's Fire totem take the wheel for a time to turn the car to the *left* to get back into the lane to ultimately drive *straight* again.

So to switch things up, let's look at that scenario in the cafe from another angle. This time, let's imagine that when Amber pushes her way back to the counter to get the barista's attention, another customer takes offense to this and yells at her, telling her to wait her turn and get out of his way.

Now, conflict is also an area where it is usually the prerogative of the Fire totem to react, but remember that her Macaw is going to forever mix Air into her Fire, meaning that Amber will usually "fight" back by presenting arguments and facts; where another person might just shout back at the man, Amber will explain hotly why she is in the right, that she has already waited her turn in line and that fixing a wrong order takes priority over new orders, thank you very much. However, in this case, Amber might also choose to discourage the Macaw's influence in order to avoid an argument with a stranger, and so drawing on the Aldabra Tortoise's immovability would be the key to tempering her anger and defensiveness. Both strategies would be reasonable defensive shifts if done unconsciously, and reasonable offensive shifts if done on purpose.

158

But we can take it a step further, and in so doing, draw in her other two elemental totems. Let's say the other customer takes his attack too far and begins to insult and degrade Amber, calling her ignorant and rude, and making it personal by calling her ugly and fat; another customer laughs and she is humiliated. Her feelings are hurt, she is embarrassed, and she is confused as to why someone would be so mean over something so inconsequential. Different people may react to conflict differently, with more anger or more arguing. But for Amber, her strong Water totem, the Brown Bear, is what takes control when her feelings are hurt.

However, Bears are not good at conflict resolution. She tells the man he is being rude, but it takes everything in her not to cry, and once she gets her coffee she leaves immediately and doesn't speak to anyone else for the rest of the day. A Bear will ignore things until they are deemed a threat and threats are dealt with by a deadly blow of a bear-paw; ignore or destroy works 99% of the time. But for that 1%, when something gets past that formidable defense and actually hurts a Bear, his instinct is to retreat and hide, to hibernate until it's better. Amber thinks about the confrontation all afternoon, brooding on it, trying to work out why it happened, trying to sort through her feelings on it, unable to get much work done or focus on anything else until she resolves a situation that, in this case, is unresolvable because that stranger is now long-gone.

Now remember, it is perfectly normal for someone to feel pulled closer to the emotional Water totem (and away from the Air totem) when something happens that makes them sad; that's exactly how it's supposed to work. And it is still perfectly normal for this to happen often if someone's Water totem is larger or in some other way more influential than the Air totem; perhaps Amber is just a person whose emotions run strong and deep, and that's simply an aspect of who she is.

The situation becomes a problem, becomes unbalanced, if she is pulled towards that Water totem so often that it is affecting her life, or so strongly that she is unable to balance herself for a long time afterward. Let's say that she becomes so withdrawn after the encounter at the cafe that she can't concentrate at her job, and her boss has to confront her about poor performance that afternoon. Being an emotional person is fine, but if her Air totem, Mountain Goat, is all but lost and she can't make good decisions because she's unable to use her head, then we would consider her unbalanced.

Left to their own devices, without conscious intervention, Bear is nearly always going to overpower Mountain Goat when they are pitted against each other, because Mountain Goat is a smaller animal and a Goat's head-butt won't do much more than irritate a Bear. Left unchecked, over time, it could even potentially pull Amber further down into sadness or depression or whatever strong emotion is taking control. If things become exceptionally imbalanced, I can even foresee Bear becoming so stressed from "driving" all the time that he withdraws and Amber becomes numb, depressed, and left at the mercy of a hibernating Bear and Mountain Goat billy who wants to spar but has no opponent and so goes around goading other people into ideological arguments to feel validated (feeling "right" is better than feeling nothing, apparently). In this situation, Amber would definitely need to make an offensive shift in Air's direction.

Resolving this imbalance would require conscious intervention, meaning appeal to Mountain Goat's abilities as a leader, protector, and group motivator, and learning through him the difference between a fair control of space and bossy aggression against others. Such a leader will know how to organize and prioritize what is important enough to keep around and what needs to be kicked out; he can help prioritize what issues (and corresponding emotions) are significant enough to be dealt with now and which should be passed-over and let go. By invoking and trusting in his instinct to be a leader, he can lead Amber out of her emotional crisis, presumably in a methodical and rational step-by-step kind of way. In turn, Bear can be politely told that he can either follow the Mountain Goat or withdraw to heal if he absolutely must, but that he will not be permitted to drive the whole bus off the road every time he is inclined. (If Bear is telling Amber to sit and listen to depressing music and smoke in the stairwell until the workday is over, and Mountain Goat is suggesting he can lead them all out of the darkness by answering one email, addressing one issue, completing one simple task, or by another small progressive one-at-a-time step to get her through the day, then he holds the key to restoring balance.)

Your totems that are positioned opposite to each other are organized that way within you for a reason, and the corresponding totem will always know best how to deal with its counterpart— you just have to trust it.

Now, just for giggles, let's return to the incident at the cafe but change the scenario and give Amber a Rattlesnake totem in Fire instead of a Macaw. What happens now? When she discovers her order was wrong? When the other customer confronts her? Consider the characteristics of the Rattlesnake according to the Five Identifying Questions. It's obvious he is likely to rattle if not strike, but out of aggression or fear? And how can appealing to the Aldabra Tortoise help her find balance?

It is a perfectly natural reaction of the Fire totem to take control, to pull you toward itself and away from Earth, when something happens to make you angry— again, that's what's supposed to happen. If you are angry or really upset, you're probably in a situation that requires immediate action, perhaps even self-defense, and sometimes in life it's more important that you engage your fight or flight reaction than contemplate long-term consequences. If Amber's Rattlesnake strikes at every small provocation, that is probably simply its nature, an aspect of her character that may save her as often as it gets her in trouble. It does not become imbalanced until her hot temper impacts her life. In the same way, the appropriateness of every totemic shift you make will be a judgement call that only you can make.

I'd like to end this sub-section with some thought exercises for you to work with. You don't necessarily have to take it to the level of detail I did with Amber, but take a moment to imagine how a person with each of these totemic alignments might behave— and do a little research on the animals if you're not familiar. For each animal, consider it first in Earth, then in Air, in Fire, in Water, in Light, in Dark; then as Lord, as Lady, as Primary.

- Arctic Wolf
- Tree Frog
- Bison
- Kookaburra
- Ibex
- Saltwater Crocodile
- Pink Dolphin
- Sun Conure
- Grasshopper Mouse

I will repeat that defining what is and is not a good solid state of balance between all of your totems is something relative to each individual person, and something that can only be learned in time through continually working with your totems. My other half, for example, typically seems more "together" than I am, and for the most part I feel this is a result of his Primary Wolf (as an alpha female) being such a good natural leader. His Lord and Lady totems give solid advice, but don't often overstep their bounds, and the rules for when they can step in and lead feel more clearly defined. His Lady, the River Otter, is charged with interjecting the need for silliness and play (i.e., a healthy bit of chaos) when Wolf's need for order and rules becomes so pronounced that he forgets to have fun; however, Wolf rarely fights Otter's pull and allows the shift without (much) conflict. He will interact directly with his elemental totems very infrequently, if ever, leading to the conclusion that they each play their parts at the appropriate time with little fuss.

Meanwhile, my totems do not necessarily "play so well" together, but I do not consider myself an unbalanced person. Jaguar just does not have the same instincts to create rank and file amongst the passengers riding in his bus, preferring to let everyone do their own thing a little more freely like a "free-range" parent. This leaves my Lord and Lady open to air their views and advice in stronger or even patronizing tones that can create conflicts in purpose, especially considering that both Lion and Elephant are trying to take control with unique leadership styles. And it leaves my elementals much freer to exert their own colorful influences, leaving me less focused and a little more prone to be pulled from one interest, idea, or mood to another. But at the end of the day, while I may appear unorganized or flighty to some, I am not dysfunctional; I get done what needs doing. And anyone who is (or who is close to!) a highly creative person might agree that forcing too much "order" onto such a person is counterproductive to the creative process. (Cats need to be cats, after all).

Some of you may have gotten the impression that I lean heavily towards Air, and in fact my Air totem, Magpie, has a more active presence in my daily life than even the Lord and Lady might in other people. This, at least more so than anything else, has personally been my largest area of totemic imbalance to reconcile. Magpies are active, energetic, highly intelligent and creative animals — but so too are Ermines, my Water. Yet when faced with conflict, a Magpie (like any bird) will dismissively fly away and above its opponent, while a weasel feels compelled to retreat or to viciously fight. In nature, sometimes corvids hunt weasel pups— and sometimes weasels raid corvid nests. Magpie is larger, but both are small sized predator/omnivores and they have a predator/prey relationship with each other in both directions. Yet Magpie has hugely dominated my personality, and this is due to Ermine's instinct to hiss and dive into a hole while Magpie simply roosts higher in the tree whenever they are in opposition. Unconsciously stuffing one's emotional side into a hole is obviously rife with opportunity for larger problems, such as depression, anxiety, and anger — which is exposed explosively in those times when Ermine chooses to stand and fight with all the viciousness a Weasel can muster.

For me, resolving one of my most prominent inner conflicts is a continual process of actively seeking the Ermine and honoring and listening to her input, of reminding the Magpie that his voice is only one among many, and that despite their good intentions, reminding both that neither is in charge here. For anyone, we feel this is a good strategy for resolving most all totemic conflicts. That is, identify the issue, recognize which totems are involved, and honor their contributions to your life and acknowledge that they do so with good intentions. And then you will choose which totem's influence will be followed and *do it*. This is a process accomplished by your human *Will*, which we will now discuss.

Chapter Five:
Evolution of the Self

At this point, the reader might have a very important question: if this path of totemism is defined as accepting all aspects of the self as valid and important, where is there room for self-improvement? This is a very important point to consider, because even as it may seem contradictory at first, in fact learning, growing, and evolving as a person are important components of our path of totemism.

Human Will

To understand self-improvement within our path of totemism requires discussing the concepts of human thought and choice. We all likely understand at an intuitive level that human minds operate differently than those of all other animals. Those differences, as it turns out, are crucial to understanding our essential selves and our own relationship to our nine totems, as I will explain.

A recent experience with a friend and some wild owls coincidentally occurred just at the right time to be included in this sub-chapter, exactly where such an example was needed. (Serendipity can seem counter to rationality but I find sometimes it's best just to roll with it.) As often happens, my reputation as "the totem lady" caused this friend to ask me for help interpreting the odd behavior of some Great Horned Owls near his home who were awake and active during the day. As I always do, I explained our basic understanding of totems and the place of animal spirits in the greater scheme of things, both of living individuals and as metaphysical concepts, and essentially told him there is no one meaning inherent in seeing any specific animal. (Most people are far more familiar with the geomancy system of interpreting animal spirits and expect me to say something like: "Seeing an owl means secrets revealed, or is an omen of misfortune," or something to that tune.)

Rather, I explained that if he felt the experience had some significance for him, he should enter into a meditative state and seek the Owl itself for further information. Maybe there was some message meant specifically for him, or maybe more likely the Owls were acting for their own independent reasons. But if he found the event significant, it might be because it spoke to something going on inside of him. If he felt there was something to be learned from it, then there probably was. [12]

I pointed out what I felt was the most prominent aspect of the situation: Owl is an animal with an innate elemental connection to the Dark, so its decision to be awake and active during the day (i.e. Light) is likely reflective of an abnormal situation, caused by or in response to a reversal of opposites; we have been experiencing an absurdly warm winter this year and seeing temperatures more befitting late

---

[12] I am somewhat amused by the notion of asking someone else if something is significant, if it "means something" to see this or hear that — especially in a spiritual or metaphysical context. Feeling that an event carries significance is the same as feeling that something is beautiful— that is, it is a *subjective* experience, an emotion unique to you, and it is absurd to seek validation from another person for a matter that exists within your own heart. It is not for others to say if it is or isn't if something strikes your heart as carrying higher meaning or spiritual importance. The question you should ask is *why*, not *if*.

spring, and it has been upsetting the normal balance of animal behaviors. The element of Dark hides things, both the hunter and the hunted, while Light reveals them; an Owl's decision to risk giving-up the cover of Darkness in exchange for the ability to see more in the Light may be what struck my friend as personally significant on an instinctual level. However, after I personally took a bit of time to ruminate on the situation, it struck me as the perfect way to introduce the pagan concept of the Will and how it functions within our path of totemism.

The concepts of sentience, self-awareness, and/or free-will are usually referred to simply as "**The Will**" within many magickal paths. Humans have choice in how we act, and we are aware of this choice and understand that we have it. It is the uniquely human ability to understand our lives objectively, to know that we exist in an abstract sense, to make complex decisions factoring-in a variety of ideals, options, ethics, concepts of cause-and-effect, and a sense of time that differentiates past, present, and future. For pagans, this ability is considered one of our most special and important blessings from nature; it is the defining factor of our humanity and to us it is sacred. We call this ability **The Will**.

Animals also have the ability to choose, and some of the more intelligent have some ability to consider consequences in a limited way, but in general animals do not understand the broader concept of complex choice that humans do. *They do not have human Will.* An animal's choice is simply whether to follow its instincts or to not; animal willpower (with a lowercase "W") is instinctual only. A Raccoon is a clever creature and can contrive complex strategies to feed himself, but he is a loner who thinks of himself first, and he cannot choose to adopt the pack hunting strategies of canines, the safety of Penguin's life-long mating strategy, or a human's concept of personal property boundaries that label pilfering the garbage as "theft." A Dog cannot understand "right" and "wrong" or feel guilt for her sins the way humans do; she simply feels stress from two conflicting instincts, the first to eat the forbidden food left unattended in the kitchen and the other to avoid displeasing her pack leader. She will never make the creative leap to come up with other options— such as to lie about it or rationalize the theft in the way a human child would. An Owl can choose to hunt at night or it can choose to hunt during the day, but there is never an option where it does not hunt, where it does not behave as an Owl — or rather, where it behaves like another animal that is not an Owl.

To put it another way, a Raccoon is influenced by Raccoon energy, a Dog by Dog energy, and an Owl by Owl energy. But in every case, there is only *one* animal energy within them affecting and influencing their choices. That is, *non-human animals do not have totems.* **Our nine totems within us are reflective of, and exist as a direct result of, our unique power of human Will.** They are the wider breadth of influences and complex ideas within us affecting how we think, behave, and make choices.

Before this incident with the Owls, I had understood that non-human animals always acted from the influence of their instincts, but I did not fully understand that they still employ the idea of *choice*— the choice to bow to the influence of instinct or to fight against it. Now, the idea of human choice, based in human Will, will always be infinitely more complex. Yet, we too nevertheless choose either to obey our instincts and inclinations or to supersede them. Just because it is an Owl's nature to hunt at night doesn't mean he cannot decide to do differently for his own reasons. But an Owl cannot decide to listen to Dog or Raven or Stag energy because there is none within him. Humans, however, can allow themselves to be led by the influences of any one of their nine different animal voices. But they can also decide to listen to none of them— to choose instead to listen to a different, external energy that comes with the face of a spirit guide animal— by means of human Will.

The key here, the all-important caveat to this bit of information, is that the ability to over-ride our animal instincts and influences when necessary hinges on our awareness of those influences in the first place. I'm sure we can all think of numerous people who seem blissfully unaware that they are being led down one path or another by strong unconscious, instinctual, or emotional pulls— be that by anger and fear, a lust for base and simple pleasures, or the approval of others— and to the outside observer their eyes are clouded and quite unaware that they aren't acting from a clear mind. The most clouded of these people are the ones who have never thought much beyond how they look, beyond becoming popular, or beyond getting laid. They might as well not be human, for all that they live by animal instinct alone. A person on the path of the wise, or who is attaining wisdom by whatever other means, becomes *aware of the self* in such a way that he or she can see plainly the many voices, impulses, and drives within the soul. And being aware of them in the first place allows the wise person to *choose when and how* to best make use of the many voices of their totems.

Beyond Nature

Our core personalities, our essential selves, are built of the nine separate animal energies of our totems. They are ourselves, and we will always be who we are. It is difficult, if not impossible, to fully discard or shut-out the voices of our own souls and I will never understand the people in this world who feel our mission in this life is to do exactly that, the Buddhist or Hindu who dismantles the Ego, or the Christian or Muslim who denies the self as sinful and who gives up their own Will for that of their God. Nature survives by diversity, adapts through mutation, and it is a proud lesson for the vibrant, living green pagan heart that your soul is unique for a reason. Mother Nature made the oak different from the ash and the willow, and she wants each to grow from seed to sky, to become tall and proud and beautiful, to the best that each is able. So, too, is every man and woman a unique creation that is to be embraced, loved, celebrated, and not dismantled in obedience to another.

And so, it can seem, the line between learning to love the self as it is and learning to grow into something more can seem hazy or unclear. Whether those nine voices are wisdom to be heeded or animalistic instincts to confuse the human mind can vary circumstantially, and it is not always an easy question to answer, to know when it is best to do one or the other. The important distinction to be made is between teaching yourself to be the best "you" you can be and denial of the realities of the self in an attempt to rebuild it. This goes doubly-so if you are remaking yourself according to someone else's standards. Allow for evolution of yourself beyond initial boundaries as need arises, but do so without compromising yourself. There is a difference between natural growth and forced reconstruction, as well as between peaceful acceptance and stagnation.

And more, there can also be an important difference between what might be a perfectly legitimate and functional state of balance for *you* and what larger society may permit. We will discuss this idea in much further detail in the closing thoughts of this book, but a heavy truth of this life, with which one must come to terms, is that who we naturally are— our core personalities as outgrowths of our totems— isn't always compatible with life in this modern world. Had you been born in another place or time, following your instincts might have been a perfectly acceptable, even highly desirable, way to live a balanced life. But the same instincts that might have made you a very successful medieval monk or blacksmith, viking warrior or midwife, mammoth hunter or shaman— may very well contribute to you being a terrible cashier, college student, IT technician, call-center operator, or an otherwise socially-isolated clock-puncher. Sometimes it may be as mild a symptom as being accused of being too serious, too aggressive, too empathic, too quiet for the tastes of those around you.

Now, sitting back on your laurels and finding pride in your "outsider" status and charging forward in your mediocrity is certainly a popular option. However, though it does not always work, there exists an alternative option: learning to evoke the instincts of one of your totems more suited to the situation, an offensive shift toward a totem you wouldn't choose normally but who may be better suited to thrive (or at least survive) in the cubicle or standing in front of a projection screen giving a report on this month's numbers (or whatever the hell people who work in offices do). In this case, it wouldn't mean that how you behaved before was unbalanced internally; it means you have *found* balance, *calibrated* yourself to your environment, while still listening to the instincts of your own essential self.

My mother-in-law raised my husband on this bit of practical wisdom: *actions repeated form habits, habits repeated form character.* Clearly, she didn't mean the exact same thing we do when referencing "character," which to our totemic tradition has meant an immovable and permanent aspect of yourself, rather than a more malleable expression of your self-disciplined self, which she intended. But nonetheless, the wisdom rings through clearly. If you do not like the way you act or react in a situation, exercise your human quality of Will to change it. ***A conscious offensive totem shift, in time, will become habit, will become an instinctual defensive shift.*** You have not changed who you are, but you have changed to become a better expression of yourself.

There is another important concept within paganism known as "the **Gray**" or "being Gray," and in a wider context it refers to the hard truth that no rule, especially of ethics, behavior, or human culture, can remain good and just without allowance for exceptions. There can be no justice when laws are absolute, as the almighty Captain Picard once said. And nothing in Nature, in life, is absolute (except for death— and taxes, as the joke goes). Nothing is ever as clear as black and white, and knowing when to reap and when to sow, when to love and when to hate, when to punish and when to forgive can only be understood in its season through complex wisdom, through being Gray. So too, in this situation, does the philosophy of being Gray apply: I cannot tell you when it is and isn't appropriate to follow your nature, for any guideline I lay down would have exceptions, and the truth for you as an individual would be found someplace in the middle.

However, even as I cannot offer a rule, I can offer a suggestion: return to the question of balance, of finding functionality within yourself. It is true that your totems are set within you in such a way to make you as you are, and to provide you with what you need to be the best version of yourself you can be. But, as the tired adage goes, nobody's perfect. It is a rare individual indeed whose soul is already complete, for a person's totems to instinctually know everything their bearer could ever possibly need to know for this life. You can not know everything there is to know, and as your totems are you, it follows that neither can they. Sometimes, we still do find that some things are beyond our reach, and that none of the nine tools in our tool belts are quite right for the job.

If you find yourself in a situation in which the chorus within you seems inadequate to the situation ahead, you have tried working with them and all they have to offer, and yet you still feel off or otherwise dysfunctional, I would suggest it might be time to seek knowledge from outside of the essential self: to enlist in the aid of a spirit guide.

Spirit Guides — Coyote's Lesson

According to our path of totemism, a **spirit guide** is a metaphysical animal form whose tutelage can help fill the gaps in areas wherein your instinctual totemic energies may be lacking; they come to you to address a specific problem and so your association will be temporary. In a simpler sense, a spirit guide is like a patch, covering a hole in your instinctual knowledge with something you can use to grow and learn, a way to overcome the weakness implied in that totemic lack. Often they may share qualities with a totem that cannot project its voice, and the Guide presents as a larger, stronger, or louder animal than the totem to help push the lesson forward— or simply to get your attention in the first place. In any case, while they are not considered proper totems as they do not compose an aspect of your essential self, you can learn a considerable amount from them and become quite close to them— over many years in some cases— and it is not uncommon even for people very well-versed in metaphysics and magick to confuse them with permanent totems.

I have introduced the concept of the spirit guide by suggesting they be sought in times of uncertainty or other distress after working with the primary nine has not produced the desired result. However, it is also just as likely to happen backwards, that an individual will be approached by the spirit guide animal first, and only later become aware of just why they have come. If you suddenly find yourself very aware of a certain animal, or drawn to it in an inexplicable way (as was described in uncovering a totem in Part Three, Chapter Two), it is important to pay attention and address it. For while you may not yet be aware of your own need on a conscious level, part of you may still be well aware of your own lacking and so you were drawn to that animal spirit to help cover that gap.

This process can be especially tricky during the beginning of your quest to learn your totems, as a spirit guide may spend quite a bit of time working with you before you learn its true nature and it can be very easy to confuse it with a totem. In fact, the need to find one's totems by itself may be enough to draw a spirit guide to you as a facilitator — requesting just such a Guide will be one of the methods to revealing your totems I'll provide in the Rituals Appendix. I promise things will get easier once more of your totems are known. In this instance, I find my more assertive approach to spirit communication to be most helpful: if you are uncertain of the animal's role, I see no reason why you can't just ask it.

As an example, I have two spirit guides whom I have worked with on-and-off for several years: Coyote and Grizzly Bear. In both cases, these are animals who came to help amplify a neglected or otherwise overlooked quality of one of my true totems, and in both cases, I didn't fully understand this until I had spent some time working with them both. According to other traditions of totemism (as well as, perhaps, the greater anthropological concept of the word) both animal entities would likely be considered my totems, especially one who has been with me for as many years as Coyote has. Nevertheless, I have come to know them both well and I can say with some certainty that they are *not* totems as we have defined them in this book; they are not aspects of my essential self, in whole or in part. While they both came to me to highlight certain aspects of my true totems, they also carry characteristics that are clearly foreign to my essential self.

To express it in a more colorful sense, totems are like family and spirit guides are like friends who can become like family. Such a friend can be regarded by you as family, and perhaps even loved more than some of the biological family you have. But no matter how close you become, you will never look at such a friend and see yourself reflected in them, see the shape of your own nose or the color of your eyes in their face, in the way you might with even the most disliked and rejected family member. I am confident that, with time and experience, you will be able to feel the difference between a close spirit guide and a true totem in a way that rings true without confusion.

In the case of my friend Bear, he showed up after a particularly traumatic job loss and career shift to speak for my smallest totem, the Ermine in Water, and show me the healing benefits of temporary, metaphorical retreat into the earth as well as the strength and power that can be summoned when defense is necessary. He comes and goes as he is needed, usually in the role of protector when I just can't mentally get past how small Ermine is. He serves as a mirror, or more aptly a magnifying glass, for key qualities of my Water totem that I sometimes forget.

Coyote's role in my life has been far more complex, and as he has made his wishes known in regard to this book, he has provided me with a detailed and nuanced example of the purpose and value in a spirit guide. As one would expect of him, I cannot pinpoint exactly when he showed up; all of a sudden one day I looked around my studio and it hit me that I had been collecting and reproducing coyote symbols and images for several months to the point that he had his mark spread all around the room before I even noticed him. But nevertheless, once acknowledged he has never really left, only faded in and out of prominence over time; he has walked with me for years and shows no intention of leaving any time soon.

Coyote came to help me address the issues of anxiety and fear by embracing the reality of the randomness of nature and the implicit lack of control that comes with living. He came to help me better understand an aspect of my Jaguar Primary totem. Now, one may not necessarily think of animals such as Jaguars as exemplars of what in metaphysical studies is usually dubbed "chaos energy," but they are, and Coyote's lessons have helped me to gain deeper understanding of how the idea relates to the wider animal world.

You see, all animals have within them a set of what we humans might call "rules" that dictate what the animal believes it can and cannot do; these are all forms of instinct and genetic behavioral predisposition that affect how that animal believes it must live and the world must be. Such rules create discipline, structure, guidance, security, and order within the animal's life, but they also limit the animal's creativity when it comes to problem-solving and crisis management. To bring back an example I used earlier, we might say that for a Wolf it is a "rule" that intelligent animals "must" live in cooperative, hierarchical social groups, and a Wolf simply cannot conceive of a life without a pack. Usually, this is a source of comfort and strength for a Wolf, but again as we discussed, it can also limit Wolf's ability to thrive without one. Animals with more specific diets, who can only live in certain ecosystems, who *must* live a certain way, are all therefore limited by these rules they must follow.

In contrast, animals with the fewest rules have the most flexibility when it comes to survival: they tend to be omnivores, able to eat nearly anything; they are widely dispersed, thriving in the heat and the cold and the urban world alike; they can get on in groups or alone; they grow canny as they can hunt but also be hunted. Humans observe this flexibility, this creative survivability, and fear it; they are used to the idea that animals have predictable behaviors and when it seems one is capable of anything it's labeled mischievous, too clever, untrustworthy. Evil. *Chaotic.*

However, a pressing and repeatable lesson for the gray pagan heart is that that "evil" is an invention of the human mind, and though "chaos" is a valid concept in both the scientific and metaphysical world, within the hearts and minds of living animals there is simply the ability to live with fewer restrictions, with fewer rules, and with such creative freedom comes the growth of powerful and often unpredictable intelligence. But as one should expect, nature will always balance itself, and that type of intellect has its price. One cost of chaos is uncertainty, as one becomes aware of more potential outcomes for one's actions. Another is malcontentedness, as the ability to get by as easily on less as on more begs the question of the value in anything, including meaningful work. These "rules" we speak of provide the framework in animal minds for how they define contentedness or discomfort, joy or sadness, success or failure. And when a game does not have rules it can be difficult to remember why we play.

Human folklore has its poster-children for this type of chaos animal. The Native American Coyote is often the first to come to mind, followed closely perhaps by Raven and Spider. Depending on where you live, you might instead think of Coyote's English cousin Fennec the Fox as King of Mischief, followed by his local compatriots Badger, Hare, and Rat. You might even think of Coyote's Aussie cousin the Dingo as the champion "sneaky bastard," with wildcard feral player House Cat and the Ibis, the garbage-eating "bin chicken," also coming to mind. But outside of human lore, we can see more clearly Coyote's lesson of chaos at play in a much wider variety of animals. We can additionally see the element of chaos is not simply present or absent, and occurs in different animals in variable amounts depending on just how many or how few "rules" within them they "must" follow.

In the Jaguar's case, he carries more rules than Coyote; as a large animal he is never prey, and he is an obligate carnivore. Yet despite this, Jaguars as well as their close cousins the Leopards are regarded as exceptionally adaptable, creative animals. They must eat meat, but meat in nearly any form will do, including domestic animals, the kills of others, and human garbage (Leopards in Africa have been known to raid garbage cans in urban areas no differently than the common Raccoon in America). As hunters, they are exceptionally proficient; they will eat any animal they can fit into their mouths and they can catch almost anything they wish. They mate casually and with little fanfare, yet can form strong bonds of friendship that last a lifetime. So long as there is adequate food and basic shelter, they can survive nearly any conditions.

Coyote's lesson, in part, is that nearly any animal that is omnivorous, or that can scavenge, or that must catch prey while escaping being prey, or that has flexibility to live any old way so long as it has something to eat and somewhere to sleep, will have to deal with much of the downfalls of chaos energy as discussed above. But is has also been just as much his lesson that it is irrelevant whether or not the local human culture casts the animal as "the mischief-maker" in their lore. Bear is an animal that carries a considerable amount of animal chaos, as is Raccoon, Sea lion, Parrots and Crows as well as many other birds, rodents, and mammals somewhere in the middle of the food chain. A Koala lives in one place and eats a single food; his anxieties are a matter of having what he needs or not, and when he has it, he is content. **But the more an animal must creatively *think about how it will live* the more it will inevitably cause *existential discontent* in a human who bears it as a totem— that is, the more chaos it will have.**

When one sits down to research a totem, one will no doubt find a large and potentially overwhelming amount of

178

information to digest. Yet, no matter how much you think you've learned, there can always exist the possibility that you are overlooking a key component of their personality, their energy, for a variety of reasons, including your own cultural biases. Animals in nature might know full well to fear the wrath of a weasel on the war-path, but human eyes are prone to see only the cute and the fluffy. I have never read anything anywhere about the Jaguar that would suggest that he should be associated with the metaphysical concept of chaos. (Half the books I own still insist on making "black panther" its own separate entry!) Yet he *is* a chaos animal— to some extent, nearly all cats are. To miss this point is to miss-out on understanding a large part of why I am the way I am.

A final but important point to keep in mind when dealing with spirit guides: not every tendency of their animal characters will necessarily be appropriate, helpful, or healthy for you to emulate. And it is important to remember the qualities a spirit guide has in common with your totems can vary, from nearly all of them to practically none.

At the onset, this may seem unimportant. After all, shouldn't it be a good thing that such a spiritual teacher has traits or skills or ideas that you do not that they might share with you? The issue lies in just how you interpret what they have to say. They do not speak *for* your soul, as totems would; they speak *to* it. Therefore, some of what they have to say can amount to well-intentioned bad advice. Every tendency of every one of your totem animals represents an existing side of your psyche, personality, and soul— even when those of one conflict with those of another. When a totem shares its wisdom, gives the advice that you should heed the instinct he or she represents, you can be certain the behavior is natural to you. The question to ask is whether the behavior is appropriate and helpful *in relation to your current situation*, not whether it is good for you in general. Remember, because your totem's behavior is simply a reminder of what you already are. But when a spirit guide shares the same wisdom— advises you to follow its lead toward a new instinct— there exists the possibility that this might not be a healthy decision for you.

The best example I can give in this instance is my continued association with Grizzly Bear. While he and Ermine share many similarities between them, there are many important differences (and coincidentally, size isn't the one I'm going to talk about). All weasels will utilize the burrows of the rodents they hunt and remake them into their own cozy dens, and when danger strikes, an Ermine understands the advantages in retreating into any available crevice in the earth until said danger has passed. The reader can see how this is similar to, but distinctly distinct from, a Bear's practice of hibernating through the entire cold season. The difference is a matter of duration and of the conditions needed to justify reemergence, of simply waiting until the coast is clear versus withdrawing from the world until conditions fully change. If Bear had his way — that is, if I were to follow the lead of Bear totally and without reservation — he would be content to see me retreat into my own space, my own comfort zone, until the conditions of the outside world changed to my liking— however long that would be. But though he means well, neither Ermine nor any of my true totem animals (aside from the Snake) ever hibernate and instead generally continue to endure and work through the cold and/or dry seasons they face. For an Ermine or a Jaguar or a Lion or a Magpie, withdrawing into their den for *too* long means starvation, not salvation.

A similar lesson lies with Coyote. While his words regarding creatively adapting to an ever-shifting world have been invaluable, it is important for me to never forget that Coyote is able to enjoy, dare I say even rejoice in, the adventure of not knowing what's around the next corner precisely because of his ability to roll with all the punches. But a

Coyote has skills that a Jaguar does not: namely, a Coyote can utilize a variety of hunting strategies that include pacing, or the ability to scent prey, track it across the landscape, and run it down. A Jaguar, on the other hand, is instinctually an ambush predator, one who waits in hiding for the prey to come to it. Coyote can eat a wider variety of foods, including insects and some vegetables. And a Coyote is perfectly comfortable hunting alone or as the leader or a follower in a team. [13]

In a human character, an ambush predatory totem (such as my Primary Jaguar) leaves one able to seize opportunities when they arise, but less able to conceive of a goal and devise a realistic and adaptable strategy to achieve it. Ambush predators consequently spend a lot of time knowing what they want but waiting around for the right opportunities to develop to seize it, such as when I knew I wanted a new career but instinctually assumed finding one was a matter of waiting to pounce on the right opportunity — rather than creating my own opportunities. My standards for living are not necessarily high, but I require more to live than someone who might be perfectly comfortable living in an RV or a one-room apartment with no furniture other than a mattress, a wood pallet, and a toaster oven, for example. And anyone who has ever had the audacity to tell a cat what to do has no doubt found themselves on the wrong end of the claws— even if the cat knew the other person was right all along— so following another for the sake of convenience is not an option.

---

[13] It is known to scientists that groups of Coyotes will willingly join and follow a lone Wolf in need of a pack, to benefit from his protection and skill at coordinating group hunting— and mate with him to produce offspring that carry the best of both species; research the "coyowolf" for more information on this extraordinary show of adaptation.

In short, while it is valuable to understand the chaotic nature of the Jaguar, it is wrong to ascribe it the same level of adaptability as Coyote, and as such it is erroneous to presume that a Jaguar can learn to find the same amount of fun in riding the rollercoaster of the unknown. As before, to follow the instinctual instruction provided by this spirit guide would be to ask the Jaguar to enjoy a level of uncertainty that he is not necessarily innately equipped to handle. And it would mean asking myself to enjoy the chaotic nature of living rather than simply learning to ride it out in a healthy way, and to off-set anxiety by better understanding what I can and cannot control.

And Coyote's most prominent lesson of all has ironically been the most helpful. Unlike a totem that follows you from the cradle to the grave, if a spirit guide's advice ever outlives its usefulness and you realize you are better off without it, you are completely within your rights as a bearer of human Will to politely decline its contribution and move on. There is no better way to gain the upper-hand on chaos than to tell Coyote (if you will excuse me) that he needs to fuck right off— at least until the next time I need him.

PART FIVE:
Rituals and Exercises for Revelation and Communication

As has been stated previously, there are numerous ways to uncover one's totems. For many the path to discovery is something only the individual can blaze, and only a unique approach will feel suitable. For someone who is approaching the path of totemism from an entirely psychological and less spiritualistic context, that path may be as simple as a prolonged period of research and critical thought. Someone else who travels the meandering and many-forked road of eclectic metaphysical or neo-pagan spirituality may wish to initiate the process only through the rituals or spiritual methods of their own choosing.

However, for those who would benefit from my assistance, the following chapter explores some techniques that might be of service, both for initial totem discovery and for continued communication throughout your journey with those totems.

We will focus on these types of metaphysical exercises as they are easy to use and can be used quite companionably with totemism:

- visualization and manifestation of intent
- shamanic journeying and/or guided meditation
- raising/casting a magick circle in the Wiccan style

I will discuss what these techniques are and how to utilize them in this section. I have also written outlines for specific rituals that you may follow step-by-step. Those can be found in the Rituals Appendix.

Chapter One:
The Totem Wheel — Visualization and Manifestation

If someone does not already have some impression, hint, or inkling about which animals might be totems, it is my opinion that the best route for them to explore is a more passive one: declare your intent and give the seed a chance to grow. If you feel you have some idea what direction you need to be looking, by all means, pursue a more assertive approach with fervor. But without some genuine indication of what you're looking for, you run the risk of trying too hard when trying to "force it," of squeezing your brain in such a way as to latch-onto the first random animal you think of, or one you might really want or really not want as a totem— or just the last animal you saw in a commercial.   As we have talked about before, it is important to recognize the difference between a true connection and just a desire for a connection; equally important is the difference between a true connection and random imagery generated by your imagination.

With this in mind, I feel the road I can best suggest is "putting out there" your intent and request to know your totems, honoring them the way that feels most appropriate to your heart, and then leaving it alone for awhile. There is wisdom to be found in the ability to step aside for a time, let things rest and resolve, and return later with a fresh mind and heart— as opposed to working the thing to death in a single sitting. It is also the crux of the metaphysical method of manifestation known within the wider neo-pagan community as "intent-based" magick.

The method of intent-based magick I will provide here will focus around what we call a Totem Wheel. Its design will help you focus your intention on what you want (the revelation of your totems) but allow you the freedom to step away, take a breather, and give your mind space to relax and become open to impressions from your spirit. The Totem Wheel is a variation on the common "vision board" practice, but it is also a form of meditational aid, similar in concept to things like mandalas. It can also become a handy tool to further explore your relationship to your totems, and will later serve as a means to help deepen the bond between you.

The Totem Wheel addresses the question of how one can honor or show respect to one's totems in a visual way if they are yet un-revealed. Recall I spent a bit of time explaining how displaying images of your totems in your home and work-place is the best way to honor them and incorporate them into your life; this chart will work as a stand-in for your totems until you have faces to put to them. And once you do have those faces, you can add them into the wheel design and continue to use it as a meditational and study aid. The **Totem Wheel** is a map of your nine totems that visually represents the elements and concepts your totems represent and their relationship to you. The design is a wheel with a central axle and six spokes, with circles containing symbols of each totem around the wheel and at the center. It echoes many existing metaphysical constructs such as a Celtic Sun wheel, the Wiccan/neo-Pagan Wheel-of-the-Year, the neo-pagan symbol for the element of Spirit, a variant of a Native American Medicine Wheel, and the Buddhist dharmakara. (See: Fig 2A)

You may scan and print-out the Totem Wheel I provide here, re-draw and color it yourself, or perhaps paint it on a

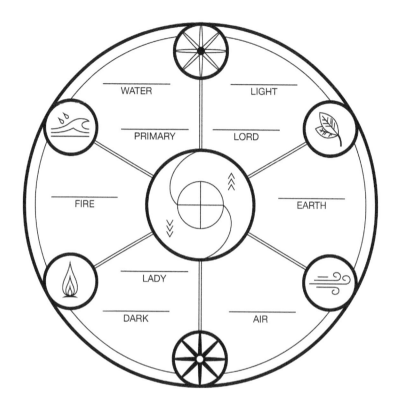

Fig. 2A: Totem Wheel

piece of hide or cloth if you want to get fancy. You can change-up the symbols if they don't feel right to you, just so long as everything is represented. When a totem becomes known to you, draw an image of the animal or write its name next to its circle; if a totem is already known, you may do this from the start. Depending on your feelings toward a cluttered aesthetic, you may wish to consider making two Wheels, one that is more neat and formal and another on paper on which you can write notes. I find that a meditation aid doesn't work as well for me if it's over-cluttered, but other people have had good success with the more modern concept of the intention board which is usually nothing but words, so apply your own judgement. Either way, you will need to leave space to write a few things under the representation of each totem.

Spend some time thinking about the different nine totems, how I have described them, and what these concepts mean to you. Hang your Totem Wheel in a prominent place in your home, or better, in a place near to where you meditate, pray, or just where you feel comfortable and at peace.

When you feel ready, take a moment to perform this simple affirmation ritual; I feel it is one of the most foundational and important, and is thus the only one included here in the main body of the book instead of being left to the rituals appendix (Appendix One). First, ground yourself (if you are not already familiar with the process of grounding, you will find a guide to the process with the other rituals.) Calm yourself, take several slow and deep breaths, pray for the blessing and guidance of Divinity as you understand it, feel you mind clear of distractions and your soul find a moment of clarity. Sit or stand before your Totem Wheel and recite the following:

The Declaration of Self

I Am
And I seek to know myself

I have come to a place in my life's journey where I
would know who walks with me
I have come to a time when I would know my
totems

Totem that is my true essential self; Totem of the
Mother, Totem of the Father; Totems of Earth, of Air,
of Fire, and of Water; Totems of Darkness and of
Light;

In the right time, in the right way,
in love and in light,
I have come to honor the spirits of my animal-self
and declare
my intent to learn,
to listen,
and to live in harmony with what
I Am.

After you have voiced your request, leave your Totem Wheel hanging at your altar or sacred place and continue with your day, at least for now. Repeat this affirmation *daily*. You'll want to remain open to any impressions you may receive, but don't force it; if nothing comes to you for a period of time, even days or weeks, don't be too concerned and try to remain patient. However, it is also quite possible that you may begin to be aware of at least some of your totems not long after you declare your intent; make note of any strong mental images, dreams, or experiences you have.

Now, once you *do* know a totem, you are ready to use your Totem Wheel for a secondary affirmation: to formally acknowledge your totem and its role as a face of your most sacred essential self.

After you have researched the Five Identifying Questions for each newly discovered totem and spent some time thinking about its nature, I want you decide what its five most dominant characteristics or qualities are (for you—there are no wrong answers). You may write those qualities here in the space provided, but I also recommend you incorporate them into your Totem Wheel in some way.

Characteristics of Earth Totem Animal

_____
_____
_____
_____
_____

Characteristics of Air Totem Animal

_____
_____
_____
_____
_____

Characteristics of Fire Totem Animal

_____

_____

_____

_____

_____

Characteristics of Water Totem Animal

_____

_____

_____

_____

_____

Characteristics of Light Totem Animal

_____

_____

_____

_____

_____

Characteristics of Dark Totem Animal

_____

_____

_____

_____

_____

Characteristics of Lord Totem Animal

_____
_____
_____
_____
_____

Characteristics of Lady Totem Animal

_____
_____
_____
_____
_____

Characteristics of Primary Totem Animal

_____
_____
_____
_____
_____

Once the characteristics for a totem are complete, insert them in the blank spaces in the affirmation for that totem to learn more about your essential self. One affirmation is included here as an example, and the rest are found with the rituals in Appendix One. In Wicca, the ritual of circle begins with calling Earth, so here is the affirmation as though written for the Earth totem as an example.

Affirmation of the Earth Totem

I am
Through my flesh, I am the Earth within me. I am the soil, the stone, and the trees. I am myself.
I am the (totem) within me. And I honor myself.
I am _____
I am _____
I am _____
I am _____
I am _____
I am the (totem)
I have come to know my true self
And I give gratitude, acknowledgement, love to myself, my essential self, my sacred-self, and I *accept* myself as
I am

You must incorporate the totem as part of yourself and understand that their identity is your identity. You must go beyond recognizing the totem spirit for its own sake and understand that you have become reacquainted with a part of your own soul.

The feeling of discovering a totem will come as an epiphany, as the realization of a profound truth, but one that on some level you knew all along. Do not worry about ambiguity; once your true totems come into your awareness there will be no doubt in your heart or mind. You are not meeting someone new, but rather reuniting with an all-but-forgotten old friend.

A Totem Guide

If you would like to uncover your totems with a more assertive approach but are uncertain what direction to take your quest, another suggestion I have is to enlist the help of a spirit guide specifically tasked with leading you to your totems. As we discussed previously, a spirit guide is an animal spirit that is not a totem but that comes to you from outside of the sacred self, and that comes into your life to teach you about a subject to which your totems may be inadequate. In this case, it is your own connection to and understanding of your totems that is lacking, preventing the natural flow of energy between you. It is an attractive opportunity to draw a facilitating tutelar spirit to you: a totemic spirit guide or **totem guide**.

Exactly *what* animal spirit responds to your request for a guide will be reflective of your current mental and emotional state and is not necessarily a matter for your choosing. *However*, it is completely within your realm of rights and abilities to formally request that such a guide manifest itself right here, right now. That is not to say that its help will be swift, or its messages clear and easy to interpret. But a bearer of human Will has the natural right to request a spirit guide show itself promptly— for this or any other task, for that matter. I have provided a ritual for requesting a spirit guide in the Rituals Appendix if you would like to make use of it. Your totem guide will likely be the next animal that comes into your awareness after you have performed our (or any other) ritual, prayed or meditated for such guidance, or otherwise declared your intent that your Will be done.

So how does one work with such a spirit guide teacher? If you decide you wish to pursue learning shamanic journeying (which will be discussed in the next chapter) then your totem guide is the perfect entity for you to practice seeking and learning from within the metaphysical landscape of that venue. But if you do not wish to learn journeying, the ways in which you may find yourself instructed by your guide could be a little more varied and difficult for me to predict and therefore describe.

To understand how your guide can help you (either with finding your totems or any other task) I always find the best first step is starting at the beginning: research the animal, and begin to answer the Five Identifying Questions regarding their niche in nature— their feeding and breeding habits, their social grouping, etc. Be open to any impressions of similarity between aspects of the animal and how you feel now at your place in your journey to seek your totems. Is the guide speaking to your current feeling of confusion, frustration, or stubbornness? An Aurochs may well be reflective of you stubbornly standing in your own way, and as you learn how he is moved, you too will learn to step aside. Is the guide speaking to what you should instead seek to cultivate? A Hawk might be saying you are getting too caught up in the details, and that you will find clarity in stepping back and looking at the big picture. A Horse might be telling you that you require the assistance of a knowledgeable group, or to otherwise heed the wisdom of those more experienced on the subject; whereas a Bear might be telling you to hold strong and follow your own instincts for how things are and should be.

I cannot tell you exactly how your totem guide will teach you; his or her lessons will be tailored to you and how you are able to understand what they have to give. Learn about the animal, honor the animal, and if you begin to receive mental images or impressions of the animal— especially when you are praying, meditating, dreaming, or otherwise in a sacred mindset— listen to what it has to say, and learn its animal-speak. It will give you what you need and point you in the right direction.

It is also worth pointing out that your request for a totem spirit guide could also simply draw one of your own totems to the surface, and that's ok. Remember that a spirit guide is there to teach you something that does not come to you naturally and instinctually through your totems— so when you actually do possess this knowledge, and just don't realize it, the totem that possess that knowledge is going to be the better teacher for the job. It's also fully possible that you may not realize your totem guide is one of your totems until it reveals so some time down the road. Spirits, unfortunately, can be tricky sometimes, and the only sound advice I can give you some days is just to trust your gut. Seek, and — eventually, though the path be straight or winding— you will find.

Chapter Two:
The Shamanic Journey

If you are ready to progress even further on your search and in your totemic work, it might be time for you to learn **Shamanic Journeying**, or the mental/spiritual discipline of active meditation. A shamanic journey is useful for initially seeking the totems, and I have designed several you may use for this purpose. However, it is also a useful way to communicate with your totems at any time, now or many years down the road.

Now, most people have heard of meditation and are at least vaguely familiar with what it means; essentially, both meditation and shamanic journeying are similar disciplines of the mind used to cultivate peace, calm, and heightened and focused awareness, but their distinction lies in their goal: generally speaking, **meditation** seeks a state of mental stillness, while **shamanic journeying** seeks a sense of travel or movement throughout the inner reaches of the spirit. In both instances, the mind is trained to be clear of all distracting, intrusive "mundane" thoughts and receptive to introspection, and is primed to interact with the totems within the playground of the mind.

Technically speaking, the modern western concept of "**guided meditation**" is more a shamanic journey than proper meditation, at least as far as Eastern traditions like Buddhism and Hinduism would be concerned, as the focus is on experiencing a series of visualizations, and traditional Eastern meditation would discourage embracing such active imagery as a distraction from the true goal of peaceful, empty stillness. But ultimately, I'm not going to quibble about the vocabulary, because that's really all it is. You may call these exercises "guided meditations" if you prefer (even as you would be "guiding" yourself). Nevertheless, the reader should be aware that the discipline of modern- or neo-shamanism has its own traditions and practices associated with it, and when one speaks of shamanism as a whole, there is far more to that tradition than practicing guided meditations.

To start, first recognize that there is a difference between a practitioner of **neo-shamanism** who identifies as "shaman" and a practitioner of an indigenous tradition (including that of the Saami people of Scandinavia from whom we get the word) who might also identify as "shaman." For most people within the neo-pagan community, a **shaman** refers to any person who interacts with and receives information from the spirit world directly, as opposed to through the interpretation of a religious authority, sacred text or ritual, or other outside media, often for the purpose of healing; most would also consider a shaman to be someone who creates their own rituals, practices, and general spiritual methodology through their own inspiration rather than accepting one of an existing tradition. [14]

A shaman may or may not use the methodology and cosmology provided by the founders of the tradition like

---

[14] It's similar to how one person might consider a "witch" to be any person who performs magick, creating change by manipulating spiritual energy by Will, while someone else may insist only classically trained Wiccans may use that title; there is no one right answer, only different opinions on proper usage.

Harner [15] and his contemporaries, which is what I refer to as neo-shamanism and what I will discuss below. Similar to our own totemic tradition, much of neo-shamanism is inspired by several traditional cultures but also built on the personal experience and knowledge of its creators. It is all-together modern in origin, and it has become a useful tool to be used by any spiritual practitioner, regardless of belief system, simply because *it works*.

Now, many practicing shamans (including myself) would agree that the neo-shamanic traditions fall more into the realm of guidelines than actual hard rules, as is the case with the pirate's code, and I personally believe that any instance in which a person enters into a altered or meditative state of mind and has meaningful interaction with what is found within the self has had a shamanic journey— regardless of what they did to get there. As you experiment with the example exercises I have provided, keep in mind these basic teachings of neo-shamanism, but don't be too concerned if your experience doesn't follow the map exactly. Your milage may vary.

Among other things, in Harner's neo-shamanism the metaphysical realm (that is at once of the spirit *and* of the mind) is referred to as the **non-ordinary reality**, or **NOR** for short. It emphasizes dividing the landscape of the NOR into a **three layered world**: the Upper World, Middle World, and Lower/Under World. This is a way of categorizing your experiences by characteristics understood unconsciously by all people, quite similar to the characteristics we observe in our totems and Jungian archetypes, except neo-shamans stick with just three: dark/past/primal in the Lower

---

15 Michael Harner (1929-2018): anthropologist, educator, and founder of the practice of what he called "core shamanism" which was foundational in the development of neo-shamanism. Often known by his first book, *The Way of the Shaman: A Guide to Power and Healing*

World, light/future/ideal in the Upper World, and the reality of the present in the Middle World.

A person metaphysically "enters" these Worlds by entering a quiet, clear, meditative state and visualizing themselves traveling upward, downward, or laterally across the metaphysical landscape (which is usually experienced as some sort of natural landscape) and exploring, seeking interactions with entities, or other such experiences with intent to find spiritual answers, healing, or other resolutions. Neo-shamans observe that a wide-variety of religious and mythological traditions, including many pagan, indigenous, and even Abrahamic and Eastern traditions, will also divide their concept of the "spirit world" similarly into three layers (or multiples of three, like the nine in Nordic lore), again suggesting something similar to Jung's collective unconscious at work.

Neo-shamans provide a variety of ways to enter the NOR, but the most commonly suggested is by drumming— though variations on rattling, chanting, singing bowls, etc. will also work. The practice becomes a means of *self-hypnosis*, in which listening to the repetitive sound allows the practitioner to ignore and therefore bypass the present-tense chatter of conscious thoughts and access the part of the mind that produces dreams— the part that thinks in symbols, metaphors, and impressions— and that is often better able to understand what we truly want or need than we're aware of. This state of mind is often called a **trance** state, and is essentially a state of wakeful dreaming, of allowing your unconscious mind to dream while you are relaxed but still awake enough to interact purposefully with the dream.

Consequently, a trance is more "awake" than **lucid dreaming**, controlling of one's dreams while fully asleep. It is also distinct from **astral projection**, in which the intent is to project the soul *out* from the body to travel the astral planes, rather than travel *inward* to the place where the soul and the spirit world intersect, which is the goal of a journey.

The benefit of the self-induced trance state is the total control one has over it— as compared to, say, being hypnotized by another person, or by entering a trance through hallucinogens. If at any point in a self-induced shamanic journey you become uncomfortable and want to stop, all you have to do is calmly return to yourself; you can get off the boat any time you want. If you are in a particularly deep self-induced trance, suddenly jarring yourself awake feels pretty similar to being suddenly woken-up from a deep sleep. It can be pretty disorienting, but for a healthy mind, there should be no harm.

Many books on neo-shamanism warn people quite dramatically of the possibility of spiritual harm that can befall a person who is shocked out of the NOR too quickly or otherwise incorrectly, usually resulting in something called "soul loss" in which part of you is "left behind" in the NOR (or at least feels like it is). In all honesty (and this is just my personal opinion: take it for what it is), most of that is hype to sell the thing; much of it may also be leftovers from the cultural traditions that inspired the practice, assumed but perhaps never fully challenged.

BUT, I want you all to listen to me carefully: I agree that such "soul loss" (i.e., psychological trauma or harm) is theoretically possible, but only so for the *experienced* practitioner— that is, it is my professional opinion that it's not physically possible for a mentally healthy *novice* shaman to enter into a trance state on their own that is *deep enough* to cause any such problems. The ability to get *out* of a trance state is the opposite side of the coin of the ability to get *into* one; therefore, by the time you have amassed enough practice at journeying to get into a very deep trance, you will have an equal amount of experience in waking up from one, and any aforementioned spiritual calamities can only occur in the deepest of trances. In my experience, in the beginning an individual is far, far more likely to have difficulty relaxing enough to embrace the trance state of mind in the first place. If you are mentally healthy, please don't concern yourself; you're going to be fine.

Those who *do* have mental illness of some type should proceed at their own discretion; I simply do not have enough experience with such situations to be certain of what is safe and not safe for such a person to do; when in doubt, I would ask your therapist or healthcare provider. However, I'm talking about heavy things like schizophrenia, dementia, PTSD, and psychosis presenting risk of "soul loss"; your run-of-the-mill suburban anxiety or insomnia are probably unlikely to cause any real affect. And while disorders of personality and mood such as narcissism, bipolar disorder, or borderline personality disorder will all but assuredly color-over shamanic experiences with the crayon scribblings of the disorder's influence, (e.g., a narcissist being told by the spirits that he was born perfect and requires no spiritual improvement whatever), I do not believe there is risk of any psychological harm presented in a shamanic journey, and only the risk of receiving inaccurate information.

The possibility of a "bad trip" does exist for those new to shamanic journeying, but it does not lie within the practice, it lies within the self. That is to say, if you have darkness within you, don't seek it until you are ready. If you have experienced trauma, anxieties, fears, have bad memories or pain or other bad news in your mind that could be a bad time to face, use common sense: don't seek it in the NOR until you're ready to face it. It may not even be the worst idea to exercise caution around your Dark totem until you're ready to face and accept your own darkness, but only you know how dark your darkness really is, so that's on you to reconcile. Depending on what you have had to face in your life, the same might be true with other totems —such as the Lord or Lady if you have had a toxic or abusive relationship with your parents, for example. It is my personal belief that truth ultimately cannot injure, only show us what *is*, but that doesn't mean it can't hurt like hell. Thankfully, unlike in the ordinary reality of the real world, if you don't like what you're seeing in the NOR you can just wake yourself up, take your football, and go home.

Now, one of the larger stumbling blocks when it comes to shamanic journeying by yourself is producing that drum-beat. Personally speaking, I have difficulty staying seated upright when I journey, let alone keeping a steady beat on a drum; it's like rubbing your belly and patting your head. Many of the books by Michael Harner suggest that the traditional or trad-shamans in the Amazon rainforests (from whom he derived many of his ideas for neo-shamanism) would always enlist the aid of assistants who would drum for them. More modern shamanic teachers, meanwhile, take a far more pragmatic approach and often include CDs of drumming tracks with their books. Both approaches are appropriate in different circumstances, but unless you are very comfortable with the person you ask to drum, you may find it a distraction to have them just sit there watching you. If you have the opportunity to perhaps take a class or seminar led by a more experienced shaman, then he or she will be able to prepare and maintain the atmosphere and metaphysical space for the participants by their drumming in such a way that journeying will be far easier. But if you are doing this by yourself, I would recommend that you just find an audio file of shamanic drumming online and listen to it with earbuds when you are ready to begin your ritual. If you put "shamanic journey" or "shamanic drumming" into YouTube or most streaming music services it will give you dozens of tracks you can listen to and test-drive. When you find some you like that work for you, download them for future use—and please pay for the files to show honor to the ones who composed them. Consequently, karma is an active force in the metaphysical community.

Be aware that most neo-shamans (and those who compose tracks of neo-shamanic drumming) will briefly increase the pace of the tempo towards the end of the recording; this means that the track is almost over, so you will need to begin taking steps to return to the ordinary reality— otherwise the sudden lack of sound may jar you awake against your will.

After that is taken care of, all you will need is a comfortable, quiet place where you can work undisturbed. If you keep an altar or sacred place, or otherwise have a place where you go to meditate or pray, go there. Lie down on the floor with a pillow or prop yourself upright in a comfortable chair. Don't lie in bed; you don't want to be so comfortable that you fall asleep. Distractions from the ordinary reality will yank you out of a trance faster than anything else, so set yourself up to win from the start; close the door, turn your phone to silent. If you plan to use one of the journeys I provide, I would also recommend you familiarize yourself beforehand with the steps I lay-out for each one. It is not possible to read and trance at the same time, so again unless you feel very comfortable with a friend giving instructions aloud to you while you do this, you will need to have the whole game-plan already in your head.

When you have completed your work, always allow yourself the kindness of waking up from a journey slowly and gently, just as you would on a lazy Saturday morning. Sit up-right to help wake yourself, but don't move too quickly; turn on any lights only after you are ready. Listen to your body and wake-up in the way that feels healthiest to you. If you feel a little drained or otherwise out of sorts, have a snack; eating is a very old and tried-and-true pagan remedy for spiritual fatigue.

You may wish to sit thinking about what happened to you for a time, but I highly recommend that you make notes of at least what you consider to be the most important aspects of your journey, because just like with a dream, no matter how vivid it feels in the moment you will more likely than not soon forget a lot of it. You may also wish to remember the details of the scenes you were shown, as you can return to the same sacred places in the NOR to facilitate communication with the same metaphysical entities.

An Interjection . . .

At this point in the exercises, I would like to proceed under the assumption that you have accomplished two things: one, that you have found your totemic spirit guide animal (or a very assertive totem animal who is ready to do the job), even if you haven't had much by way of interaction with it; and two, that you were able to enter a trance state and have an experience in the non-ordinary reality. If you have not, then you may want to re-visit the shamanic journey exercises and try again. If you aren't one-hundred-percent sure that the animal you found is truly your Guide, that's fine; and if you aren't one-hundred-percent sure that you "really" entered the NOR, or that your experiences there were "genuine" and not just your imagination, that's fine too. (Remember: the line between the two concepts is better ignored than examined, especially at an early stage.)

What I'm looking to get past is where someone just sat there listening to the shamanic drumming and nothing happened besides a mental review of the narratives I wrote, where "I don't know, you didn't tell me" was their answer to the observational questions I set throughout. If you are that person, if you really could envision and imagine nothing unique in addition to what I provided— then you really need to spend more time day-dreaming, frankly. Because if you are a fully-grown adult who doesn't know how to use their imagination, I legitimately don't know how to help you. Please, with love: I'm going to have to insist that you put down this book and pick up a good fantasy novel like Lord of the Rings or Harry Potter and come back when you remember that part of yourself. I'll wait.

. . .

But if you are still with me, I'm hopeful that at this point you are at least beginning to see the value in exploring what is within you through shamanic journeying. Yes, it is a means to explore the spirit world, however you understand what that is; but at the same time it is also the best tool I know of to explore the inner landscape of your mind and soul— the home of your essential self. It is a matter of seeing what is already inside you, of taking what at some level you already knew and turning it inside-out so you can really see it. Sometimes realizing that you already have an answer to your own questions is just that easy— and just that hard.

However, I am also aware that journeying (and/or guided meditations) isn't everyone's cup of tea, for a variety of reasons, perhaps unrelated to a lack of imagination. If that is the case for you, and you are sure you don't want or need to try any journeys, I would recommend ignoring the journey exercises and continue your search for your totems by trying the Totemic Circle ritual concept discussed in the next section.

Conversely, if the idea of things associated with magick or witchcraft traditions such as Wicca are unacceptable to you, knowledge of casting Circles is also not necessary to proceed along a totemic path (though your refusal of knowledge is your own doing). Neither is it a case where knowledge of one is necessary to proceed with the other, in regards to Shamanic Journeying and Circle casting. They are simply the two best methods we have amassed for communication with the spirit and the sacred self.

Chapter Three:
A Totemic Circle

If you have spent any amount of time within the pagan or broader metaphysical community, chances are good that you have at least heard of the ritual of "casting a circle." For some of my readers, an explanation of what a circle is and why it is performed should be unnecessary. But as with many other things we've covered, I am proceeding under the assumption that not everyone here is a practicing pagan, and so before we do anything else, we must briefly review what we're dealing with to get everyone on the same page.

Technically speaking, a magick or ritual **circle** is an area of space marked out or otherwise set aside with intent to raise metaphysical or spiritual energy within it, to create sacred space within it, and/or to provide spiritually protected space within it, to perform sacred rites therein; spiritual powers are called upon to bless, empower, and/or protect the sacred space within the circle and assist with carrying-out the work and the rite performed. The powers vary by tradition, but usually include the four elemental powers of Earth, Air, Fire, and Water, and some face of dualistic divinity expressed as the Lord and Lady. Some people may choose to cast a circle in the same location each time, such as in a grove of trees or around a largely permanent altar; others, whenever or wherever they deem necessary. It is sacred space that you erect as needed, and put away when finished. While other religions may erect brick-and-mortar temples to house their sacred spaces, think of a

Wiccan circle more like a pop-tent you carry with you for whenever you need shelter. Its clear and straightforward structure is also useful, as it helps practitioners mentally separate and focus on the sacred work taking place within the circle as a clear liminal experience and ignore the mundane regular world outside of it.

I will provide specific steps on how to cast your own totemic circle in Appendix One, but as always, remember that my directions do not have to be followed to the letter, and as the saying goes— you may do you, and make adjustments as you see appropriate. But the basic order of operations for casting a circle is as follows:

1) An appropriate place is selected (or reused) and spiritually cleansed, blessed, or sanctified. This can be done according to any tradition or preference.
2) A circle is drawn around the space either mentally or by using a magickal tool such as an athame or wand, and sometimes by also walking around the space, while envisioning and invoking a line of sacred energy at the edge of the circle. Traditionally in Wicca, this is done clockwise (or "deosil" in the lingo). All those involved will stand within this circle for the entirety of the rite.
3) Each of the four Elements are called upon, at each of the four cardinal directions, to hold, protect, and empower the circle; they are often referred to as "Quarters." Sometimes they are called just as energies, and other times through embodying sacred entities such as the Wiccan Watchtowers, the four Winds, Archangels, or other Guardian Spirits such as animals. Traditionally, one begins with calling Earth in the North, Air in the East, then Fire in the South, and Water in the West, but this does vary by tradition and practitioner.
4) The deity or deities are called. Traditionally, a representation of the dualistic sacred masculine and sacred feminine are called, either through a god and goddess pair from pagan cultures (Odin and Frigg,

Zeus and Hera, etc), or a less specific expression such as the Earth Mother and Sun Father or Greenman, or even just "The Lord" and "The Lady." In many Wiccan traditions, proper circles are raised by both a priest and priestess, and they will invoke the essence and invite the Lord and Lady to share the body of one another, but this is not necessary. Monotheists may also simply call "God" in whatever form they prefer.

5) Sacred energy is raised and the purpose of the ritual is expressed. This aspect of the circle is the most flexible. It is when you declare why you have cast a circle in the first place— to raise a spell to make something happen, to honor the versions of deity you worship, to celebrate a sabbat or other sacred day, to call-upon a spiritual presence for help— and raise the sacred energy necessary to make that happen. This can be done through mental concentration, sacred sound such as chanting or drumming, and/or prayer. The idea is to fill the interior of the circle full to bursting with this sacred energy and intent. When it reaches a peak, release it all at once into the universe toward its goal.

6) A libation is consumed. Typically, this involves consuming "cakes and ale," or some sort of bread with some sort of alcohol, but what foods specifically are used is not set in stone. The intent is two-fold: it is a means of honoring one's deities and sacred spirits by sharing food with them, and it is also a means of grounding and regaining balance and strength after the spiritual exertion of raising and releasing energy in the previous step.

7) All sacred powers that were called upon are thanked for their assistance and released, and the circle is taken down. Typically, it is believed most appropriate to (politely) *tell* the elemental guardians to leave, but to *inform* any faces of deity that they are free to "go if they must, stay if they will," as a form of respect to higher beings who should not be bossed about by a mere witch. After releasing the powers that were invited, the

circle itself is taken down by walking around it in the opposite direction (counter-clockwise, or "widdershins") or otherwise repeating the actions taken to raise it but in reverse.

Despite its origins with Wicca, other witchcraft traditions, and other ceremonial magick traditions, use of the ritual circle in this form has been expanded in its usage by a wide variety of contemporary metaphysical practitioners and traditions, and has been used at least at some point by nearly every practicing pagan. Part of the reason why is its flexibility and adaptability, as it allows any god(s) and/or goddess(es) of any belief system to be called upon without changing the basic structure or purpose. Further, a great many traditions and belief paradigms use (or at least acknowledge) either elemental energies and/or sacred directions— and if not, I know of no belief systems that prohibit it. (I even have a very free-spirited Christian friend who feels no qualms about calling Jesus into her magick circles! And Enochian or Angel Magick is a tradition in its own right.) In contemporary times, the Wiccan circle has seen so much imaginative reinvention and broader application that it's not necessarily incorrect to think of it — now, with apologies to traditionalist Wiccans— as simply a spiritual tool that can be used by nearly any belief structure, not unlike yoga, meditation, shamanic journeying— or totemism.

So at this point the reader is obviously aware of some similarities between the structure of a Wiccan circle and the positioning of one's totems according to our totemic tradition, minus a few tweaks here and there. This is a good point to remind said reader that while it is true that our system is a modern creation, it is built upon several existing metaphysical patterns that span many independent cultures and belief systems — and the structure of a Wiccan circle is one such pattern. While traditionally,

Wiccans only call four elements to a circle, there is no reason one cannot call six, and include Above and Below; in fact we have seen circles cast this way many times. Especially when a circle is raised in this way, it resembles a sphere around the practitioner— a structure not at all unlike the way your elemental totems metaphorically "sit" around you at any given time. When the Lord and the Lady are called to the center alter or invited to share our space or our bodies, then we have the Divine Male and the Divine Female on either side of us within the circle. And when we acknowledge the sacred center point— you, the person performing a sacred rite— we have the sacred center.

And we can take things a step further. In the same way traditions such as Wicca will call specific entities such as Watchtowers or Winds to sit as guardians of the energies of the Quarters, and in the same way someone might choose to call a specific god and goddess pair such as Brigid and Lugh to bless and oversee the sacred work therein, it is fully reasonable for a modern totemist to call and evoke *each of his or her own totems* to sit at each position when casting a circle. We refer to this as a **totem circle**. As each of your totems represents your soul's own personal connection to the elements and the qualities of energy they embody, it is our opinion that a totemic circle is the most direct means a person has to access, hold, and manipulate the forces that are invoked in a magickal circle.

There are many other benefits to casting a totem circle in this way. For one, it is a means to better visualize and experience your metaphysical relationships to your own totems, to "see" yourself in the center while surrounded by the forces, concepts, energies that are expressed in your animal self. For another, it can provide valuable tutelage for someone who may experience difficulties summoning the elemental energies, or maybe just that "certain one" that's always trouble, in a magickal context. And for the energetic veterans out there, it provides more than a window into understanding the depth and breadth of the elementals; it provides a direct portal between yourself and the energies, keeping in mind that your totems represent *your unique connections and pathways* to those energies. You relate to the element of Fire through your Fire totem, as it is the part of your soul that *is* Fire, so there is no one better than the Fire totem to show you what Fire can really do.

Conversely, casting a totem circle when any of the totems are still unknown can be a very direct way to uncover and learn those totems. If you were to invoke South by calling "my totem of fire" (without an animal to name) then you are essentially opening a direct pathway between yourself and the fire energy. You will be able to see and *feel* down through that connection and have a considerably less obstructed view of what animal lies between yourself and the infinite elemental— especially while you are surrounded by sacred energy in spiritually protected space.

However, please be forewarned that casting a totem circle does carry some liabilities. *A totem circle is not only powerful, but intimately personal for the one casting it.* Each of your nine totems are *you*, are an aspect of your very soul, and I would consider it very wise to exercise caution when choosing whom you invite— literally— into your soul. A totem circle is fine for just yourself, and can be a significant thing to share with a close friend or loved one, but inviting anyone else would put the caster into a position of intense vulnerability. It is the sensation of being naked, magnified many times over. I mention this specifically because circles are sometimes rituals that are shared with a group, with a coven who practices together, or even in public space, and I don't want the reader to feel that casting a totem circle needs to be anything other than an invite-only affair. Know yourself, know and understand what you can handle and what you are comfortable with, and act wisely.

Someone who has done any additional reading on the subject of totems may have come across the idea that it is inappropriate, even dangerous, to reveal to others what your totems are, as they hold personal esoteric power that might be misused by those who wish you harm, or that otherwise might "give your power away," to put things how a Wiccan would. Clearly, as I have mentioned all of my totems in this book, I do not share this sentiment. However, my totems do each carry proper personal names, and we (my totems and I) consider *those names* to be what holds the sort of personal power intended when this discussion arises, and not just the type of animal they are. (Consequently, a list of all of my totems as well as my husband's can be found in Appendix Four.) Personally, I feel there is little risk in talking about the animal itself (provided the listener isn't in a position to cause harm by discrimination against pagans, of course), but I save their personal names for the expression and invocation of their more intimate spiritual power. Anyone who asks is usually told that Jaguar is my totem, but only two people on this earth know his name. However, this is just my personal view, and is not necessarily shared by all totemists, including my other half. How much of yourself you feel safe and comfortable sharing with the outside world is a personal matter, unique to you and your life's experiences — and perhaps even to the predilections of your totems themselves— and you will have to learn for yourself where you draw that line.

PART SIX
Advanced Introspection

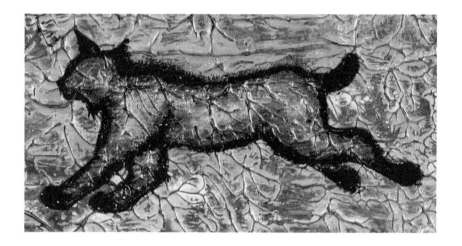

At this point in our shared journey, dear friends, if you have considered my advice and taken it to heart, if you have made an honest voyage into the sacred inner layers of your soul and found there the many faces of yourself, you can rightly claim that you walk a path of totemism. You may not know them all, and you may never know all there is to know of them; see that the learning is the progress of your life's journey, and that the desire to understand is its own resolution. From here forward, you can learn as much from them, if not more, than from me or anyone else.

From here, we will be proceeding under slightly different context. Here you will find an introspective look at some questions and some ideas involving a somewhat more advanced perspective of the fundamentals of the path of the totem. Much of what will be discussed is theoretical, ideas based in knowledge but hypothetical in terms of evidence. Much of the lack of data on some of these topics lies with the fact that there simply aren't enough people in the world who know their animal selves in the detail required for us to answer these questions— or at least who have shared that knowledge with us. However, I hope you will find these topics insightful and be able to apply them to your own journey in some meaningful way.

I would also like to highlight the reason *why* these topics have remained in the hypothetical for my other half and me: our lack of knowledge on how totems are understood and experienced by the demographics discussed, which include children, multi-generational family members, non-Americans, survivors of trauma, and members of the LGBTQ communities. We have had some discussions with people from these demographics when available, but just not enough, and not in enough detail to move our observations from the realm of pure theory into a more comfortable and concrete observation.

While up until this point I have gently reminded the reader that the information conveyed concerns our personal tradition and is not open for debate— from this point forward I would welcome feedback from readers (of all stripes) to add to our body of totemic knowledge.

Chapter One:
Emergencies vs Trauma — Totemic Crisis Shifts

One of the most beautiful and valuable properties of the multi-totem structure is its ability to adapt to changing circumstances. As we discussed previously, your uniquely human property of Will gives you the ability to choose one behavior or reaction over another. It also gives you the ability to instinctually, reactively, or emotionally change from the influence of one totem or another without you having to think consciously about the process at all. It is reflective of a normal, healthy, balanced mind to shift from the influence of one totem to another to ride out the dips and bumps and other challenges of living a life on this big blue rock.

But for some, life brings more than rough-patches; if it turns into trauma or abuse, it can cause a more serious psychological shift as an adaptation to living with that pain or fear or darkness. It doesn't happen to every person who has suffered abuse or trauma, and it doesn't happen the same way every time. But sometimes a person can experience an event so difficult to cope with that their totems may shift in reaction to it— and they never shift back. We refer to this as a **crisis shift**. For example, it is possible to encounter a scenario in which one totem, let's say the Lord or Lady totem (though it could be any of them), has "taken the driver's seat" within a person's soul and stayed there so long it's taken on the functions of the

Primary totem more or less permanently and become the de facto "driver."

In this situation, it can be very difficult to find common ground with a new totem seeker if they feel they are certain about their totems and unwilling to consider otherwise, but the subject bears hearing out, as my husband and I have seen it happen numerous times with several individuals. While it is only fair to say that we can only speak with one hundred percent confidence about our own totems, we are as certain as we can be that we have seen this happen in others. Of course, such a person seeing an potential crisis shift in themselves would require a high level of honest introspection and an earnest desire to confront and move past the trauma, which not everyone is prepared for or even able to do, and therefore they are likely to never understand this crisis-shift has happened—or admit to themselves that is has.

Unfortunately, it's a sobering thought to consider that nearly everyone in this world has experienced something painful, awful, and traumatic at some point in their lives. However, a totemic crisis-shift is still a relatively rare thing to encounter. So how does this work? I cannot with any certainty say what sorts of trauma are "enough" to trigger a crisis shift and which are not. It is almost certainly going to be different for each person, and it would be no different than in the field of psychology where it just isn't clear why witnessing the same horrible event might give one person PTSD and another not. We have often encountered people in the pagan community who have suffered and survived many types of terrible abuse, which I personally cannot even fathom, and yet their essential selves ring through clearly and in natural order. Meanwhile, another person who indeed has experienced a totemic crisis-shift may have "only" suffered an oppressive or emotionally unavailable parent— something that would seem objectively to be far less severe.

It should never become a contest as to who had it "better" or "worse" when discussing trauma, as every individual copes differently. So similarly, if you are a survivor, please do not assume you are necessarily "more likely" to have your totems out of order in a crisis shift; conversely, if you argue that "other people have had it worse than me," don't necessarily rule yourself out.

So how exactly does one go about discovering a totemic crisis shift if it is such a subtle thing? There are two ways we see it expressed, usually at the same time. The first way is one that will be far more obvious to an outside observer: the individual is insistent that their Primary totem is an animal that does not at all match the character of their personal energy or personality. And it must have gone well past the point where the individual is green to totemism, or just hasn't put the work in, and is simply incorrect and very stubborn about it. These are situations in which the person has been involved with metaphysics (or at least other spirituality) for some time and claims to have known of their totem "for years," and yet everything about their demeanor and body language, their tone and what they do and do not say, their awareness of the group and attitude toward it, the unconscious essence with which they interact with the world— suggests an entirely different animal than they claim. When they do express characteristics of the professed animal, it reads in some way as forced, adopted or put-on, fake, or insincere— or tinged with an undertone of fear or strain as though it is difficult to hold onto. After working with totems as long as we have, you learn to "smell" these things: the distance between a person's character and their Primary totem animal should be very short, and it is simply not as complicated a connection as the excessive prolixity of this book would make it appear.

There always exists the possibility that they are just wrong and very stubborn. But I begin to become suspicious once I see the person's reaction to such a suggestion. Do they chuckle or huff and just politely shake their head? Or do they become defensive, protective, even aggressive at the suggestion of the "wrong" animal? If I am wrong then I am simply wrong, and an incorrect suggestion doesn't harm anyone, so what do they have to get so defensive over? If the conversation begs the question, "Who are you trying to convince? Me, or yourself?" then I do wonder if something within them is out of order. Sometimes we are simply dealing with a person who doesn't know how to handle what they perceive to be an "attack on their beliefs." But other times, they are pushing aside a little voice inside of them suggesting this basic white witch has a point. It may even be directly influenced by the crisis totem who has assumed control and is unwilling to abdicate power.

The second and, unfortunately, much more subtle indicator that a person might be "driven" by a crisis totem is what I'll have to call profound imbalance. This would have to be something beyond someone not having their life together or their ducks in a row, and well beyond the chaotic dysfunctionality of your typical manic pixie train-wreck. I'm talking about someone whose entire personality seems to have been skewed, twisted, or altered by their traumatic event or abuse into something you feel instinctually is abnormal, a person who could well be described by the Southernism "he just ain't right." They are angered by things, or scared of things, or stressed-out by things that should not logically inspire those reactions. This state of mind will almost always be coupled by the person denying or deflecting the suggestion that they are in some way unwell. In this case, no animal information would be necessary— either that inferred from the projection of their energy and personality, or from their own account of metaphysical relationships— their true totems would not be visible. Someone who seems out of touch with a healthy mind-set, to be hanging on to the precipice by their fingernails, would clearly be in no position to see their true

Primary totem. Whatever secondary totem is helping them cobble-together something that approaches functionality would likely be terrified of the consequences of giving up the driver's seat — and would likely do whatever it could to prevent further disruption within the person's soul.

Of course, that last paragraph especially makes it sound like I am only referencing very dramatic, visible types of trauma, like surviving rape or returning from combat, and that really is not the case. As an example, the most common type of crisis totem I have personally observed at work in others is the Lord totem taking over within a woman who has suffered long-term abuse at the hands of a man, either a father or a husband. That abuse doesn't have to have been physical or sexual either, and in fact psychological abuse might very well be the key here. But what happens is a woman is taught, at an unconscious level, that femaleness is weak. Maybe their father was overbearing and dominating, maybe there was an oppressive religious element involved where they learned a woman must obey a man the way a man obeys God. And maybe their mother never stepped up to protect herself or her daughter from those ideas. But at some point in her life, this woman could no longer see potential worth or power in the female aspects of herself and so began to repress much of her true self and cling to the masculine as the only aspect with any value. It is far, far too common a mistake for a woman who's coming into the pagan world discovering the Divine Feminine within for the first time: she calls out to her "power animal" and the one who shows up is her Lord totem. It was drilled into her from a young age that femaleness was secondary to maleness, so within her, maleness had no choice but to assume the driver's seat.

It can be difficult for these women to face the suggestion that their true power and identity may yet be untapped beneath their pain and the lesson of unworthiness, and that the animal spirit who has guided them in dreams and meditations, who has stood up for them and spoken up through them when they needed defending, is not the face of their true essential self— he is but an incomplete fraction of it.

I have also seen similar situations with men. Sometimes, it is drilled into a young boy by a father-figure that anything female is weak and weakness is unacceptable, so their Lord totem eclipses all else as part of their struggle to reconcile with toxic masculinity. For others it could be from their relationship with their mothers, who might have been neglectful, distant, or abusive toward them or to their fathers— or perhaps she stood by and did nothing while their father abused them. Or perhaps they unconsciously rejected the influence of their fathers so much that they identified *only* with their mothers.

Parents, spouses, and the interplay of sex/gender often have the strongest influence, as they affect us so profoundly and often so early in life and play such a big role in how we understand ourselves; usually it is the Lord or Lady totem that takes control as a crisis totem, and as they are the most developed after the Primary, they can do a decent job and be difficult to spot. But it is also possible for a child to learn early that only anger and violence can protect them, so the Fire totem jumped forward, or they learned to repress all emotion as harmful and the Air totem took over. What an explosively unmanageable — and suffering— child they would have been. I have seen videos of people born and raised in cults and fundamentalist religious compounds and tried to see in their eyes if the harsh dogma of their world has forced the Light totem — or the Dark — to become implanted where individuality should have grown and flourished. In theory, any of the nine totems can assume command as a crisis totem.

Now, at this point, an astute reader has questions, and one of them is likely: what can be done about all this? How do you get the person's totemic alignment back to its natural order? But I'm afraid my answer is going to have to be a shrug of inexperience. A person who has a crisis totem in place of their true self has psychological trauma and needs the aid of a psychiatrist; suggesting otherwise would be above my pay-grade. I know the world is full of people who introduce themselves as "shaman" who claim the ability to pull toxins from your body and blow darkness from your mind, but if such magic exists in this world, you're not going to find it charging by the hour and asking for a Google review afterward. I'm not going to lie and suggest I can provide a path toward healing for a person I've never even met— anyone who says otherwise is selling something. Healing the essential self cannot be done externally, and it cannot be done casually. Such a person likely has years of hard work ahead of them to find peace with what happened, and only then can the true totems be identified.

This leads into the other question a reader might have: what if this method of coping is working well enough for the person? Do they necessarily have to correct it? After all, what difference does it make what their "true" totem might have been? If the one that has assumed prominence has functioned in that role for so long, why not just accept it as the "new" Primary totem?

My answer would be no, no one ever "has to" do anything, especially with regards to the spirit. Depending on the person and what happened to them, they may neither want to nor be able to face the trauma, and if their mind has found this way to get through life, then I would wish them well and leave them alone. The only important information to take away would be that they are missing out on valuable lessons about themselves, that there is a healthier and more honest way for them to live; there is a core part of their personality they likely have not seen since childhood and they may well owe it to themselves to give it a chance to flourish. But, as I said, much depends on the individual and the extent of their trauma. If they don't want to, or insist they have no reason to, then leave it alone.

In a situation in which a crisis totem has played the role of driver for so long, it really does beg the question of whether it is appropriate to simply call it the "new" Primary totem. After all, anyone who has done any further reading on totemism has likely encountered the belief that totems come and go simply as they are needed, that they are not permanent and can change many times throughout a lifetime. I have attempted thus far to make the point that the core of who you really are never changes, meaning that your totems always remain the same. But what do we do when it seems the "core" totem *has* changed in this way, at least in a functional sense?

Really, we are getting into such fine detail about the semantics that my response is a technicality. But I would insist that the situation is not unlike a step-parent who has assumed the role of primary parent for most of a person's life. A "true" or birth parent can contribute nothing (or worse than nothing) to the growth and well-being of their offspring, while a responsible and loving step-parent is the one honored with the title of "mother" or "father." They may have been your parent in every sense of the word, but yet there is still the technicality that they are not your "real" biological parent. And even if you never know them or choose to have nothing to do with them, there *is* knowledge about yourself to be found in knowing who your "real" mother or father is. It would be like that with crisis totems. Although, I will say that in some situations the shift may not be so functional or organic; the metaphor would change to a grandmother who has no choice but to assume the role of mother toward her teenage daughter's offspring, or an older brother who has to grow up too fast because he has to assume the role of father to his siblings. The situation suggests a level of stress put on the one who stepped-up, some degree of sadness or tragedy, and an imperfect fit within the role. It may be functional, but it is simply not ideal; as with a crisis totem, it is not natural.

Now, having said all that, we also encounter a situation I call a **lesser crisis shift**, which involves someone learning inappropriate and/or unhealthy reactions to situations, or where life has taught someone to respond to situations either with the wrong totem or with an inappropriate action on the part of that totem. And while true crisis shifts are rare, many people make lesser crisis shifts and have unhealthy coping mechanisms in one area or another. They are a lot easier to spot than full crisis shifts, but still difficult to change, as they represent perhaps a limited number of learned negative behaviors in a sea of personality that may or may not have serious impact on a person's life.

Now, it's true that how you react to things is a unique aspect of your personality, and for most issues, there are always several different but perfectly valid ways to respond — i.e., there are more than one totemic shifts that would be considered a healthy and balanced response. Rather, a lesser crisis shift is when the totem that responds is obviously and inarguably *wrong* for the situation, producing behavior that is unhealthy and possibly detrimental for the person.

For example, if someone is shown love and affection by a friend and they respond by getting angry, I would consider that a lesser crisis shift. Typically, responding to love is the prerogative of the Water totem— to reciprocate, to get embarrassed or uncomfortable, or perhaps to become a little afraid. Or, passion or lust might be reasonable reaction of the Fire totem, or perhaps the person interprets their friend's affection as emotional vulnerability and the Mother (or Father) totem steps up to take on a parental role, to try and take care of their friend and make certain they also feel loved and cared for.

Anger, however, is a clear interjection of the Fire totem— in a negative and presumably harmful way. It's weird and inappropriate, and it's a difference most of us should be able to see even as it's difficult to express exactly why it's so wrong. It's simply an inappropriate way to respond. And of course there could be other totemic shifts that would be just as wrong, such as Earth jumping in to shut-down the person emotionally, or the Dark totem showing up to try and take advantage of that friend's vulnerability.

Almost always, such an inappropriate response has been learned, or rather, taught to the person by stressors, pain, or trauma they have experienced, or modeled to them by others such as their parents who had similar dysfunctions — a situation similar in character to that which causes a full crisis shift. One does not need to be a professional psychologist to see anger in response to love as a defensive reaction, to push the friend away because of a perceived risk of being harmed whenever feelings become too strong, or perhaps even due to a fear that the expressed feelings are a trick of some kind. When a person has been hurt in a traumatic way, a totem learns to shift into position to respond to every such situation as a threat even when it's not.

The good news is, a lesser crisis shift does not necessarily have to be as difficult to deal with as a true crisis shift. First, one must return to the question of balance and functionality — does the behavior and inappropriate shift affect your quality of life? If so, address the situation the same way you would any totemic imbalance: identify the animal qualities of the totems involved, understand why they are responding the way they are, and appeal to their counterpart positioned opposite to them to counteract their influence and pull you back to center. In this case, however, you will need to take an additional step: choose which totem you would like to respond instead of the crisis shift totem and appeal to it, focus on it, and purposefully invoke it in an offensive shift in those crisis situations. In time, with repetition and with conscious appeal to the totems by Will, you can train yourself to correct a lesser crisis shift into healthier behavior.

Chapter Two:
Other People's Totems

Enemies, Friends, and Frienemies

Depending on the predilections of your center three totems, you may or may not think of yourself as a "people person." My experience with the wider neo-pagan community has uncovered a fair number of us who prefer our pets to people, because only one of those speaks a language we understand. This is all fair, because after all as I pointed out, we seem to collect a higher than average number of solitary predator people without much instinct for fitting-in with the flock or the pack. Most of the time this may all be well and good and we can structure our lives to suit our own comfort. But realistically, as human beings who need to interact with the human world, we find ourselves in situations in which we simply *must* interact with "certain people" we would rather not (coworkers in the office, extended family around the table at Christmas, etc.)

Here is where understanding your totem's role in the natural world takes on its most practical application: if you're not getting along with someone, especially when there's no clear reason why and you just "don't click," there is almost certainly a totemic, an animal, reason for it. If you are a Crow person you may think of yourself as a clever, witty person with a biting sense of humor. But someone who sees you as a loud-mouth or a know-it-all is likely to have a totem that sees Crow as a nuisance, for example any large hunting animal he steals food from, such as lions and wolves and bears, or very small animals Crow might sometimes try to eat such as lizards, mice, or smaller birds. If you are a Dog person and quite used to the idea that you are fun, friendly, and that most people like you, you may be either disappointed or insulted when someone won't engage with your banter. But someone with a smaller animal may only be able to see you as a hunter instead of a friend, or they may be a solitary animal that doesn't socialize much at all, despite your instinct for it (visualize a puppy trying to get an uncooperative cat to play with it). And worse yet, I'm sorry to say that someone with a Wolf or Coyote totem may very well think of Dog as an idiot, a child-like fool with no shame, whom they would prefer to avoid— or forcibly put in his place.

Of course, it would seem that in order to make these deductions the other person would need to know and communicate their totems, but that's not necessarily true. Once you know yours and have spent some time thinking critically about how all the different *kinds* of animals fit together into the greater fabric of a natural system, you will find yourself able to make pretty astute guesses, either from the metaphysical energy the person projects or from simple deduction based on their behaviors. I will say that unless you know a person very well, or unless someone's totem is exceptionally keen on being seen and known by all, you will likely never be able to guess the exact species of someone else; guessing the animal's *kind* is as close as you can usually get (reference Part Three: Chapter Four if you need a refresher on our concept of *kind*). The *kind* of Primary totem animal they have is usually enough for understanding totemic interactions in this sort of situation.

Avoid the urge to label any person you find difficult with totem animals you simply don't like or that you think should be associated with terrible people — "rat!" "sheep!" "pig!" All totem animals are equally valid, and it could well be no more their "fault" than yours that the animal energy between you doesn't harmonize. And be aware there is also an equally good chance that the problem is entirely *you*, not them.

Now, as conventional wisdom goes, knowing is half the battle, but in this case it is *only* half the battle— the other half is understanding what you can do about it. You may very well understand *why* you and your braggart uncle don't get along— because he is some type of song bird who can't stop squawking and you are a Fox who understands the virtue of silence — and there's a very small part of you that wants to just eat him. But what do you do? One of the defining features of bird energy is that their ability to fly gives them a unique relationship to the hunter/hunted dynamic: danger can be avoided by flying away, so they would prefer to know about all potential threats out there rather than hide from them. Birds don't feel safe when they're hidden, they feel safest when they are *seen*— because they in turn can see who's watching. (Consequently, this is why most natural performers are Bird people, those crazy folk who say crazy things like, "I feel so safe when I'm on stage," when that would be the literal definition of hell for a Cat person— or Fox.) When you combine that with the fact that Foxes eat small birds, it might feel like a no-win situation.

However, there are ways. You can always decide to avoid the person, or to fight them. But I feel the most practical solution, and the most mature, is to seek a way to make interaction with them less combative and more productive. When you are driving on ice, turn *into* the slide, as they say. It ultimately doesn't matter who is "the real problem" when *you* make the decision to become the solution. One way is simply to find your peace with it; it really does make a difference to see a person as simply projecting the natural instincts of their totem, instead of seeing them as willfully behaving "wrong" according to the instincts of your own, and sometimes just knowing so is enough to make them seem far less offensive.

Another way is to purposefully draw on the energy of *another* of your totems, one that can harmonize better with theirs, who can show you how to better understand them and behave around them in a more productive way. Jaguar may have no basis for understanding Stag's desire to take over the herd, but Elephant does, even as the two herd structures are not exactly the same. Maybe you have a bird of your own somewhere in your nine who will let you banter and brag a bit about a few of your own accomplishments in a playful contest with your uncle, at least until Christmas is over. If he really does have a small bird totem, you may find he is not only not offended, but that he's been expecting that from you all along— because birds enjoy seeing who can squawk the loudest. If he reacts defensively and tries to challenge you or put you down, you need to reevaluate your guess, as that could be more befitting the behavior of some type of hierarchical pack or herd animal.

A third way you can use totemic wisdom in these situations is to appeal to the other person's totem directly. Using whatever method you prefer, whether that is journeying into the NOR, another kind of metaphysical ritual, or simple meditation, seek out the other person's center totems, and do so with an earnest heart. Project your request to end the discord and your honest desire to understand the person better. You can even do it intellectually, and spend some time studying and seeking to understand the ins and outs of how and why their animal *kind* does as they do. The more you understand the person's behaviors as a reflection of their innate animal way, the more you understand the person.

Always remember: very few people in this world do things they believe are "wrong"; rather, life has simply taught them a very different definition of what is

"right." Once you understand this truth, you gain power and control in almost any situation.

Now, you can also take this idea to the conceptually opposite, and more positive, side of the coin; this same technique can be used to better understand your friends and loved ones. For one, it will help you get to know them better, more intimately, with a higher-degree of understanding than you otherwise could. It can help you see just why you enjoy each other so well, why you "just sync" with their personality. You will no doubt discover very quickly that you tend to draw certain totemic *kinds* to yourself, and there are many *kinds* that always do seem to show up together between close friends, lovers, and within families. We will discuss the ins and outs of these relationships in the next chapters.

And of course, inevitably you will find yourself at the intersection between the two ideas just discussed: conflict with your loved ones. Clearly you would never want to avoid them or write them off in this case, so bridging the gap is the only healthy solution. And if you are going to be emotionally intimate with someone, and especially if you are going to share your living space, know now if you don't already that those small areas of static between you can mean the difference between a happy home and an ongoing argument over the same reoccurring non-issues. "I love her so much, I just don't understand why she *has* to do 'The Thing' all the time!" It can happen just as often with parents, children, close friends, and other family.

A good, mature, healthy way to bridge the understanding between you and the other person is to do so at the animal level. Get to know their totems as much as you are able, and when they do something you don't understand or that rubs you the wrong way, ask their totem to explain why they did it. As before, it is quite likely they aren't doing it on purpose to annoy you, and are instead simply following the inclinations of an animal who understands life a bit differently than yours does. If the other person is metaphysically aware, all the better, as that bridge is so much more easily built if both are fully aware of what needs to be done and why. But if the other person is not and has no understanding of totems, you can still use the insight you acquired to plan how you can discuss the problem with the person if they are willing to work with you. And if they are not willing, you'll need to consider the problem might be with the relationship itself.

The best examples I can pull here are from very close to home with my totems and my husband's. While Panthers and Canines are similar along many respects — adaptable, large apex hunters— one of their most obvious points of deviation is the topic of leadership. There is a good reason some Native Americans honor Wolf as a teacher. The alpha male and female of any pack will coordinate a variety of tasks for the pack, and even middle-ranked members who look to the alphas for guidance will share in educating the pups. The leaders are responsible for showing the others "the way" of their pack, and it is the responsibility of the others to learn and follow "the way." Our problem is that cats do not have a single "way" of doing anything, and it sure as hell isn't one they were taught by someone else. Now, don't get me wrong: Panthers (and other solitary predators) understand perfectly well the concepts of education and teaching, and learning from another when you don't know how to do something is fine. But the problem lies in perception. An adult Wolf can live its whole life following its leader and never once feel they are valued any less as an individual. But there is really only one time in a solitary hunter's life when they accept a student/teacher relationship: when they are cubs learning from their mother. Once grown, a Panther teaches itself, on its own terms.

So on a human level, the problems arise mainly in the attitude of a given suggestion. The canine person sees the feline person performing a task differently than he was taught to do it (read: incorrectly) and sees it as his responsibility to the pack as a whole to make sure everyone has knowledge of the most efficient and reasonable way to do things. Meanwhile, the feline person understands there to be multiple equally valid ways to do something. But more, what the Wolf is *providing* as a helpful suggestion for everyone's betterment, the Panther *receives* as a bossy, even patronizing correction— leaving Wolf to wonder what he did that was so offensive.

And sure, these kinds of issues could just be talked out, but the difficulty involved at a human level is in maintaining a clear, open mind and heart that is willing to listen instead of sussing out who is right. Most of us unconsciously believe our own way of thinking and doing is the "right" way— that is the influence of our own totems— but if we aren't aware of this objectively, it can be difficult to get around ourselves. This is where direct interaction with the other person's totems come into play: more likely than not, the other person isn't even consciously aware of *why* they do what they do— *but their totems are*. Meditate or enter the NOR and ask their totems to show and explain their ways so that the behavior of the human they're attached to makes sense to you. As with before, few people wake up in the morning intending to offend or hurt others. Some may do so with selfish intentions in mind, such as to express dominance to inflate a flaccid ego, or because they seek protective vengeance from what they perceive as attacks that may not really exist. But largely, you are more than likely simply trying to mesh two conflicting aspects of your animal characters, and it takes human intellect and Will to determine how to create a workable balance. The canine needs to appreciate that the feline feels respected when allowed to do things their own way, and that is worth more than ensuring things are done "right"; the feline needs to appreciate that nine times out of ten, the canine is simply looking out for them and sharing knowledge.

In time, a curious thing will happen. You will likely develop a relationship with the totems of your close friends, lovers, and family that will very closely resemble one with a long-term spirit guide animal. We can see how several related spiritual and metaphysical concepts will blend together: spirit guides come into our lives to help us learn things that are not instinctually part of who we are, to help better ourselves; people come into our lives not only to teach us lessons we would not learn otherwise, but to share in our lives and complete us in a way in which we didn't even know we were incomplete. We are most attracted to people who are much like ourselves, and yet who have talents, wisdom, ways of thinking, or other admirable qualities we do not; spirit guides exist to help us gain knowledge of instincts we do not naturally have or that we may have in a smaller quantity.

In a way, it would not be incorrect to say that our loved ones are the physical manifestations of what will be our most important, long-term, and beloved spirit guides. Wolf has become my spirit guide as much as Jaguar has become one to my other half. The special people in our lives become an important, and essential, part of our totemic spiritual journeys towards wisdom.

The Mating Game

As much as I have professed my distaste for the idea of totemism being simplified into some sort of system of geomancy, I am even more cautious of it being used like your auntie's newspaper zodiac, as a system that gives you a few vague traits and predictions about yourself based on your animal *kind*, culminating in saucy suggestions as to who you should and should not shack-up with— *"If you are a Rodent person you are shy but industrious, and are well-suited to be paired with some small Reptiles, Amphibians, Fish, Birds, and other ground-dwelling creatures; avoid Snakes, Raptors, and small to medium-sized terrestrial hunters."* It sounds like something that should be printed on the back of a Chinese restaurant menu, yet inevitably the subject comes up at every live event once the idea of certain *kinds* being compatible is mentioned.

Nevertheless, totems do, in fact, play an enormous role in all aspects of our lives including our romantic and sex lives, and there is value in discussing how the different *kinds* of animals interact in this regard. However, please do not misunderstand this section to be a list of "do's" and "do not's" in regard to romantic harmony. Remember everything we have discussed thus far about human Will and the ability to supersede or circumvent our instincts as necessary. There will be challenges and benefits to every combination of totemic pairing. Though some patterns have anecdotally proven themselves to be more beneficial or challenging than others, the lesson of the Gray applies here, in that there will always be exceptions to the rules. It all comes down not just to the influences of our totems, but how we decide to act on them that matters in the end. What I'm trying to get around here is a situation where it sounds like I'm saying you and your partner "should not" be compatible, and that is truly not the case. For every trend of interaction I will discuss, there will be a successful couple out there to prove me wrong— and *that,* consequently, is the most important point here. There are no *kinds* of totems that "cannot" pair in a successful relationship, only pairings that will produce *more* or *fewer* challenges.

All of that being said, however, it is also very true that a great many people in this world, if not damn near most of them, have chosen their mates without any knowledge of totems whatsoever; that is to say, they have done it entirely without knowledge of the influence of their respective

239

animal energies. They may not necessarily know exactly why they click with a certain sort of person, or why they have separate "types" they prefer for relationships and another for flings. Another person may find themselves involved in essentially the same bad relationship over and over again, unsure of why they can't find "a good one" because everyone they date is a substitute for their father. Another might understand at a deep intuitive level that they have found their soulmate only moments after first meeting them. This is where we see certain patterns emerging.

The first and foremost place to begin understanding such interaction is once again the Five Identifying Questions (Part Three: Chapter Five) and the discussion of ways totems will thus interact with one another across the metaphysical aisle. In a general sense, these same trends will express themselves between the totems of two people, but unlike an internal struggle within a single person, the interaction between two separate people will be exponentially more complex because their Primary (or most expressed) totem will always have eight other energies behind it adding further nuance and possible influence on thoughts and behaviors. You will still see the same basic sorts of interactions — a smaller animal will be intimidated by a larger animal, or an herbivore may be disgusted by a scavenger, etc. — but it takes on a new dimension with the additional element of human romance, attraction, and sexuality.

So after all that blather, what are the trends of such attraction? Within the pagan and larger metaphysical community (so to mean: among people who have some idea what their totems are) we often see the following: large solitary predator with large social predator; large or medium herd animal with same; raptor or intelligent bird (parrot, corvid) with small omnivore or predator; raptor or intelligent bird (parrot, corvid) with bear; large/extra large herd animal with large social predator; small herbivore with same; medium-sized predator/omnivore with same. Especially prevalent among the spiritually wise is the pairing of raptor/ intelligent bird with Bear, and a large solitary predator, usually a large feline, with a large social hunter, usually Wolf.

Now, while there are several *kinds* that seem to get along best with others in a similar category, it is a rare thing to see a successful partnership between people with the same Primary totemic *kind*— and almost never the same totem— and this can seem counter-intuitive at first glance. That is, one might think that two people with Primary Horse totems might be ideally suited to get along, but that is rarely the case.

I cannot for certain say exactly why this pattern of partnership exists, except to remind the reader that we humans require a partner that *compliments* and even *completes* us, not one who is exactly like us. While it may seem logical at first glance to date other humans whose totems seem similar to our own or that come from the same ecosystem, when we are looking at it from a spiritual, metaphysical standpoint (that includes the psychological element implied in the metaphysical) we come to see what matters is *harmony of traits,* which I will explain. We would see a Eurasian Hare person pair better with an American Box Turtle (another small sized ground dwelling animal) than an Eurasian Kestrel (an animal from the same part of the world) or an American Cottontail (another of the rabbit *kind*).

Our example of a Horse person is better suited to pair with a Deer, Elk, Goat, Bison, etc.— provided that one is predisposed to be a herd leader while the other is predisposed to follow, or that both animals have both male and female leadership in their herds. And while Horse is on the cusp of being just a bit too small, extra-large herd animals like Bison or Elephant who usually only lose the young or the old to predators might get along with a social hunter such as Wolf or Orca, provided they have a strong spirit and Will to lead, though probably no herd animals (save perhaps for an exceptional Elephant) are large enough to pair with Lion/Lioness. Meanwhile, the Horse person will likely find they instinctually place all other Horse people permanently in the "friendzone."

Of course, a pairing could also fall into the category I would consider one of the more volatile: when both animals are leaders or alphas with different, incompatible leadership strategies, or when leadership structure is otherwise incompatible. A Mare might be content to allow a Stag to lead if his methodology proves functional (even if inconsistent), but a Stallion might not like it that a Doe expects some degree of independence for part of the year — and that she will subject him to a yearly evaluation report. A nanny Goat may feel safe enough beside her big, strong Ox to follow him into battle against a large predator, but Ox risks losing her if he does not respect that his much smaller mate sees threats differently and is as disposed to run from danger as to charge it. An Elephant bull and a Bison cow may likely find themselves quarreling because each expects to see more initiative to take charge from the other, while a Bison bull and an Elephant cow might quarrel because each expects to be the dominant one in the relationship.

However, it should be noted that this issue does take on a different dimension when it comes to same-sex couples. A man who has relationships with other men (and who identifies as a man) will still have a female Primary totem— and vice-versa for women. Therefore, if both or either partner has a social/sex differentiated Primary totem, it is important to consider how those animals themselves get on in same-sex groups. Two lesbians with Elephant and Bison totems might get along perfectly well, as both of those animals have all-male "bachelor herds" that follow different social rules from the "main herd" of one dominant animal (male for Bison, female for Elephant) and the breeding females. Two gay men with Lynx and Fox totems would face no issues different from those of a straight couple with the same totems, seeing as those animals don't have sex-differentiated characteristics. People who fall in the middle of, or outside of, more traditional gender identity may be more likely to have Primary totems similarly without sex-differentiated characteristics, and might do well to avoid a Stag or a Doe of any persuasion who might unconsciously try to box them into a more binary identity.

We have often seen successful human marriages in the pairing of intelligent birds (corvids/parrots/raptors) with either a small omnivore/predator or with a Bear, despite the initial oddity. One point in favor toward such a partnership is that Bear is usually an omnivore, and when he does hunt he is too large to consider even the biggest birds to be food. Corvids and Parrots do live in a flock with a complex social hierarchy, but dominance is expressed differently and shifts so fluidly it is likely incompatible with any animal for whom group leadership is a largely permanent or long-term position. Rather, long-term relationships for such birds are their mates, the same as with Raptors who do not form flocks, giving them all many temperamental qualities in common with solitary animals. Bears are solitary and maintain individual territories, and when they come together to mate it is usually with one of the same bears from previous seasons whose territories overlap with their own, laying the foundation of having the same mate or mates every year that can easily become monogamy, serial monogamy, or committed polyamory in a human. And their omnivorous lifestyle gives them an intellect not dissimilar in character, and nearly equal to, such a bird.

To understand if two animal totems will be compatible in a human partnership, imagine the animals attempting to live side-by-side one another on some hypothetical landscape, putting geographical distance aside for the moment. Are those animals competing for the same foods? To hold the same type of territory? Is one looking at the other as a potential meal? Does one run away from the other? Do they snarl and fight? Or do they simply lift their noses to each other, perhaps walk in tandem for a time, while at the same time maintaining their own lives? Can they peacefully coexist? Coexistence, harmony, is the keystone requirement we're looking for here, the metaphysical equivalent of comfortable silences and happy, quiet nights together just watching TV— the bedrock of any solid relationship.

Predator and Prey — Attraction vs. Connection

One of the most important totemic relationship interactions we need to discuss is the unique and colorful interplay of the predator with the prey, the cat and the mouse. This is a dynamic that often shows itself in other modern totem books even if no other relationship types are discussed, and it would seem that the insight to be gleaned from such interplay goes back into ancient, ancestral wisdom, well past the overly complex needs of the modern dating scene.

One example is the lessons of many British and Irish myths, built upon the metaphor of the hunter and the hunted, the hare and the hound or the bowman and the stag, of the hunted in turn leading the hunter, and on both growing strong and canny and better for their interaction. The relationship can grow into a wider metaphor of challenges or goals that are set by the one who would be claimed for the one who would pursue that prize. The hound chases the stag, and the stag leads the hound where he wants him to go. The stag fights for the right to the hind by fighting the other stags, and the hind chooses the stag who beats the others. The queen sets a quest to find a husband superior to other men, and the man who wins the challenge assumes his right to the queen— and her kingdom— as his reward. It is a powerful, perhaps infinitely complex metaphor for our lifetime's worth of challenges from nature, from Fate, from the gods, from ourselves, the way they intersect with our own choices and free Will, and the continual evolution of the Self through want, choice, training, trial, victory, failure, and learning.

So, then, I must ask my astute readers: what would happen between two people whose totems interacted as hunter and hunted? In the short-term? How about in the long-term?

Now, to clarify: I am referring to a consensual sexual and/or romantic interaction between two people who have a predatory animal and a prey animal as Primary totems. I am *not* talking about rape, or of targeting sexual partners non-consensually. When I reference this dynamic of predator/prey energy in a romantic partnership, I am speaking about the metaphysical and magickal ramifications of forging a long-term relationship under such conditions.

Rather, an otherwise healthy and consensual partnership built upon a predator/prey *totemic* energy dynamic can be incredibly useful on a lot of fronts, as well as a lot of fun. It becomes a creative partnership, a productive one, an emotionally exciting and intellectually challenging one. Your interaction is exciting, passionate, interesting, a fiery back-and-forth of thoughts and ideas and creative output. I would recommend that every person bless themselves with having such a relationship in their lives, at least once, for while it may be challenging to maintain— the proverbial 'wild ride'— you will grow as a person in a sense that cannot be achieved any other way.

But such a relationship is not the foundation of a healthy marriage. Yes, I know I said earlier that there is no totemic combination that makes it *impossible* to work as a long-term romantic relationship, but more so than any of the others (combined), the hunter with the hunted will raise challenges that are exceptionally difficult to work with—and are often insurmountable. I do not want any friend or relation to feel singled-out in this work so I will not name specifics, but my other half and I could count on two hands the number of failed marriages and relationships we've seen that were based on a totemic predator-prey relationship. You need the benefits of this sort of relationship in your life, but you would be wise not to marry it.

However, that is a thing much easier said than done. For every failed relationship we can name, the counterpoint arises that the relationship blossomed in the first place, so there must be something to such a pairing that makes a great many people believe it's a good idea. That reason is attraction. It would be easy to say a hunter/hunted dynamic produces lust, but such a word is far too limiting, as the energy between two such people can be far from merely sexual; it can be intellectual lust, emotional lust, a desire to be around that person that can very easily be confused with the sort of deep, spiritual connection you'd expect to have with "the one." Obsession is another word that comes to mind. But it is *attraction*, not *connection*, and there is a difference.

As an apex predator, I have only experienced this sort of relationship from the hunter's perspective. (Any instances of intimidation I've felt from another person's totem are based in other types of fear, not that of prey). The feeling is of intense interest, of a desire to "figure out" the person, get them to teach me everything about the unique and beautiful way they think and believe and imagine, and if they are complicated in a way I have never seen before, all the better. The Jaguar's usual foods in the wild are animals like Capybaras, but if you take a moment to search the Internet for wild Jaguar videos, you'll see they fall into two camps—

successful normal hunts, and funny interactions with unusual animals they don't usually hunt like Anteaters and giant, aggressive River Otters. There's regular, easy prey— and then there's interesting, challenging prey, prey that could bite back. I love the bite-back kind more than any other game or puzzle.

But unfortunately, at a human level, this means there will come a point where I've "figured out" the other person, I've leveled them, I've worked out how best to challenge them to think and to grow, I've decided how smart they are, how right or wrong they are. And while I will continue to care about this person, it means I've figured out how I would "defeat" them, the way I would go about hunting this unusual prey. Once I've worked out how I would go about trying to eat the Porcupine, there will come a point where I either have to try and do it — that is, challenge the person, outwit them, and win — or withhold my desire to challenge them and possibly grow to resent them, through no fault of theirs. It's not something I choose, it's just the way it happens. In severe cases, I have had to step away from friendships for this reason.

All of these relationships for me have been friendships with other women, and they were difficult enough without having to add the element of a romantic, sexual relationship— which I can assure the reader would absolutely have happened had the Anteater in question been a man.

However, my other half has helped me to understand that I am not able to fully appreciate the energy of a predator/ prey relationship through my Primary totem, and so at a personal level I am missing much of what it has to offer. Jaguar is an ambush predator, one who usually waits for the prey to come to him, to get into position, and simply chooses when or if he will strike— and if he misses, the prey runs away and the hunt is over. This is very different from the process of tracking prey, of sighting it, studying it, initiating the chase, following it, keeping up, keeping pace, adapting as it changes direction, observing its cleverness, and of exercising your own wit and Will to keep to their heel and close the distance. And even if the prey wins, there is value in the exercise, in the practice— and you can always keep trying.

A Wolf, like a hound, doesn't necessarily hunt just for hunger and enjoys the chase for its own sake. My other half enjoys a friendship like this with a friend we have (whose Primary totem is unknown; we suspect Giraffe and an Intelligent Bird in her center three). Some people would say their banter has "chemistry." And that assessment isn't wrong, but that chemistry just isn't romantic. It is the interplay of a Wolf and a clever animal who gives Wolf a run for his money.

In a way, a good chase between predator and prey isn't really so different than a relationship between a teacher and a student when both are engaged, committed, and excited about the topic, so it's no wonder to me it's something an alpha Wolf naturally understands. The master leads and instructs the pupil, and as he grows, the pupil instructs the master. For anyone interested in assuming a teaching role (especially, perhaps, in a spiritual context) it is advisable to study the interplay of the hunter and the hunted to understand how best to engage with a pupil— or a teacher. Sometimes, Jaguars do stalk prey, even if it's only for a little while, and it's something I'm working on keeping in mind in regard to my writing and teaching.

But back on the subject of romance, a romantic relationship with a predator and prey dynamic is a mistake that's easy to make, especially toward the beginning of a new relationship when it seems like such a good thing that you find them so engaging; you can't go a few minutes without thinking about them, or texting them, when you're together they occupy all of your attention— and they are great in bed. But that's the nature of the interaction of predator and prey energy: *it is never still.*

If you put a Hawk and a Squirrel together in our hypothetical natural landscape, or a Snake and a Frog, or a Wolf and a Deer, they will never be entirely comfortable together. The prey will always be a little concerned around the predator, and the predator will always be a little aroused around the prey. Even a domestic Cat and the family Dog have this problem: a puppy and a kitten can grow-up together, seem the best of friends— and yet if the Cat runs too fast across the living room the Dog will chase it. It's not a decision either makes, that's just the way of things.

Between two humans, predator and prey energy can be exciting, engaging, challenging, stimulating. But if two people cannot walk across the landscape together, quietly, calmly, in mutual respect, they will never fully relax around each other. They will always feel pressured to keep the other, to impress them, to entertain them, to challenge them, to covet them, even to fix them, all for fear of losing, consuming, or being consumed by them— and never be able to quietly *be* with them. Without that peace, the relationship between predator and prey is doomed to perpetual hardship.

Chapter Three:
The Power of *And*

Before we proceed any further, we need to take a step in a different direction. A large part of the path of the wise, of the spiritual journey toward understanding of the sacred self, involves a reconciliation of opposites. In some situations, the differences between those opposites are nearly irreconcilable, such as between people with predatory and prey totems trying to build a harmonious romantic relationship. Yet other times, such as between *yin* and *yang*, the Lord and Lady, or oppositional elemental energies on reverse sides of our totem sphere, the very energy that makes them oppositional also holds the seeds of their most potent and special magick. Sometimes, what opposites create when they combine can be their greatest strength as well as their greatest weakness— at once.

It can be a confusing cognitive journey. This reconciliation of opposites goes so far beyond the comparatively simple interactions between totems. For example, if a person is trying to fit everything I have just said in this book thus far into an existing world-view, it can can produce some difficult questions:

What really are the totems? Are they independent spirits or just ideas?

Where do they come from and why? Aren't they really just a product of my imagination?

How do they fit into the beliefs I already have? I'm a Christian or Wiccan or atheist and I have no desire to change that.

I understand that for some people it can feel like finding sure answers to these questions are necessary to proceed forward with totemism. Human minds like neatness, order, and categories for all things — and believe me, I totally get it. I'm very linear and logical myself, it's nice to meet you.

Yet, I have observed throughout my life that this type of totemism speaks to something deep within people. As I have mentioned, it is not at all uncommon for a person with no connection to pagan, metaphysical, or pre-christian religious traditions to nevertheless have intuitive, often very strong, opinions on their own totem animals. Consequently, this was even true for both my other half and for myself before we became pagan. It's a rather straightforward connection, unworthy of such stressful consternation.

For purposes of addressing these difficult questions of opposites, as well as any others one might encounter along the broader path of spiritual discovery, I would like to suggest a philosophy of sorts that might offer a solution. Later on, I will also discuss in greater detail some larger concepts within our type of totemism and how they can be addressed with this philosophy. It's called **and/and**.

The idea of and/and comes from a segment of contemporary British neo-pagan thinking, from groups that seek to connect themselves to the true pagan or pre-christian ways of ancient Britain, and not necessarily with Wicca, which, while also closely associated with its birthplace of Britain, is a much more modern invention. It is an idea that found me through works of Elen Sentier, which explore the ancient practices of deer worship through the Reindeer goddess Elen of the Ways (found in the book of the same name: *Elen of the Ways*). To be perfectly honest,

I'm unsure how prevalent these ideas actually are among the population of British pagans as a whole, but for me they rang true and have helped me help those spiritual seekers who possess more questioning and linear minds (including my own).

The idea of **and/and** is one important lesson learned when becoming spiritually wise or knowing, (known as being "canny" in the tradition), and it states that the physical world and the metaphysical world operate by different rules, different logic. Most of us are exposed at some point in our educations to the Greek philosophy that contradicts this, that says the same rules of logic and reason that exist in the physical world should also apply to ideas and to the process of rational thinking in general; some of us may have even taken courses in philosophy and might recall exercises in which logical statements are organized like math problems, to the tune of "If we hold idea A to be true, but it contradicts idea B, then we can assume idea B to be be false. If we know idea C says the same thing as idea A, we can assume it to be true," etc etc. Often this type of thinking is is referred to as following Euclidian logic, following mathematics. To the canny, it is known by the shorthand designation of "**either/or**" thinking. *Either* idea A is true *or* it is not, and if idea B is true then idea A is not, etc etc.

It is true that our concepts of "thoughts" and "the mind" are metaphysical constructs themselves, but we run into some uncomfortable problems when we try to apply either/or logic to most other metaphysical ideas, which especially in a pagan context really means a *spiritual* context.

For example, I have some vivid memories of a class I had to take in college that was taught by the philosophy department head. He was attempting to force a room that included many anthropology majors to accept either/or logic in place of **cultural relativism**, or specifically the idea

253

that the actions of an individual should only be judged moral or immoral by the standards of their own culture, and not by the standards of the observer. We understood this to be anthropology's attempt to simply *observe* other cultures while keeping judgement based in Western values out of a report. You see, in the past, anthropology as a discipline has had something of a problem with this very thing, labeling cultures and practices negatively in ways that sometimes had real consequences: for example, a single ethnographer's characterization of the Yanomami of Brazil as violent, head-hunting "fierce people" was used as an excuse by the Brazilian government to forcibly take their lands.

However, this professor saw our discipline's attempt at non-subjective observation as political correctness run amok—an attempt to be "nice" to everyone that would ultimately hinder our ability to think critically, to see what was actually real and not real, good and not good, in all of humanity. I remember him standing at the whiteboard trying to get us to admit to his way with a thought experiment: "In this scenario we are given two choices: either the soul goes to an afterlife OR it is reincarnated. If one is true, the other cannot be true. You cannot say both beliefs are 'right'! You can say a culture has *a right* to an incorrect belief. And until we know one or the other is true, we can say either group *could* be right. But *if* one is true, the other *has to be* false! It is wrong. *You need to be able to say someone is 'wrong'* — not 'bad' but 'wrong'—when they hold a false belief." It was something of a mess, as you can imagine.

Today, over a decade later, a lot has changed, and I understand a little more where he was coming from. There's a lot of social evolution happening right now, and I often do see people neglect to think critically in their rush to be accepting and non-judgmental, especially concerning hot-button topics like gender and sexuality, feminism, cultural appropriation, and how to eat in a way that is the most healthy, ethical, and environmentally friendly. It's easy to forget that our own search for truth can and maybe *should* be a separate thing from being kind and tolerant of others as they walk their own life paths. *You can think someone is wrong and still respect them.*

However, despite his best intentions, my professor *was* still wrong, and here's why: his entire argument rested on the single word *if.* Yes, *if* we could objectively prove that something definitive happens to the human soul at death, it would prove false all other beliefs. But *so what?* Matters of the spirit are just not like science, where we can gather hard data and replicate experiments; they are by-and-large ideas and feelings, they will never be "proven" one way or another. In class, I pointed out to him that he treated the idea of a soul as a known constant when it absolutely is not, as he was forgetting there are an infinite number of ways to understand a soul as both a singular — and plural — entity, cross-culturally, including those who don't believe in its existence at all, meaning it actually *was* possible for both *or* neither option to be "right." His word-equation might hold true on paper, but there was no real-world scenario in which it was realistically possible to "prove" an answer.

While we might be able to eventually prove some aspects of some religions to be true or not, matters of the spirit are by-and-large *subjective* concepts, based in personal experience, and are not usually experienced or understood the same way by all— even when multiple people share the same belief structure. A hundred people could observe the same rainbow, and maybe only one person feels it is a sign from the spirit world. Does that make that one man "wrong" because none of the others felt it was a sign? Does that make the ninety-nine others wrong because they missed it? Which is right? What is true? In fact, to the canny, it is entirely possible that both are true.

And so in this roundabout way I bring us to **and/and**. *The laws of the spirit world are different from the laws of the physical world.* When we look at the dream world and the world of visions and traditional, sometimes shamanic ways of interpreting them, we come across the idea that one will see things there as backwards, reversed, or "upside-down" from how they really are— but that is just the tip of the iceberg, a superficial side-effect of a much deeper construct. In the spirit world, the metaphysical world, things that *appear* to be contradictions, opposites to each other, can *also* be equal to each other, the same. Similar to the scary world of non-Euclidian geometry Lewis Carrol tried to express in creating Wonderland, the spirit world is a place where what seems "constant" is not constant, where what is "normal" is not normal, and where things like pocket-watches and chess pieces can be infinitely complex metaphors *and* random imagery with no meaning at all— at once.

The idea can be applied to so, *so* many ideas within religion and spirituality, and it resolves so much **cognitive dissonance** (or that uncomfortable feeling that comes from having two conflicting ideas at once) that is honestly unnecessary. We have been taught to believe that if ideas conflict then only one can be true, but that is not the case— not with the spirit, anyway.

"God" or deity both objectively exists *and* is a construct of human imagination and does not exist; it is both a singular entity, the pagan All or the Christian God, *and* it is many entities, the face of individual human experiences of *darshan*, in every culture on earth. The Lord and Lady are oppositional and opposite to each other, encompassing the diametric nature of the masculine and feminine *and* they are the same being, showing the singularity of the human soul. Human beings are inherently good, altruistic, and kind, *and* they are also inherently evil, selfish, and violent. The courses of our lives are governed by our choices, our human free Will, *and* they are guided by Fate, by a higher pattern of existence outside of our control. Death is the end of this life *and* it is not the end of who you are; part of you will cease to exist *and* part of you will move on *and* different aspects of you might go to different places. All religions have irreconcilable, fundamentally different beliefs about walking a spiritual path *and* they all provide a map to the same enlightenment. *And.*

Therefore: you can be a Christian, a Wiccan, a Buddhist, an atheist, or an eclectic Whatever-ist *and* a totemist. There is no rule that says you cannot be both, and at least one rule (this one) that suggests you should. Totemism is a totally independent system of belief *and* it is only one piece of a larger puzzle of understanding yourself, the universe, and whatever is in between.

Religion itself is simply a weird byproduct of human culture, used to control and confuse the populace, that should be regarded as both dangerous and silly. *And* it is an important aspect of being human that is a fundamentally necessary and sacred part of who we are. The Lakota *Heyota*, the "contraries" who were clowns *and* spirit-men who walked backwards, understood this. Respect religion— *and* laugh at it.

Chapter Four:
Totems and Children

The reader, at this point, might well be tired of hearing me repeat the idea that one's totems are unchangeable because they are with us since birth. This is true, but there is a strange aspect of this truth that arrises when we are dealing with the totems of children. You see, it is inadvisable to try and discover the totems of children because their totems are not set yet; only a developed adult personality has nine visible, distinct totems, and a child does not because its personality is still developing and growing.

Hopefully the reader can see why I chose to cover this topic only after discussing the philosophy of and/and, as we are getting into a cognitively squishy area with some seemingly circular logic. The energetic patterns of the totems are set within a person from birth, because a person is human since birth; totems reflect a person's essential self, who they are at their core; *but* an infant is born with little personality, and most of "who they are" will grow as they grow, influenced by experience, environment, and genetics. You cannot see the totems with clarity until the person is grown, finished developing; how the person will turn out cannot be foreseen as experience depends on choices made by Will and developing circumstance; *yet*, the totems *are* the Will within the child and will affect how they respond to those circumstances and makes those choices. How a child develops is greatly affected by the adults around him or her; *yet*, it is difficult to alter the person a child would grow up to be, especially on purpose. Totems are a manifestation of the human soul and are with a person from birth; *yet* the soul itself is something that grows, learns, and changes as a person grows up, and so too are the totems something that develop with adult maturity.

Really, if we're getting down to the nitty-gritty of it, the totems of children are not set at all. They exist as a sort of proto-entity, there but not fully there, with presence but not definition, with room to shift in one direction or another along with a developing personality. The totems are set within a child in the sense that no one really has the power to change who they will grow into, any more than a person can change the genetic predispositions they inherited from their parents or the memetic behaviors they will learn from them. We want to discourage the notion that one gets to *choose* totems, for themselves or others, or that one has any control over what they are, and so we say "they are set from birth." But they are set only in the sense that a child is going to grow-up to be who they are going to be. The statement should, from this point forward, be mentally read with a small asterisk at the bottom, meaning "please see footnote for additional information."

Here is an area in which my other half and I really wish we knew more pagan families, so that we could have the opportunity to observe how their children's personalities— and totems— develop and grow. Because one thing we have noticed is that a child's Primary totem will almost always be of a similar *kind* to one of their parents— but often also with some characteristics of the other. We believe this may be related to the genetic, biological tendencies they inherit from both. If the mother is a Saker Falcon and the father is a Brown Bear, their child's Primary totem is either going to be Bear-like with some Falcon tendencies or Falcon-like with some Bear tendencies.

But because every life experience is unique, that proto-entity will be shaped and molded by circumstance to become unique totems— and each of that child's siblings will come out a little differently, despite having the same parents. The mother's Falcon makes any type of raptor, from a tiny Kestrel to a giant Eagle-Owl to a fun-loving Rock-Hopper Penguin, easily possible. Or perhaps the child takes more after their father but inherits the hunting spirit of their mother, and becomes a Polar-Bear—or perhaps he rebels against her influence and becomes a gentle, vegetarian Panda.

When we add adversity to the child's life (and who has escaped from that?) we add further influence. Maybe one or both of the parents were over-bearing or emotionally aggressive, making the child grow into a Kodiak Bear to protect himself— or a tiny Peregrine Falcon who can fly away without being seen. Perhaps the mother divorces and re-marries a man with a Wolf totem who tries to put order into his step-children by dominating them— and the child grows even farther away from his Bear-like core and becomes a Wolverine man, aggressive and always on the defense. Things can get even more complicated when we add additional older people into the young child's life who influence who they'll grow up to be, from step-parents to grandparents to even older siblings. It can be further complicated if a child has an unhealthy or broken relationship with their birth parents and other adults assume a role of strongest, primary role-model; we have a friend who has the same Grizzly Bear totem as his grandfather, because his grandfather was the only stable and responsible parental figure in his life.

But the point I am trying to make is that the child of a Falcon and a Bear is never going to grow-up to be a Snake, a Squirrel, a Lobster, or a Lion. An individual child is only able to be pushed so far in one direction or another, and nothing can change their core identity. That is, your upbringing will influence what sort of "you" you will grow-up to be, but it cannot change who "you" are.

When a child is growing-up in a relatively comfortable and secure family environment, it is certainly possible to see signs of their dominant totem (its *kind* if not a specific species) at an earlier age. This is usually an area in which we rub parents the wrong way when they are absolutely certain that their nine-year-old's totem is this or that. And I'm not necessarily going to argue with them— because they may turn out to be absolutely right! But it *is* important to know that even if a child shows tendencies toward a totem animal at an early age, that child is not a fully developed personality and there is *still time for a shift to take place.*

This is a situation in which I feel Sir Phillip Pullman's *Dark Materials* series provides a good comparison. In the story, people's "daemons" or souls are shown as visible animal characters, and their forms are fixed in adults but flexible in children. The main character Lyra's daemon shifts from one animal to another depending on her situation— though because she is an older child, she has noticed that her daemon is appearing as a ferret more often than not, and many wonder if that is the final form it will take, though they recognize that something big could still happen to change it. In the real world, my husband I have not observed Primary totemic energy in children to shift quite so fluidly as all that, and in general it's more common to just see it as energy with vague or undefined form, but the general premise is pretty sound: children's totems aren't set yet and so there is nothing of value to be gained in trying to define them.

Another point to consider is that my husband and I have also observed that the totems of a child's parents (or grandparents, siblings, or other family members) can also take-up the role of guardian (a type of spirit guide) for a vulnerable child. If someone is certain they see or sense an animal hovering around a child, there exists the possibility that it may represent the protective tendencies of their mother or father, and not necessarily a unique aspect of that child's developing sacred self.

At any rate, that does leave us with one important question: when do we consider a person "grown" enough to accurately discover their totems? There is no easy answer, I'm afraid. It's obviously not at thirty-five when someone is finally married with children and a mortgage. I'd like to be able to supply a nice and easy rule like "at puberty" or "when they leave home" or "when they start making their own doctor's appointments" but hopefully the reader can see how that's problematic. We don't have a single metric in our society that measures adulthood; even in societies that do, it is possible for a person to meet that metric and still mentally and emotionally be a child, or to have not yet met the metric but be an adult internally nonetheless. A person is an adult when they simply . . . are no longer a child. And that has always occurred at different ages for different people. I've met some pretty mature thirteen-year-olds and some pretty immature twenty-five-year-olds. It's a subtle thing.

Actually, I might even go as far as to say a person is an adult *when their nine totems have fully developed.* They *must* have their *own* answer (albeit simplified) to the questions of "Who are you?" and "What do you want?" When they get there, you'll know; if you have to ask, they're not there yet.

Mother and Father as Lord and Lady

At this point, after reading the previous chapter or perhaps even earlier, the reader may have developed a very important albeit specific question regarding the Lord and

Lady totems, which I will finally address now. If we consider the amount of influence the center totems of our parents (or parental figures) have on our developing totems and essential-self, *and* if we also consider that the Lord and Lady totems within an individual represent their concept of the ideal man and woman often as demonstrated by their parents, where exactly do we draw the line between the two? Should we assume that a person's Lord and Lady totems will be similar if not the same as their mother and father's Primary totems?

The answer will be in the details (do I ever supply any other kind?) and can be a subtle thing to sort out. The place to begin is within a memory of an epiphany that every adult should have had: the day you realized your mom and dad were "just people." When you were a small child, you might have been aware that your parents had personal names like other people, but that was largely irrelevant to their identity as "Mom" and "Dad" in your eyes. They were beings that were larger than life, almost entities, that represented a significantly large portion of your experience and understanding of the world. Children don't think about their parents as being anything other than parents, but their reliance on that relationship allows their opinion and view of those parents to eclipse reality.

But then there was the day you realized that wasn't real. Maybe something happened that showed you a human fault, maybe it was just that you were growing up, but it was like a curtain had been pulled aside allowing you to see behind the scenes. One day you realized that "Mom" and "Dad" were just "Emily" and "Jack" or whatever their names are, two human people not so different from yourself who have thoughts and ideas and personalities and failings outside of their role as parents. "Dad" may have easily commanded the monsters to vacate the closet, but "Jack" always wondered if he was doing the right thing when he punished you or gave you advice.

That is the difference between your Lord and Lady totems and the Primary totems of your parents. Your Lord and Lady totems will grow from your subjective experience of what a Mom and a Dad are; your parents' actual, personal totems are what you can't see until you've grown-up a little.

So, to address the question: in most ways, no, Lord/Lady totems are not directly related to one's parents' personal totems. And yet, to tie this idea to the and/and philosophy, there will still be a thread of continuity between the two; most people do not parent from a place far outside of their core personalities. If you become learned enough in the ways of totemism to feel comfortable discerning your parents' totems, there is a good chance you will see some shared characteristics between your Lord/Lady and their Primaries; you could likely see a similar thread connecting your Primary to your grown child's Lord or Lady.

The best example I can pull is, per usual, from my own life. As I have mentioned, my Lord totem is a Lion, an animal who is the leader of his family yet who shares that responsibility with the lead Lioness, who protects and indulges his cubs even as the Lioness is the hunter, and whom I like to envision is happiest sitting back proudly, watching his healthy family playing around him on the savanna. That was my experience of fatherhood. My Dad's Primary totem is a Dog— a far cry from the mighty Lion to be sure. And yet a Dog (taken as a sub-type of Wolf; see the later chapter on domestication) as well will protect, indulge, and instruct his pups, and he shares responsibilities with a lead female. It is not so hard to see a proud papa Dog content in the exact same scene, indulgently overseeing his tussling puppies. A Dog and a Lion are not necessarily similar animals, certainly not of the same *kind*; and yet, they are not completely dissimilar animals, and my experience of their dominant, most important characteristics are not so different at all. The difference itself is a matter of relevance: when a Dog bravely chases away a scary monster, to a small child, he can be as big as a Lion.

Media and Other Influences

Another area of discourse that benefits nicely from a recent discussion of and/and theory— as well as a subject that flows well from the discussion of children's totems— is the subject of exactly *what* influences in a child's life will shape their developing totems aside from parents and other family members.

As I have brought-up before, some questions to ask when one is at the earliest stages of totemic discovery center around childhood experiences: favorite animals, early animal interactions of significance, animals featuring prominently in dreams or in nightmares. They may also show themselves anywhere from a favorite "safety" stuffed animal to one's favorite book or cartoon. It's something that we can often easily see with the perfect clarity of hindsight; while there is always room for a few "surprises," you will likely see more than a few quite familiar animal faces in your spread of nine, faces that could likely be traced back to familiar bedroom wallpaper, collectable figurines, and favorite picture books.

But of course, we must again return to and/and, as an astute reader no doubt is asking a question of the "chicken and the egg" variety: is a child drawn to certain animals *because* they are signs of emerging totems, *or* are the child's developing totems *influenced* to conform to the animal images surrounding them? The answer, unfortunately (at least for the rationally- minded) is both; the child is drawn to the animals that resonate within them, *and* the animals in turn shape the child. It is another aspect of the circular, as opposed to linear, relationship that exists

266

between aspects of the self within the context of the spirit world.

I think I would be hard-pressed to find someone who knew me as a child who would be surprised to learn I have a large cat for a totem, let alone three large cats in my spread of nine, considering among other things my early obsession with the Lion King. And it should similarly surprise no one to learn that I often experience my Elephant as a Mammoth, considering the gravity of influence Jean Auel's *Earth Children* (or E.C.) book series has had on my life, both professional and spiritual. Readers should take note that I first read these adult books in my early teenage years, but I was still very much an underdeveloped "child" despite the "teen" attached to my numeric age.

However, it could easily lead the reader to a third aspect of the and/and conundrum; what if, when you were looking "deep inside yourself" for totems, you just picked animals you simply connected to early memories and fond experiences? A love for "The Call of the Wild" or "Balto" may not necessarily point to a spiritualistic connection to Wolves or Dogs, and one instead could simply associate those animals with good feelings and happy memories, right?

Even as I can see clearly (with that hindsight we talked about) the "origins" of some of my totems, it is not so cut-and-dry. Despite a love for Lions, Tigers, and other large cats, I can't say there was ever a time when I gave Jaguars a second thought (I probably assumed they were the same animal as Leopards), despite him growing to be my Primary totem, and I honestly had more of an affinity for Cougars than anything else and she is not a totem of mine at all. Someone familiar with the E.C. series might easily see how both Mammoth and Lion draw directly from those books, but Bear and Horse are just as important within that series and they are nowhere to be found in my nine. Wolf, who also has a role in those books, only just barely gets a pass and a position of spiritual prominence for me as the totem of my life-mate, but is not really a part of who I am without him.

So what is a parent to think if their child gets behind the latest re-boot of Thundercats and longs to be Cheetara when she grows up? Children certainly choose their activities based on more than a simple, ineffable "affinity" that is easily linked to spirituality, don't they? Can simply following a fad fandom have an affect on a child's developing totems? That depends. On the one hand, it could just be that they enjoy the cartoon or belonging to the community of fans and riding the wave of pop culture. But on the other hand, our childhood obsessions do have a way of becoming significant events in our lives in their own right, and any experience of significance has the potential to affect the person we will grow into. It's simply not something we'll be able to understand until it's already happened.

Family, Tribe, and Self

There is a final area of thought on the subject of influences on the developing totems of a child that requests our attention, and that is our modernity. Specifically, how our contemporary Western lives have affected our relationship to the spirit world, to Mother Nature, and to our own souls; I think it goes without saying that while we are the same animal, the differences between us and our progenitors of the ancient, almost archetypal past are significant, and they go beyond our meaningful disconnect from the land and the natural world. What *does* happen to the mind of an animal when it is removed from its native environment?

Quite a few things, to be sure. But with the human animal, it creates a human soul far more independent— and unique — than any other that came before it. This is an area in which my other half and I can only speculate, but we believe strongly that the totems of people in the past were much more connected to, and influenced by, the totems of their families and tribes.

Contemporary people each carry a pattern of nine totems unique to ourselves that represent the breadth of that uniqueness, but we are also raised from the cradle in an environment that demands individuality and sees personal expression as a virtue; we expect teenage rebellion as a normal, even necessary, stage of life. Even within homes and communities that teach conforming to a norm we still see the pattern, as the process of "conforming" implies augmenting and adjusting attitudes and behaviors to fit a standard that would be scattered more freely across the board when left untouched. If anything, Westerners are defined by our individuality, and especially in America, every growing child is encouraged to blossom into a unique special flower, taught that each has "something special" to share with the world.

And aside from ego, this individuality has a purpose in our society. After all, it is a competitive world we live in, and anything that differentiates you from the rest of the herd can make the difference in getting noticed at school, getting a job, or getting a date— when there can potentially be dozens, if not hundreds, of people with identical qualifications vying for the same goal. Ours is a consumerist, capitalist tribe; success is usually dependent on your ability to sell the unique "product" that is yourself.

But when taken against the whole of human history, this is not normal. Humans are a competitive, status-driven animal to be sure, but this trait is expressed differently in tribalist societies. Firstly, for any individual there would have been fewer people around to compete with; secondly, success was more often a community, not individual, goal. There was less purpose to individual success that came at the expense of others, or that excluded others, as the success (and survival!) of any given individual was usually *dependent* on the successes of his group. Even as we are talking about an uncountable number of distinct cultures here, stretching back over many thousands of years, it is a pattern that is still observable to anthropologists today (and perhaps understandable intuitively by all) that tribal, traditional societies value(d) the success of the individual more as a means to advance the success of the community as a whole— and only then would they consider advancing their community above *other* communities or tribes.

Therefore, when growing-up within such a society, a child (and their developing totems) had far less incentive to express something unique and far more reason to mimic the patterns of people around them. One's elders were the exemplars of how to live successfully, and the source of a cultural identity that one strived to uphold. Teenagers coming of age on the formative savannas of Africa or on the frigid steppes of ice-age Eurasia likely had little reason to "rebel" from the influence of their parents and elders; it was likely considered a compliment, not the insult of modernity, to tell someone they had grown-up to be exactly like their mother.

My other half and I believe that, over time, one would have likely seen the emergence of the same totemic patterns over and over again within the same communities. This would become even more likely if said community lived in a time and place where living was not so easy, favoring the success and survival of certain personalities over others. For example, societies that saw regular warfare would not support a preponderance of smaller, more timid animals such as Rabbits, favoring instead the larger and stronger animals, like Wolves and Bison; societies that required intricate cooperation between members for complex community activities like raising earth-mound temples or farming on terraces likely saw much fewer solitary predators and favored the pack and the herd that carried the ability to get along, etc etc.

In such a situation, we believe it would have been far more common to see the same totems (or *kinds* of totems) "passed on" through the generations through families and clans. If such a totemic influence proved very successful or was otherwise well favored, you could see the same animal looking after whole lineages of people. And depending on an individual's cultural relationship to the common animal, it could show-up as the Lord, Lady, Light, Dark, or even Primary totem to nearly everyone in a community— or at least a sub-group within a community.

Consequently, here is where the anthropological definition of a totem (which we covered early on in the book) intersects with our totemic tradition: *group totems, or as I should more accurately call them here, **family totems**, were likely much more common to our ancestors, but are usually absent in modern Western people.*

We believe this may also be why ancient cultures who did name personal totems were still less likely to recognize more than a single Primary totem each: if everyone in your Clan had the same Cave Bear as their Above totem, for example, it would likely be recognized and acknowledged in a different way than as a personal tutelar spirit.

Sometimes when my other half and I are speaking about totems in a public setting, someone will bring up group and family totems— "I am part Cherokee and Grandad said we were Panther Clan. Is that one of my totems?" someone might say. Or, "What about traditional nations who all honored the same animal— like the Lakota with the Bison? Do we consider that a totem?" Undoubtedly, when you are reading about any traditional or pre-Christian society that has a special connection to an animal spirit, you might ask a similar question, especially if you are yourself related to one of these groups. How does that fit into the system we have established?

All I can say on that front is a resounding *maybe*, coupled with a stern frown and a shake of the head indicating my doubtfulness. It *is* possible, but in my experience, unlikely that you carry any totems that are inherited directly from your heritage— even if you happen to be a descendant of the First Americans. You may belong to a tribe, but tribal life today is just not the same thing that it was a thousand years ago, and even if you really want that relationship to amount to something, it just doesn't come through the wash as the same thing your ancestors experienced, and therefore it did not affect your developing psyche in the same way. This is especially true if you didn't find out you were "part Cherokee" until you were an adult and you began researching spirituality outside of your basic-bitch white girl upbringing. (Cue that one person who'll immediately raise their hand and insist they are the special exception; no you're not, sit down.) Think about it critically: do you know anything at all for certain about your great-grandparents, or great-great-grandparents, aside from perhaps a name or a nationality— if that? How much influence, then, could they have *really* had on shaping who you grew-up to be? Most of us (especially in America) remain quite ignorant of our ancestral heritage until we spit into a tube and pay $100 to map our DNA by mail. Unrelated best friends and their families, church pastors or other religious leaders, and influential school teachers have more influence on us by a thousand yards.

However, as a final point on this topic, I do need to clarify something. It is absolutely not at all uncommon for a person to have one or more totems that seem to *represent* and facilitate a connection to a culture— to which we may recognize a genetic or spiritual relationship— or simply a region or part of the world. If you are an American with Irish ancestry and you feel that the Mare as your Lady totem represents your connection to the goddess Epona and your Celtic heritage, that is perfectly legit, especially if you feel your inner Celt is an important aspect of your sacred-self. All things considered, it's honestly pretty common for totems to come from parts of the world we feel connected to in some spiritual way.

What I *am* saying is that *genetics alone do not produce a totem*; modern Western people simply do not experience the concepts of tribe, heritage, cultural inheritance, or family in the manner necessary to inherit totems passed along lineages.

Chapter Five:
Commonality and Relativity

Someone in the totem class always wants to talk about sea-cucumbers and it will never not be funny.

Yes, technically speaking, echinoderms are animals, but no, they cannot be totems. (There, that was the shortest answer you will ever get out of me; enjoy it.)

Seriously, though: it does bear discussing why certain sorts of animals are more likely to serve as totems than others. Considering the way that nature is constantly experimenting with ways to renew itself through mutation and variation within the gene pool, one might think at first that all animals have a fair shake; after all, I implied earlier that variation among human personalities provides exactly that.

Yet, the reality is we find that center totems especially rarely stray from the realm of mammals, birds, and sometimes marsupials, with slightly fewer reptiles, amphibians, and perhaps octopoda thrown in for good measure; when we expand outward to include the elemental totems, we can include a few types of fish and some special insects. And that may sound like all of the animals there are— except we are actually excluding a significant portion of the animal kingdom. There are those found in the water, such a staggering number of creatures that bear shells such as clams and other mollusks, boneless squishy things like our pal the sea cucumber and his kin, spiky anemones and flowery corals, shrimps and krill and crawdads, and a multitude of fish most people would see as no different from one another. On land we have a huge variety of insects no one would give the time of day. And let's not even get started on the microscopic variety of animal.

But you will never find someone with an amoeba as a totem. It comes down to the fact that totem animals represent aspects of human personalities, so *we are more likely to see animals as totems whose natures are more complex, more human.* Most mammals and birds have an intelligent, complex understanding of social structures and status that provide a human bearing it as a totem with skills that translate into a successful life in a human society. Hunting animals, your Falcons and your Rattlesnakes and your Cougars, each provide unique, but valuable, strategies for a human character to set and attain goals; herding animals provide the ability to give orders or to follow them, and on how to get along with others. Sea cucumbers have nothing to say except to slowly wriggle around in the sludge, ignore parasites, and ingest anything that gets sucked into its mouth-hole. A human with a sea cucumber as a totem would *not have the innate skills to live a normal human life.* Modern notions of cellular complexity aside for the moment and moving toward common sense, we will define these animals as **underdeveloped** animals — physiologically, intellectually— and underdeveloped animals just won't work as totems.

Consequently, the same logic must apply to the question of having plants, specifically trees, as totems. This does come up occasionally, as there have been many instances of different cultures observing plant-based totems, such as the Sweet Potato Clan of the Cherokee people— but understand, these would all be *anthropological totems*, more like mascots or emblems of a groups of people, and not like our personal tutelar totems. Trees are beautiful lifeforms, and anyone presenting the argument that they are complex creatures in their own right with energy and wisdom to impart are not wrong. But for the same reason underdeveloped animals cannot be totems by our tradition, neither can plants (or for that matter, neither can stones, mountains, bodies of water, or any other non-animal).

Here is an area in which my other half and I have had some disagreement, though in the end we reach a similar enough conclusion. We both agree that if such an underdeveloped animal *did* occur as a totem, it would be an aberration, an abnormality, or a mutation that was a manifestation of an underdeveloped, diseased, under-functioning, or otherwise malfunctioning mind. Because it would represent a person with basically no instinctual understanding of how to survive as a complex animal, I believe over time we have largely weeded out such totemic influences, through passing on successful genes and cultural memes, to the point that I would say underdeveloped totems *do not exist;* over time, we have *bred out* of ourselves all but the most successful totem animals.

My husband, however, insists that I think this way because we only ever *see* the successful people, working and living and carrying on, but that the "unsuccessful" people influenced by underdeveloped totems are still out there— living solitary lives as shut-ins never straying far from the TV in a lonely apartment, in uni-bomber-style hermit shacks in the woods— or in mental healthcare facilities. And perhaps it is even the case that such individuals are *born*, but do not survive to adulthood. He believes there is room to discuss the roles of underdeveloped, highly unusual, or otherwise "inappropriate" totems as they may be related to human mental illnesses and mental disorders, which we can alternately define as dysfunctions or unusual functionings of a mind.

Now, I'm not even necessarily going to argue against the obvious similarities between a Parrot's character and that of a person on the autism spectrum (a love for order and repetition coupled with a high intellect and difficulty reading human emotional cues, to name a few) as an example at the very most-functional end of this scale. I'm just not sure I carry the same logic all the way to explaining *all* mental abnormalities with totems. And for me, such an explanation would neglect defining who such a person was or would be *outside of* their condition, which may or may not affect them to such an extent that it takes over their whole personality. It really depends on which mental conditions and disorders we're talking about here, as they vary so widely, and how we individually understand the concept of *personal identity* — which is such a complicated concept it's enough to fill many books on its own (and has).

However, suffice it to say, if you are able to read this book and comprehend its meaning, you are a "successful" enough human that you bear totems, absolutely and especially center totems, from the more common, most developed animal categories; your elemental totems are more simplified aspects of your character and so can be less developed animals, but they must still have *some* developed traits to share with you.

I know within the spirit of middle-class Westerners the urge to be special can be strong. But I want you to look to the feathered creatures, the furry and the hairy creatures, and the scaly creatures; perhaps even look to the tiny creatures with eight legs, or six, or nothing but a fin. But you can go ahead and ignore the amoebas, the sea cucumbers, and the earwigs on your totemic quest. Eagle, Bison, Bear, Coyote, Deer, and Wolf are common totems for a reason: they produce a successful person who lives well.

Chapter Six:
Stubborn Nature

Mythical and Metaphysical

Someone walking in on us off the street might be surprised to hear the neo-pagan community speaking of their interactions with unicorns, fairies, and dragons— and wonder perhaps if they have accidentally slipped through a doorway into Narnia!

To clarify for non-pagan readers who are not in the know, such creatures as dragons and fairies (known alternately as "the fae") are in fact a part of neo-pagan religion for many, and are believed to be **non-physical creatures**. Alternately known as spirit creatures, metaphysical creatures, non-corporal creatures, or energy beings, they are distinct both from physical animals as well as from entirely metaphysical entities such Abrahamic angels, gods — or totems. Usually, they overlap with what the general population would think of as "mythical" creatures from folklore. In form, these entities are (usually) believed to lie mid-way between the extremes in that they have no physical bodies or mortality, but they can and do often live in, affect, and interact with the physical world in a way that suggests individual lives and identities like an animal or person.[16] They are not personifications of abstract ideas or ideals as most gods are, and are rather viewed as a "different" or "alternate" form of life on this earth that is simply comprised of spiritual energy only. Depending on who you ask, the concept of "the fae" specifically (by way of Celtic folklore) can bleed-over into broader categories of nature spirits, ancestral spirits, and Old Gods themselves more earthy in their nature, their concerns, and their interactions with humanity and the physical earth. Other traditions, such as those originating from West-African and many Native American systems, view their gods and spirits similarly.

Inevitably, there is always someone who wants a dragon for a totem. However, it bares addressing why these non-physical creatures cannot be totems by our tradition (as disappointing as that may be to some out there). While it may very well be the case that I cannot exclude them with total certainty, that is only because I have not checked the totems of every person on earth, and we have two strong reasons why non-physical creatures cannot be seated as totems. The first reason is according to the boundaries of our totemic tradition as we have already established. The second is an argument based in paganism's typical understanding of the nature of the reality of such entities.

To begin, within our tradition, we believe there are reasons we perceive of the various aspects of our sacred-self in animal form. As I discussed before, one such reason is that they serve us well as the face of non-human intelligence when we are seeking to understand the self objectively in sections or segments that each become short of a full human personality. But more importantly, they are also a type of non-human intelligence that *shares in the*

---

16 Very specific branches of ceremonial witchcraft may also include in this category agents of light or dark magick known as angels and demons.

experience of living life on this earth— of life in a "meat body," as it were. The various faces of all of the many different types of animals on this earth all represent our connection to different instinctual approaches to physiological, biological *survival—* and in order for them to be valid approaches, they should be rooted in actual experience. Or, to put it simply: it would be bizarre to take advice on how to live from an entity that is not a living being. Think about the Five Identifying Questions one needs to address to understand a totem — habitat, diet, social structure, mating strategy— and then try to assume such knowledge for a solely-spirit creature that doesn't eat, doesn't mate, doesn't live, and doesn't die. It doesn't work. There is solidarity between the human animal and every other animal born in blood of Mother Earth: *we walk a mortal life together.*

Further still, even if non-physical creatures are alive in their own way, it would be impossible to learn about them in a culturally non-biased way. That is, there have been no scientific reports published on the social habits of dragons, no documentaries on the seasonal migrations of the pegasus. All you have to go on are myths and stories, which as we have discussed are secondary in quality to science; you also have metaphysical and neo-pagan literature, but that usually doesn't include research conducted scientifically, either. *Creatures that exist solely in the mind's eye or that are perceived-of by the soul would carry a gigantic question mark next to the very qualities that would be necessary to understand them as totems.* Some of you might say that your own observations of dragons have been unbiased, but I doubt you consider yourself an expert, and at any rate, haven't we discussed before the fact that spirits always speak to shamans with shadows on their tongues? If all you know is what they've shown you, you can never know the full truth of their reality, can you? If all you knew of horses was what a proud Stallion spirit chose to tell you during meditation, would you ever learn that horses are stymied by curtains, or terrified of plastic bags blowing in the wind?

Now, it happens that paganism as a whole has already decided that non-physical creatures cannot be totems— it's just that many people don't realize it. If we were to first approach the subject from a different angle, and I were to ask: "Are fae *animals*? Are dragons *animals*?" one especially who works with fairy or draconic magick would absolutely say: "No . . . well, in a way yes, but not quite . . . they're in a special category, you see . . ." and then launch into an explanation similar to what I gave in the second paragraph. Non-physical or spirit creatures may be considered lifeforms of their own variety, but they are distinctly *not* animals. Therefore, they should not be considered for the job of an animal spirit. That would be like saying Odin is your totem, or the spirit of your great-grandfather is your totem, or that archangel Gabriel is your totem. *They are different categories of being.*

Of course, I would have to kick myself if I forgot to tie this idea back to what I've already said, far back at the beginning of this book: that for whatever reason, some people will perceive of their totems in a form other than animal, but as long as a connection is made and productive communication is facilitated, ultimately the form our mind chooses as most acceptable for said entity is less important; at worst, it would slow the process, affecting the clarity of the communication. I bring up this point to remind the reader that there is no *harm* in perceiving one's totems as dragons, only a loss of potential information, and I am not here to tell you that you "must" change— or that you "must" do anything at all, for that matter. As likely as not, you are seeing your totems in exactly the way you need to at this stage in your life. As I have tried to impart before, the timing of these sorts of things can seem a little suspiciously serendipitous and predetermined, but it's best to just roll with it.

However, if your mind is insistent on seeing one of your totems in an unusual (and according to the definition of our tradition, "wrong") form, I would like to suggest a reason, and through its resolution, provide further valuable insight into the workings of your own soul. That reason came to light through my own experiences with another not-quite-right totemic form: extinct, ancient, or "pre-historic" forms of animals, which I will discuss below.

Ancient and Extinct

As I have mentioned before, much of the time I have perceived of my Lady totem, an Elephant. as a Wooly Mammoth. Now, even as all mammoths are extinct, both forms of modern elephants (Asian and African) are their close cousins and their physical similarities are obvious, so I don't think I will find any arguments with putting them in the same *kind*. I have already discussed a variety of reasons why a totem may choose to communicate with its bearer through a closely-related animal of its *kind*, so one may wonder where the problem might lie.

Yet, I would like the reader to consider my arguments against non-physical creatures and apply the same critiques to the Wooly Mammoth, the Dire-Wolf, the Saber-toothed Tiger, and the Cave Lion potentially sitting as totems. Of what value is advice on how to reproduce, how to eat, and how to live in an environment that no longer exists? When the plants, the weather, and the terrain are all vastly different from what they knew, their instinctual knowledge becomes misplaced, often inappropriate to modern times and situations, and (with all due apologies to my elders for the simile) like a Baby-Boomer telling an unemployed Millennial that it surely makes a better impression to submit a resume in person than online, their knowledge is of how to live on the earth as *they* knew it — *not* the way it is now.

Of course, you may be saying to yourself that the earth hasn't *necessarily* changed all that much, and anyway, it would seem that the instinctual advice of an ice-age animal wouldn't be all that different than one from a contemporary tundra, but it goes deeper than that. Remember that the connection to the physical world is only half of a totem; the other half is a human soul, and is forged in the dark depth of the psyche, the realm of symbology, archetypes, and imagination. Perhaps in this life you may or may not have actually visited a tundra, but there are people alive today who have, and they can accurately convey every detail of it to you through books and BBC documentaries. Further, people who fall more heavily on the concretely pagan side of things understand that the metaphysical energy of a living ecological system contributes to the fabric of the earth's energy as a whole and is accessible to those on the path of the wise. It exists, now, and is *knowable*. But though scientists understand a great deal about the topography, climate, and ecosystems of the Eurasian Steppes of the Pleistocene, no human eyes have seen them in that state for 12,000 years, and so even the most educated perception still includes an element of reconstruction, of *imagination*— making it and the animals who inhabited it, such as the Mammoth, contain an element of *myth*.

And here, after all that blather, is the point I'm trying to get to: these inexact forms of totems all prohibit you from seeing things *as they are*, and instead show you *what you'd like to see*. An extinct animal, but one nonetheless of a close-*kind* to living animals, is only partially affected by this factor, and some of what you perceive will be "real" while the rest is "imaginary"; non-physical entities, meanwhile, are almost entirely clouded by perception. It is also my personal belief that extinct animals who walked the earth at the same time as humanity are afforded an easier spiritual relationship with us, and can more easily speak through a contemporary of their *kind,* whereas extinct animals from well before the dawn of humanity or any of the animal *kinds* we're familiar with (such as all types of Dinosaurs, etc.) might as well be classified as fully mythological in this context, despite the fact that they did at one time walk the earth. (Half of us still envision velociraptors with crocodile-skin rather than feathers, after all; 99% of what you think you know about them is a Spielberg myth.)

For me, this has been one of the most important lessons taught to me by the Mammoth spirit, through my Elephant, and it has been a hard one to accept. I had often felt that the Mammoth, as my Lady totem, connected me directly to my concept of the divine, the earth goddess whom I refer to as the Great Earth Mother (due to my aforementioned early, heavy influence by J.M. Auel's *Earth's Children* series, naturally). But more than that, I had unconsciously linked Mammoth in my mind with everything I had wistfully imagined about life in an ancient, pre-Christian time period; like nearly every pagan before me and probably since, I looked back to a time "when God was a woman," when healers and storytellers and wise women were respected, essential cornerstones of societies that valued the shaman, honored their connection to the earth, and lived free and innocent before bronze-age notions of sin and "the patriarchy" ruined things for everyone— and I did as the almighty Starhawk commanded and "remembering" such a time turned into "creating" it. Mammoth, to me, was (and is still) my connection to who I feel I *should have* been, the role I *should have* had— or maybe did have in some past incarnation. A shaman, a wise-woman. One who Serves the Great Earth Mother. Not some dingus writing a book. And it was entirely the fault of our backwards, polluted, confused modern world that I wasn't.

But the lesson of course is that "should have" amounts to relatively nothing but a fun fantasy. We know many of the ideas from above existed in the Americas, in Africa, Australia, in South Asia prior to the rise of colonialism, and the educated suspect such was the case in ancient Europe as well before a few successful groups from the Caucus Mountains and Central Asian steppes brought the domesticated Horse, the wheel, agriculture, warfare, and the end of the stone age. But misty-eyed myths of the Aboriginal Australians and Native Americans do tend to gloss over the ugly parts, and though my childish unconscious mind would try to argue, the Mother Earth-worshiping cultures of the Earth's Children books are idealized fiction. How much of that was real and how much was not really has little, if anything, to do with how the world is *now*.

Fantasy is fine, and the deeper sort called dreams can help shape who we are, but our totems are here to help us understand who we are in this life, here and now. I am no more a Siberian shaman in a sweat lodge than a Mammoth is likely to go migrating down the streets of Kiev. The path to wisdom lies in understanding where my soul can find its niche in the world *today*. Mammoth went bald to adapt to a changing world— stranger things have happened.

Clouded Faces

If you find yourself facing a spirit who would be a totem, or who is acting as such, who shows a face that is not of this earth of flesh and bone, there is an important lesson in it for you. I would wager my entire career as a suburban shaman that some cloud of perception colored by how you feel things "should be" is in the way of you seeing what totem animal is really there. For whatever reason, *you are not yet ready to be fully honest with that aspect of yourself.*

286

I want you to imagine how a young, proud, perhaps cocky Stallion spirit might view himself: as the most beautiful horse in the forest, so fast he is unable to be caught by any man or predator, who chooses for himself only the most lovely virgin females— and who has no need of antler-envy because he has a kick-ass magical sword growing right out of his forehead. A unicorn in a dream or in the NOR is probably a side of you that isn't ready to see a Horse's weaknesses, and so you perceive only his adolescent fantasy. Emotional vulnerability is on the opposite side of the coin from pridefulness, after all.

If you are face-to-face with a Dire-Wolf who confidently tells you that this urban world is too small and too tame to contain him, ask yourself why you are ignoring that Wolves are one of the most adaptable creatures the Great Earth Mother ever produced, thriving in nearly all ecosystems— including the urban, though perhaps you are just embarrassed to admit that a Wolf adapted to the urban world looks too much like a Dog. Most modern forms of Wolves such as the Gray existed *at the same time* as the Dire and clearly survived quite well, driving home that his boastful statement is actually an admission of weakness and that largely he is full of shit.

If you are shown a fairy, a wood-nymph, a water sprite, one of the elves or the little people, and it begins to assume a role within you that rightly belongs to a totem, you may be facing a situation in which you would have little respect for the intelligence, abilities, the *worthiness* of your true totem animal if it showed its real face— and so it first shows you another, a human or *humane* face using human expressions and human words, to prove to you there is more to its spirit power than meets the eye. A Grasshopper, a Mouse, a Sparrow, a Snake, a Spider, a Goldfish. Other animals have such large personalities that it's a wonder they can be contained in such small bodies in the physical world, and I've yet to meet a Parrot or a Pug who understands how small they really are; your initial perception of them in the spirit realm might be stretched to keep up with the volume until you are a little wiser, and you'll see types of wyverns and feathered serpents, thunderbirds, griffins, hell-hounds.

If you are certain that you are the reincarnated soul of a Druid, that assurance may be forcing your mind to only accept a system of three elements, not six— because you are certain a good Druid would have totems only of Earth, Sea, and Sky. In many ways, it is easier to ignore totems, or to have multiples speaking through the same mouthpiece, than to create extras, but if you are certain your soul only follows traditional Chinese medicine you may well prime your mind to "find" ten, due to the five terrestrial elements of Fire, Water, Wind, Metal, and Wood you are certain must exist. (Spirit guides can be nearly-permanent, if you need them long enough.)

If you are certain that you are such the burly manly-man that you have no "feminine side," or that you are such a strong, independent woman "that don't need no man" and that includes male protective spirits, you can be sure you are standing so far in your own way that your Primary totem may just concede and show you a form the same sex as yourself. (The truly wise know the line between male and female is as flexible as it needs to be.) That goes doubly-so if you are adamant that gender is an oppressive construct that should not exist and should be wiped-out; you forget what I taught you about seeing the naked truth of yourself in your Primary totem, and the face of your soul will reflect who you really are, regardless of the form of your body or what anyone else tries to force upon you— if you remain open and allow yourself to be shown.

And it comes as little surprise to me that the mythology of dragons assigns a draconic form to all of the natural elements; it feels almost otherworldly, despite being of the earth in the most primal way. Therefore, it is understandable that some people simply cannot understand their spiritual connection to the powers of the earth within themselves as anything less than magnificent, mystical, magical, and mysterious. And surely something as awe-inspiring and life-changing as discovering and harnessing the full powers of the Water elemental cannot be contained in something as terrestrial as an Otter or a King-Fisher!

Coincidentally, I do not find it a coincidence at all that it is largely those with less experience walking the path of a witch who immediately want to see their totems as dragons. It is simply because that person has yet to learn that the line dividing the metaphysical from the physical, the super-natural from the ordinary, the magical from the mundane — is a myth of perception and *does not exist.*

There is another important occurrence of and/and philosophy at play in this situation. As you progress along the path of the wise, you will learn, and as you learn, you become certain of various knowledge. Yet, if your mind and spirit are "certain" about anything at all concerning the spirit world, that insistence can and will prevent your mind from receiving new information and keep you from learning. If you are "certain" the sea is blue, you prevent yourself from seeing her as green— or, for that matter, any color at all, as she may appear in the NOR. You must learn and gain knowledge, and yet you must remain open and innocent to all possibilities. That is how you become wise.

And yes, to my astute readers: I am aware of the concept of irony as it applies here. But suffice to say, within our tradition you cannot have non-physical creatures seated as totem animals.

Chapter Seven:
The Nature of Wild— Domestic, Tame, Trained, and Feral

We humans are domesticated animals. As much as we sometimes like to imagine a life in an idyllic ancient time and place where we could live in close harmony with Mother Earth, if most of us lost our way in the wilderness, we would die. We wouldn't do any better than a pet Dog "set free" and abandoned on the roadside, because instinct can only carry an individual so far when one has neither experience nor education in how to live as a wild animal.

And yet, there is a disparity, an area of mental oversight in our conversation of the nature of wildness. With an unbiased heart and an open mind, consider: is domestication *wrong*? Is it *bad* to be a domesticated animal?

I understand the potential reaction, the sense of tragedy and loss of inherent beauty that comes at the suggestion— especially compared to the mood of my own Foreword. But I want us to consider what the concept actually means, and in so doing, provide ourselves with the most practical and perhaps useful suggestions for how to utilize one's instinctual totemic tendencies to our greatest advantage. When life in the human world is the only option, an animal that has adapted to life in that human world is a *successful animal*. When the only other option is a dead animal, that starts to sound like a win to me.

Of course, outside of metaphor, what we are more likely dealing with is an anxious or depressed animal, a socially-isolated animal, an existentially confused animal, an unhappy animal; it is a human who cannot function, or function well, or function happily, in their own life. As we speak, the zoos and circuses of the world are finally beginning to understand that so many animals— Elephants, Sea lions, Orcas— cannot live in cages. A Cheetah will die of its own anxiety in a zoo— but a House Cat will sleep contentedly on your couch. Given the options, which one would you rather be? There is no "wrong" answer here, only your own.

It can be a confusing thing: is domestication the source of the problem or the solution? As we search a little deeper down into the concept, I want you to keep in mind that this is another— and *very important*— instance of and/and philosophy at work. If your natural instincts, your inclinations, do not fit into life in the modern world, you will be unhappy and not understand why. But if you know, love, and respect the true animal nature of your essential self **and** embrace whatever tendencies it possesses that might allow it to flourish in captivity, you may fare far better in your every day life. The harmony, the balance, must come into place in utilizing the attributes of domestication, while recognizing and respecting the needs of the wild animal it is descended from.

And so I would like to present to the reader an additional four concepts to explore, and an additional Identifying Question to address for each of your nine totems, especially the center three.

Can it be *tamed*? Can it be *trained*? Can it be *domesticated*? Can it go *feral* again? *How well does it fare in the human world?*

292

For our purposes, we will define an animal that has been **domesticated** as one whose physiological form as well as temperament has been altered by humans, often through selective breeding to favor desired traits. In contrast, an animal that has been **tamed** has been taught to accept the authority of humans, often by being raised by them or imprinting on them, but has not been physically altered from their natural form; an animal that has been simply **trained** may still be thought of as a wild animal who has been taught to obey some commands by humans. And a **feral** animal is a domesticated animal who has returned to the wild, while retaining their altered form.

A Cow is a *domesticated* animal, bred to be fatter and more docile than their wild ancestor species such as the Aurochs. A pet Conure or Ferret is a *tamed* animal, as they are bred in captivity and raised by humans, but they have not been physiologically changed (or much changed) from their wild counterparts. A Dolphin at a zoo or a Lion in a circus is a *trained* animal; they have been taught a few commands and behaviors that allow them to interact with a few specific humans, but they largely remain dangerous and wild in nature, even toward their handlers. A Mustang or a Brumby is a *feral* animal, a domestic horse that has returned to life in the wild, despite maintaining many of the physiological characteristics of human selective breeding.

When compared to the wild form, each of these possibilities reveal an even greater amount of valuable information about their *capacity to adapt* to changing circumstances. I understand it can feel a bit insulting — even sacrilegious— to spend all of this time learning how to revel in the beauty of your totem's wild nature— and then to ask it how well it would respond to training behaviors in a zoo. But when we look with a *pragmatic* rather than emotional eye, we reveal nothing more than *another aspect of its nature*, another tool in its tool belt when it comes to survival. Some animals can adapt to a wide variety of temperature or weather variation, while others can deal with food changes or scarcity. And some animals can adapt to life around humans better than others.

An American 'Possum is a damn good surviver. It can survive in the forest, it can survive in the alleyway— and it can survive pretty darn well curled up on the rug by the fireplace. And if that means he has to do a few tricks for a bit of high-value food, so be it, seeing as that's a pretty good trade. He gets shelter, food, protection, and affection all in exchange for loss of control over his own movements, loss of the ability to bite anyone he pleases, and perhaps even loss of the ability to mate and procreate. (Hey, you can't win 'em all.) But in exchange, he may live twice as long as he would have in the wild, entirely in relative luxury. From a human perspective, it's a matter of priorities.

Wolfish Logic— It's All Adaptation

I need to take a moment to tell a story to further drive our point. Anyone who's been reading around the Internet in the last few years may have run across the new "there are no alpha wolves" concept. Depending on what you read and where, you may have been left with the impression that the entire idea of "alpha Wolves" — or of Wolf society being organized hierarchically by expressed dominance— was somehow recently proven "wrong." Somewhere in olden times, someone studied Wolves and came up with the alpha concept but didn't realize the animals' natural behaviors were disrupted because they were confined in a park or something. That wasn't "natural" behavior at all! That was "prison" behavior! All this time it's been a matter of humans projecting toxic masculinity onto an innocent animal who simply lives in cute little families of Daddy, Mommy, and babies with no nasty violence or aggression. What a happy and uplifting story that contains no political ulterior motives whatsoever!

Seriously, never get your science from two-minute videos on social media. It is true that the original study conducted by L. David Mech was later amended by the author himself to reflect the fact that what he observed may or may not be "normal" Wolfish behavior as it took place among unrelated adult Wolves in captive circumstances. However, the more important error that was committed was on the part of his report's *interpretation* by the general population, who took the idea of "natural-born" "alphas and betas" and ran with it as an excuse to be terrible to other people and other animals in a variety of circumstances.

The *error* lies in how *humans* understand and relate to the concept of "dominance" — but any Dog trainer worth their Milk Bones will tell you that's a pretty common problem. What humans *think of* when we say "alpha wolf" is wrong, and indeed often reflective of unhealthy, competition-driven masculinity: domination for its own sake, authority without earned status, constant expression of challenges and submission, the beginnings of an abusive relationship. But Wolf packs have always had their own "alphas" that they understand whether we do or not, and for them an alpha is simply a *strong leader,* one who shows the others what to do to everyone's benefit because they know how to do it best. Wolves are never about the expression of dominance for its own sake, in the manner of a man who parks his BMW across three parking spaces for no clear reason. An alpha Wolf will only exert him- or herself to "express dominance" when another Wolf clearly challenges their position, which may well only happen when they begin to grow old, or if food becomes scarce; an alpha worth his or her mettle may rarely have to exert dominance at all. Often the alphas of a pack *are* the mother and father of the others, but not always; a pack will be lead by the most fit and experienced male and female of the pack, but pack size can vary according to the carrying capacity of the land

and other changing circumstances. This has not, and will not, change.

My other half would never have forgiven me if I hadn't found a way to work all that in here. But Wolfish agendas aside, it drives us right into another great example of *adaptation varying by circumstance.* The breadth of the land, the amount of prey on it, and the presence of humans are all simply variables to which the same Wolfish instincts can adapt to in different ways. Sometimes this leads to enormous packs of twenty individuals, sometimes it favors smaller packs of just a mated pair and their offspring; packs are often formed by a mated pair and their adult pups, but sometimes unrelated adults have to form a pack together; sometimes this leads to an easy pack life where all members are well fed and content to keep their rank with little fuss, and sometimes it leads to a situation where the lead male or female have to exert themselves to keep everyone in line. What is natural is the Wolfish behavior, their method itself as applied to all and every widely changing situation, and not necessarily any one situation itself.

If you are with me up until this point, check your own biases and continue on with me when I suggest that giving up the role of alpha entirely to humans was just another adaptation to a new environment made by Wolfish logic. We have all heard the pretty well-established theory that domestic Cats domesticated themselves (trading affection with humans in exchange for living in their mouse-filled granaries). But there also exists the theory that the first Dogs did similarly, with packs choosing to follow behind bands of humans as they hunted and migrated, eating the free food the humans left behind in the form of garbage, trading their protection and (eventually) their assistance with hunting for a fair share of a more reliable food source and perhaps better protection for their own pups. The Wolf in charge should be the one most able to lead and provide, and whether the idea first belonged to Wolves or the humans, in the end the Wolves stuck with it when the humans proved themselves the best "Wolf" for the job.

Of course, once in charge of the pack, the animal needs of the humans themselves began to make their mark. Alpha Wolves for the most part only expect excitable, submissive attention from puppies; only on rare or special occasion will adult pack members show affection like pups do. But humans are different, and human leaders responded very well to such behavior from puppies and adults alike. Combine that with the fact that human packs would never accept a Wolf as a leader and expected the Wolves to always follow instead of lead, and it continued to favor adults who were content to act like pups who wanted for a parent. In time, Wolves whose minds had adapted to find tail wagging, face licking, and rolling over for belly scratches completely normal behavior for adults were able to be more successful as Dogs. In time, the Wolf template had adapted so much that it became a new type, a Wolf with a permanent Peter Pan Complex. But it is still a Wolf, just one of many legitimate types of Wolf; we have Gray Wolves, Red Wolves, African Wolves— and we have Dog-Wolves. And the Wolf within them begins to reassert itself most especially when they are left to govern themselves again, when they return to a wild, feral life away from humans and the strongest Dogs take the lead again.

When the true importance of exploring the concept of domestication totemically became known to me, I had a sobering conversation with my other half. He understood perfectly the entire idea when I first said: "Despite best efforts, in a hundred, maybe two hundred years from now, there simply might not be any Wolves left. But there *will* be Dogs." Despite the fact that he has often joked that to a true wild canine totem, a Dog is a nothing more than a "stupid Wolf," the importance of the concept deeply took root, as survival of the species is, ultimately, the only true rule set forth by Mother Nature. As we chug along into what some scientists are suggesting we call the Anthropocene, the geological age defined by the changes wrought by humans, all animals, all totems and the people who bear them, will have to take a step back and evaluate what the future holds and what their survival options look like.

Which is all well and good (or, you know: *not*), but it can leave us with the question of how making such an adaptation applies to the lives of specific humans and their totems. But I can continue to use my other half as an example, because for him, surviving a career in the corporate world can be a matter of pulling on Wolf's ability to domesticate himself— and to listen to what Dog has to say to get him through the day without biting anyone.

Remember, you will be quite easily able to pull at closely related animal energies to your totems, others of the species or of closely related *kinds*. So his alpha female Gray Wolf is able to provide him with instinctual information from male wolves, from wolves who are followers, and other *kinds* of wolves, including Dog. As it happens, Dog is much better suited to take orders from someone of higher rank who doesn't necessarily display the signs of a competent leader; Wolves see such signs as weakness and question whether it is time to step in and take over the pack, but Dog's loyalty to his leader is much more ride-or-die in terms of faithfulness, and he is much more willing to forgive a mistake and give the benefit of the doubt. And Dogs, as we all know, are also much more keen to shrug-off a bad day and let a smile and a playful attitude buoy them along. So that needless, boring staff meeting with middle-management is much easier to take as a loyal German Shepard than as a Wolf; being asked to re-do the same task, solve a problem that would have been easier if dealt with a week ago, or just resisting the urge to say "I knew better" are all easier to swallow as a playful Lab who's just happy he has something to keep him busy— and a secure pack to follow.

In the same way I have advised you to draw on the influences of one of your other totems that is not your Primary if they could handle a situation better, it is only slightly more challenging to listen to advice of a close-cousin of your Primary— a domestic form who can handle this "society" bullshit better than you can.

The Zookeeper

So what exactly is the owner of a Wolverine to do? We don't all have the luxury of totems that slip gracefully into the urban lifestyle. Some animals can be domesticated, but some cannot even be trained; I myself even suggested that confinement to a cage was enough to kill certain animals outright.

If you (and your totem) are having difficulty finding a comfortable niche in the human world, and your totem does not have the benefit of a closely related domesticated *kind* to look to, I want to suggest a mental exercise designed to help you find that balance. Provided of course that you have first thoroughly researched the ins and outs of their natural lifestyle, I want you to look at the situation through the eyes of a responsible zookeeper who has been put in charge of caring for your totem animal. Rehabilitation and release is not an option, so your job is to design a habitat to house the animal as well as an enrichment program to mentally stimulate it.

What might that look like? How big does the habitat need to be— Does it need space to run? Or tiers to climb? Does it need rocks to crawl through, or foliage to hide in? Does it need running water to swim in? What about food? Will you need to hide the food in different places as a foraging exercise, or put it in puzzles? Does it need to be housed alone, with others of its kind, or with other animals? How would it respond to being on display to the public — is one-way glass required, or perhaps setting it back from the crowds across a moat? Or would it enjoy the attention too much and over-stimulation become a problem?

Consider researching how real-life zoos and wildlife refuges handle your totem animal and others of a similar *kind*; look at both the most progressive, modern approaches as well as the well-intentioned but perhaps less-than-ideal methods of the past, including those of circuses. What are the most common health problems encountered when dealing with your totem animal in captivity? Depression and lethargy? Nutritional deficiency or obesity? Stress from too much display exposure? Aggression towards handlers? Refusal to reproduce, or aggression toward others of its own species?

Every problem you uncover in exploring how your totem would fare in a zoo will uncover a potential area of difficulty you've likely experienced in your own life; every solution the responsible "zookeeper" finds for helping the animal adjust to life in captivity will provide you with a means to address those difficulties.

So let's explore some examples. An animal who needs space to run, and the regular exercise that goes with it, may experience lethargy when confined to any enclosed space, except perhaps for the largest open wildlife refuge. A Buffalo, a Horse, an African Wild Dog, a Cheetah. So a person bearing such an animal as a totem will need to understand that depression and lethargy may be reoccurring problems when confined to the closed-in stillness of the classroom, the cubicle, or the apartment complex. Physical exercise would be important, but the problem would be more difficult to solve than a gym membership.

So what is the responsible zookeeper to do? In this case, we may need to allow the keeper the ability to take the animal out of confinement for limited periods of time, so long as they are able to be controlled and recalled. Think of it like taking a Horse or a Dog out for a good run in the woods or the park— a bit of time to run "off leash" as it were. As a human with such a totem, your instincts may predispose you to feel an urge to *get out* into the wild, to roam unfettered, to be *free*. But quitting your day job and joining-up with a group of Lakota-Sioux warriors riding the open plains hunting buffalo isn't a realistic career option these days. So think like a zookeeper, and give yourself the best you can. You will need to get out into nature regularly, and don't just *sit* in it "glamping" in your RV— hike, walk, run, climb, explore. If you can afford it, or are physically able, put a National Park on your list of yearly vacations. If not, do the best you can; you will get at least some benefit from walks in your local park where you can feel the wind on your face and hear the birds in the trees.

What about if you have a hunting animal? Usually, my other half and I see the hunting instincts of totems reflected in their bearer's ability to set goals for themselves and achieve them. Some animals hunt only when hungry, such as Lions, while others must hunt to appease an instinct for the hunt whether they are hungry or not, such as House Cats; some humans create new goals for their lives only when they need a change, while others can become obsessed with success for its own sake. Some hunters scent, track, and chase down prey, while others wait patiently for the right circumstances to leap out and strike; some humans are good at conceiving of a plan and creating logical, achievable steps to attain it, while other humans will wait for the right circumstances to occur on their own and then seize them.

But for many people, the "hunting" instinct of their totems may not be so easily appeased. After all, despite what the most well-intentioned Buddhist or opinionated vegan may tell you, the human animal itself is a predator (please research the structure of our teeth, the positioning of our eyes, and the nutritional requirements of evolving our over-sized brain if you don't believe me). But hunting, as a sport, is just not for everyone. For one thing, someone who has not grown-up around hunting culture, or farm culture where animals are raised as food, may find the experience of killing an animal emotionally traumatic, even if they aren't intellectually opposed to the idea. For another, there is both ethical and unethical sport hunting available in the U.S. and abroad, and for an urbanite without access to a cousin with land out in the country someplace, the only kinds of hunts available might be paid "canned hunts" where you pay to be driven right to the animal and all you have to do is "point and shoot." Obviously, this is not "hunting" by any true or natural definition of the word; it is *killing*, which is a different instinct entirely.

If your totem is turned-on by the idea of stalking prey, but your human life just doesn't support hunting, be a creative zookeeper and find other ways, other "enrichment exercises" which might satisfy that urge. One way might be through sport in a variety of forms, in which one masters throwing or kicking something accurately at a target, or at catching it. My other half has found that wildlife photography scratches that itch, as the process of sighting and stalking "subjects" is relatively similar to stalking prey, and "catching" the animal is a matter of getting that perfect photo. For that matter, activities such as competitive bird watching with the National Audubon Society are a thing, where you are driven to find and see as many types of rare birds as possible to check them off your list. Be creative.

I would like to highlight the term again: *enrichment exercises*. The right habitat and diet are only the start; the true test of the zookeeper's ability to not only keep his animal alive but *happy* lies within the steps taken every day to satisfy as many of its natural instincts as possible, to stimulate its mind and nourish its soul to the best of human ability. When you learn your totems, ask them what they need. And ask all of them, and not just the Primary.

Look into yourself, ask your totem what it would most like to be doing right now or why it is unsatisfied with the choices you have made for your life. Then, exercise your human quality of Will in the form of self-awareness to do what you can to address your animal needs in the best way possible in your civilized modern life. At first, asking a fierce hunting animal like a Wolf or a Python or a Cheetah to be satisfied with nature walks and bird-watching may sound like a cop-out. But consider that it's not so far removed from what people do with working Dogs: if your pet is a birding Dog, you will *need* to give him retrieval exercises, and if he is a herding Dog, you will *need* to run him. And even a Pit bull born and bred to fight bulls can be a faithful, loving friend if they are exercised in the right way— and doubly-so if they aren't chained to a tree and ignored. It is not such an unreasonable step to apply the same logic to your own animal self.

Domestic Animals as Totems

Over the years, between my other half and myself, there has been no topic that has received more attention than the idea of domestic forms of animals serving as totems. A reader who may be familiar with the works of other contemporary authors on the subject may find themselves in a similar position to my husband's: that domestic animals are not "natural" forms, they are not "made by Mother Nature," and therefore cannot be totems in their own rights; rather, seeing a domestic animal in totemic context is a finger pointing the bearer towards the true totem in its wild form. Or, the short version: the belief that Dogs cannot be totems, only Wolves. Many people might understand the domestication situation to be similar to my discussion of "imperfect fit" totems such as a prehistoric or mythical animal represents an aspect of yourself you are not yet ready to face in its true form.

But notice that I chose not to speak of domestic animals in the Stubborn Nature section with the other imperfect fits. Through a great deal of introspective work and observation, both of us have come to accept the conclusion that domestic forms of animals in fact *can* be seated as totems, though bear in mind that such totems also carry with them certain liabilities not seen in their wild forms.

That largest area of contention in our conversations would always arise along the ideas of adaptation and traits. The argument went that while domestication by selective breeding might produce a few new traits (or inhibit traits) it does not create a new animal, it is not a substitute for speciation caused by evolution. (They can still interbreed with their wild forms, after all). It is not a new or independent type of animal; it is a muted form of the original, and therefore should not be regarded as separate.

Of course, keep in mind that a majority of these discussions took place before we had fully explored and codified the concepts of domestic, tamed, trained, and feral, and gained more specific understanding of the differences between them. Because it is true that a tamed or trained animal is still wild and unchanged in its form, and speaking of a tamed animal and a domesticated animal in the same conversation can create some confusion. Yes, it is true there is no notable difference between a "domestic Cockatoo" and a "wild Cockatoo" because the birds kept as pets are only tamed and have not been altered; there is only "Cockatoo" where totems are concerned. But that is not the case for all *domesticated* animals.

My other half was finally able to be swayed on the subject after we had both read a report of a study done with Dogs that explained the *unique* (highlight that word "unique") behaviors Dogs possess compared to Wolves. These include but are not limited to the ability to understand when humans point at something, a better ability to understand human facial, vocal, and body-language cues, the instinct to prefer the food of its human even when its own food is clearly of higher quality, and a much stronger instinct than Wolves to ignore unfair treatment in deference to pack hierarchy. All of this forces the issue that if Dogs aren't just muted or neutered forms of Wolves, but in fact possess *different* skills from Wolves, then they *must* be regarded as different animals— a sub-type to be sure, but a legitimate sub-type as different from their ancestral Gray as is the Arctic, the Tibetan, and African Wolves.

All of this does fit together with our tradition's existing belief of why totems must be animals: walking a mortal life on this earth as humans do. Certainly domestic animals live life in the flesh the same as any other, and can provide advice on how to live through unique survival instincts. In fact, in many situations, the energy of living domestic animals in this world well outnumbers their wild counterparts (and in the case of some, the wild form is extinct) making the domestic a more common and accessible animal to appear as a totem.

However, when defining a totem's true form, it should be noted that even when concerning comfortably domestic forms of animals, there can still be an area of ambiguity that is not quite as clear as that between Dogs and Wolves, or Cows and Aurochs, or Sheep and wild Muflon. With some forms, the domesticated animal is not quite so far removed from the ancestor, with perhaps only a few traits changed. For example, House Cats are relatively unchanged from the small African Wildcats they came from, with the only major difference being that House Cats continue to mew into adulthood as a form of communication meant specifically to influence humans. Similarly, domestic Horses have been changed in form to be taller, faster, prettier, and to have more agreeable temperaments than their wild ancestors, but mentally they are basically the same animal; the same can be said for many types of domesticated farm birds, some Goats, Rabbits, and Pigs. For that matter, there is a technical difference between wild Bison and those contemporarily raised for meat, as those have been interbred with Cows to improve temperament, and today there are almost no non-hybrid American Bison left.

As I've mentioned before, a good benchmark to use is the question of going feral: if the domesticated animal can not only slip back into the wild with relatively little difficulty, but resume the roll of its ancestral species in the ecosystem, then there may be little functional difference between the domesticated and wild forms as far as totems are concerned. Remember that even though Dogs can survive relatively well as a feral species, there will never come a point where they turn back into Wolves; areas could conceivably see wild populations of both at once. The same could be true of actual wild Horses (such as the Przewalski's) and Mustangs. But anyone from the southern half of the U.S. will know that feral Pigs resume their roll as Wild Boars with relative ease, and an Australian reader would know well that House Cats set loose in the Outback resume hunting small animals in the deserts exactly where their ancestors in Egypt left off. The details separating one from another vary according to the animal. When researching the details of a totem, one should simply consider signs of domestication no differently than others differences between one species and another of a similar *kind*.

So after all that, what does it mean to have a domestic form of an animal for a totem? I mentioned previously there are some liabilities; pragmatically, it means that such totems bring unique challenges to their bearer along with their unique skills. It comes down to this: a domestic animal has no natural role in nature; therefore, as totems, they often have more difficulty than normal achieving the functional *balance* or *harmony of self* that I spoke of early-on in this book.

Let's look at that in more detail. When asking the fundamental questions about how such an animal relates to the wild, a domestic animal has no "native" ecosystem to speak of; all of your answers to the Identifying Questions of its feeding habits, social structure, mating habits, and basic niche in nature etc. will have to be second-best-guesses that combine information from its wild ancestor with information from its feral cousins. We know that Dogs are socially pack animals, hunt small to medium sized prey, and can survive in most climates— but feral populations live only in places where they were first discarded by humans, and a good many Dogs have been bred to have unique coats for human work or pleasure more ill-suited than a Wolf's to adapt to weather, and many others carry an instinct to hunt animals only for their master's sport and not their own survival.

The keystone point in understanding a domestic totem is the inclusion of that word *human* or *master*. Domesticated animals have been altered in such a way that they *rely* on human interference as part of their instinctual survival strategy. While a strong Dog will assume the role of alpha if one is needed in his pack, all Dogs (no matter how willful) feel more secure with a strong human master taking charge; a Dog bred to hunt ducks and other waterfowl will find the task all but impossible without a hunter's gun. A domesticated Horse gone feral will always want for harmony with his animal neighbors, as there is no balanced natural relationship between Horses and other grazers who can get pushed off their own land when Horses move in. We all know domestic Sheep must be sheered by humans or become suffocated by their own wool; most all domesticated farm birds carry elaborate decorative plumage only to suit human aesthetics that would get them eaten in a second in the wild.

The unconscious template, the blueprint if you will, of a domesticated animal comes equipped with a blank space, a lacking of sorts, that is intended to be filled by a human master. Yes, they can survive without humans; but they cannot be totally fulfilled or complete on their own. Ideally, the goal of our discipline of totemism is the realization and acceptance of the entire essential self, which brings with it a pragmatic understanding of needs, interests, limits, dreams, and along with it peace-of-mind— that is, *balance* within the self. A domesticated animal totem cannot find nor provide that balance on its own. Instead, it will bring the liability of co-dependence.

If seated as a totem, and especially as one of the center three, this leaves the bearer of a domestic animal totem with an inability to find fulfillment or balance without the direct involvement of another person, rather than wholly within themselves.

The most common example I can pull is Dog, who is not an uncommon presence in the totemic world. It is not my intent to embarrass or single-out anyone with a Dog totem (many of whom are fine, successful, usually exceptionally kind individuals), but among them I do see a common, uniting factor that usually manifests itself in their choice of mate or spouse: they want for an alpha. If they have managed to marry someone who is a strong leader of some herd, pack, or pod, they can generally do quite well in life.

But I see problems arise when Dog people elect to be with someone whom they only *think* can be a good leader but is actually not, perhaps someone whose totem is large or fierce in some way but lacks leadership instincts. Here is where the defining difference between a Dog and a Wolf really shows through: any Wolf, despite temperament, is capable of coping and assuming a leadership role if a leader is needed, but a Dog forced into the same situation will be under profound stress and may not be able to cope at all. (Dog trainers, coincidentally, view most misbehavior in the animal as stemming from confusion and anxiety over just who is in charge of— and therefore *responsible* for— the whole household). I have seen too many Dog people try to *manipulate* their partner into being who they think they *ought* to be, rather than accepting them for who they are or moving on. Their partner cannot provide the sense of secure pack structure they want for themselves and they grow to resent them for it. This is the sort of person who believes they can coerce or manipulate their partner with small, biting comments, or who can shame them into being "better" by belittling them. "Why don't you just leave him, then?" "I know, right? I totally should, he's such a loser." We run into a similar problem when a Dog person tries to be alone; they see it only as a resting phase between dominant mates, not a period of aloneness for its own sake. The idea of being their *own* alpha simply eludes them.

The concept of the "Lone Wolf" is largely a myth. It's not uncommon for adult Wolves, especially males, to leave the packs of their birth and strike out on their own. But any Wolf wandering in such a way is looking for territory and a mate of his own. Unlike the human attitude we give the same name, a true "lone" Wolf is not naturally predisposed to wander alone and single, and is instead simply looking for the right mate, looking to not be alone. Wolves can cope with being by themselves because they can become their own alphas, can lead a pack of one. But whenever we see a lone Dog, we all instinctually know it must be a recent escapee, slipped under a fence somewhere, because feral Dogs never travel by themselves.

Any person who carries a domesticated animal as a totem needs to understand that some of their natural inclinations may lead them toward behaviors that are not always healthy for human relationships; even as it may be right for them, it may not be right for the others in their lives. And yes, this is true for some types of wild animal totems as well. But it is, unfortunately, more pronounced for the totem that has no niche of its own to find in the natural world; a Dog person cannot look to nature to understand their place or role among the other animals. Ultimately, however, to progress with pragmatism and purpose in their life, such a person needs to address this propensity for co-dependence no differently from any other limiting factor of any other totem: it needs to be recognized, understood, and ultimately respected and loved for what it is. Like any other quality, human Will allows you to choose which voice to listen to and when in order to find peace within yourself and your life.

The End — The Untamable

Anyone who has ever spent more than ten minutes with a group of pagans will realize that we're the biggest bunch of misfits you're likely to ever run across. Each individual's performance will vary, but we do seem to collect a large number of people who cannot, or will not, function smoothly in broader, "normal" society— the number of grown-up goth kids Wicca inherited notwithstanding. I mentioned before my tongue-in-cheek observation that a group of pagans may as well be a herd of cats. Your basic House Cat may well have domesticated itself, but any wildlife rescue will be quick to tell you that even if you raise them from cubs, *Tigers are never pets.*

Of course, not every pagan who cannot (or willfully will not) fit smoothly into broader human society is a Tiger; sometimes they are just a stripy House Cat who wants to be bigger, or more powerful, or more respected than they are. (As an aside to my fellow witches and pagans who are fond of the "we don't *really* eat babies" joke, I hate to be the one to tell you this, but no one really thinks this about us; people don't think we're dangerous, they think we're *dorks*.) From my personal observation, we are a religion that is far too quick to make allowances for our weaknesses, or to deny them altogether through alternative identity that gives the appearance of power, rather than invest ourselves in the effort to truly grow stronger. The community is in need of a little kick in the pants, a little left-handed magick given with love, which I will offer now with my closing thoughts, with all due kindness.

Unfortunately, within that larger pagan community, I have always seen a preponderance of what has only recently been given a name by Internet culture: the ideological echo-chamber. It is one thing to feel uncomfortable around strictly Christian family or basic and straight-laced colleagues, but it is another thing entirely to be unable to function around them, unable to talk to or interact with them — let alone hold-up your end of a debate with them— and to have to build for yourself a life that involves only other pagans, progressivists, vegans, light-workers, left-wingers, "all-natural" crunchy people who think exactly as you do; it is the exact same for those on the opposite side of the coin who surround themselves only with other pro-gun, pro-life, anti-government, anti-feminist complementarian, pro-kindred "I swear it's not racist, it's heritage" lineage-based magicks. It's one thing to be frustrated by opposing opinions (or even views that are, dare I say, *wrong*), but it's another to be so upset by simply hearing them that you purposefully edit people out of your life altogether, building instead a sort of self-sheltered safe-space with people that only ever agree with how you already think and feel. (And if you scowled and rumbled at my mere *suggestion* that kindred-based heathenry is often racist, you've forfeited your right to call anyone else a "triggered Snowflake" ever again, so please sit down.)

Personally speaking, I do not believe any totem incapable of adapting to life in the human world; as with so many other things we have discussed, we are simply dealing with situations that present *more* or *fewer* challenges. Still, we do come to a point where we must deal with totems, and the humans who bear them, who really give us considerable difficulty shoe-horning them to "fit in" with larger human society. Some animals can be domesticated, and their domesticated forms can become a sound source of advice on how to adapt; some animals can be tamed and trained, and made to live comfortably enough in captivity so long as their "keeper" is educated and conscientious about their needs; and we can use the concept of going feral as a barometer of sorts to gauge just how much (if any) permanent change has taken place, depending on how easily the altered form can return to natural life. But what about animals who simply *can't* adapt to the cubicle, the car-pool lane, or contentment on the sofa?

This is a question that only an individual can address for him- or herself after a healthy amount of time has been spent cultivating self-awareness and deepening their understanding of the true essential self; it takes the sort of wisdom that only strengthening our relationships with our totems can provide. Is it really true that you *can't*, or is it that you just don't *want to*? And at what point does a want become so strong that it becomes a need? I am not, and have never been, here to tell you how to live your life. Only you know what you can and cannot do, what you want and do not want, who you are and who you are not. I am simply here to offer the wisdom of my observations and the guidance of a little left-handed magick — specifically to that House-Cat who grows lazy and fat because he will not make himself explore the snow outside the backdoor and blames his condition on the idea that he is supposedly a Saber-Toothed Tiger who is too wild to be an indoor cat. If no one will date you, if no one respects you, if no one likes you— chances are pretty high the fault lies with *you*, not in other people who stubbornly refuse to see what a "nice guy" you really are.

I have learned through my never-ending research on the Jaguar and his kin that in suburban Africa it is not uncommon for Leopards to live at the edges of civilization, raiding trash bins and picking-off domestic animals and pets; in North America, the Cougar often lives similarly, as does the Jaguar himself in places where civilization and the jungle collide. There is space to be found for Clan Pantera in the human world: he drops-in when he needs something and then retreats to his solitude, but he can coexist if he respects the rules and minds the boundaries of what will be tolerated and where. It is a form of training, self-imposed, to learn how to successfully navigate the human world to reap its benefits without threat or danger. I don't believe I will ever completely "fit in" with mundane society, and I don't think I'd ever want to. But I choose to take the hard route and I will never withdraw from the human world, either; coincidentally, misanthropy does not necessarily lend itself to hermitage.

A Jaguar is not an animal that can be domesticated. With some discipline, it can be trained; but even a Jaguar born in a circus and bottle-fed by a human remains a wild, untamed animal, at risk of biting the hand that feeds him for little more than a foul mood. Please: do not mistake my above observations for the ramblings of another "love-fixes-everything" hippie who is suggesting you can solve all your problems by forcing a muzzle and leash on a Bear. I do not call myself a witch without reason; it is because I understand full well the extent and power in darkness and how both Light and Dark can be redirected to healing, growth, and betterment. I know damn well how difficult it is to force a wild animal to live in a house, to teach a natural-born shaman to give a damn about capitalism and income taxes.

I have come to understand that life is simply a matter of *what is*. There is no room for denying it for the sake of what we'd rather it be, or for rejecting it for what we feel it "should" be. View reality with clear eyes and *then* make the best of what there is. Seek out what brings joy to your soul and do it, but recognize that you also have a duty to take care of yourself and your family to the best of your ability, despite how tedious and difficult that work may be; your dream of owning your own shop or retreat or rescue means nothing to me if your children's needs are neglected.

If you take nothing else of me with you, *know* that you are endowed with the awesome power of human Will and divinely blessed by your knowledge of it. It is *unbecoming* of someone on the path of the wise to blame their own failings on their circumstances.

If the innate wildness of your totem has led you to be an artist, a performer, a writer, a dreamer; a teacher, a builder, a creator, a doer; a misfit, a poet, a music-maker, a weird person who is always just a little bit on the outside looking in at all the muggles of the world who seem so able to be happy and content with little fuss or difficulty— I want you to ignore all your natural instincts and listen to me: *you are the way you are*. And that's more than ok— it is *beautiful*. No one sits around and marvels at the mystery and the majesty in the colors of a common beast. If you truly are a Tiger, it is not your place to be jealous of the House Cat, even as he has a warm stuffed bed with his name embroidered on it.

The Lioness born captive in a zoo is the shaman born captive in suburbia. In another time, or another place, you might have had the opportunity to grow into your natural role of the medicine man, the wise woman, the healer, the seer, the one with a foot in the spirit world, the *contrary*, the full-time shaman who had no need to fit-in with the regular goings-on of your village because your concerns were of the spirit-world and your place and purpose were underscored by that "outsider" status. But also recognize that your ability to *live,* here and now, means some degree of discipline and adaptation to this reality: by putting on that tie every morning, by putting on that leash— at least for a few hours a day, before you can run free again. After all, if my other half was not willing to do this very thing to make a living for our family, I would not have been able to take the time to write this book. It *is* different when you put the leash on yourself to live, because *you* can take it off whenever you need to. And because there is never shame in living.

The path of the totem is not gentle. I know many people have come to expect neo-pagan books to be empowering, to expect a teacher of pagan ways to present them as nothing but uplifting and encouraging. But that is not the reality of *what is*. It may sell books and tickets to seminars, but it is not the truth, and it is not what you need to hear to grow within yourself. True witches, true shamans of our ancestral past, knew that a teacher must be honest with her students. And they knew that a path of honest introspection, by its very nature, can only be a difficult, lonely road to walk. I do not have an easy, step-by-step path to perfect enlightened happiness through totemism that I can lay-down before you, because no such thing exists— it would be wise to be wary of anyone who claims otherwise.

A totem is not just a source of pride, a pagan merit-badge you wear on the shoulder of your ritual robes. It is a scar that becomes a tattoo when rubbed with the ash of your trials. The truths you uncover *will hurt.* But pain, by its nature, evokes the magick of Fire; for the new forest to grow, the old must be burned away, and in order for a wound to heal it must swell and ache with heat and even decay. When you come through your trials and out the other side, **you will know.** And being *One Who Knows* is worth more than any boost of adrenaline and serotonin that comes from group hugs and happy chants.

See the world for what it is and do the best with what you have. Find *liberation*, not discouragement, in that knowledge. Nourish the souls of others. Care for them as though it were your job, even if they don't understand, even if they don't realize you're doing it, because in another time or another life it would have been your place to look after their spiritual welfare, and because in many ways, it still is. Teach. Create. Have patience. Love. Sing. Maybe someday, write a book.

A domesticated animal never ceases to be an animal. And the wild spirit of an animal never ceases to be beautiful.

Appendix One: Rituals

Grounding

Grounding (also called "earthing") is an important preliminary step before any spiritual exercise is undertaken. The term is taken from electronics, in which part of a circuit is arranged so that excess electricity is discharged into the ground to keep the system from overloading.

Within a human being, grounding your body's energy is a matter of reestablishing your natural connection to the earth, of releasing excess stress, emotions, thoughts, and physical energy so that you are relaxed, focused, mentally present, and spiritually cleansed of the clutter of the mundane. You must ground yourself before you take on any spiritual exercise or ritual. Otherwise, your spiritual experience will be clouded by all the excess "stuff" you may be carrying in your heart, mind, and soul.

There are many methods of metaphysical grounding, with almost as many varied and unique methods available as there are people who practice it. Many people ground themselves through behaviors they don't even realize are grounding exercises, such as meditation, prayer, cultivating awareness, and relaxation techniques such as measured breathing.

This is a technique that works well for me. I invite you to research the topic for yourself. You may use any technique you find or discover that works for you.

Grounding by Roots, Trunk, and Branches

Begin by sitting upright in a chair; choose one that has good back support or consciously use good posture and sit-up straight. Relax your shoulders and arms. Plant both feet flat on the floor.

Close your eyes. Breathe in deeply and slowly, hold the breath for a moment, and release it slowly. Breathe whatever way feels most comfortable to you, nose or mouth, belly or chest. Pay attention to your breaths; if your focus drifts away to something else, bring it back. Simply be present in the moment, watching yourself breathe in, hold it, and breathe out. Do this for at least five breaths, but you may do as many as you need until you feel physically relaxed and calm. Continue to breathe calmly, but now shift your focus inward.

Become aware of the earth beneath you, no matter how far down she is. Feel the support, the security of the solid ground; become aware of the gravity pulling you downward. Visualize that your feet have sprouted roots, and they are growing down, deep into the soil. Feel the depth of the great planet beneath you, dark and damp, full of stones and water and life. Recognize yourself as the child of the earth, and you are making contact with your mother, the mother of all life. The mother earth is feeding you from your roots; she pulls all negative energy and feelings out from your roots, and gives you rich life energy to pull up your roots into yourself. Pull that good energy up into your core, near your stomach.

Envision yourself growing into a tree, that your core is your trunk as your roots are growing deep into the ground underneath you. Now, shift your focus upward and envision yourself growing branches and limbs up from your arms, shoulders, and head. Your branches stretch up, up

II

into the sky. Feel the breath of the wind through your branches. Feel the warmth of the hot sun shining down on you, that great luminous being that gives its energy to all life on earth, looking out for us like a father. Beautiful green leaves unfurl and flowers bloom from your branches. You feel the wind carrying away any remaining negative thoughts or stressors. Feel the heat of the father sun nourishing you as you grow stronger.

Bring your attention back to yourself, and bring your focus back to your own breathing. Breathe in, hold it, and breathe out. Do this for at least five breaths.

Open your eyes. You should feel calmer, more present and focused, but also energized, perhaps more awake, more healthy, and ready to begin whatever task lay before you.

You are now ready to perform whatever spiritual rite or ritual you wish. You may also use this technique any time you feel anxious, unfocused, or otherwise in need of being centered and balanced— or reconnected to the magic of the natural world from which you came.

Totem Wheel

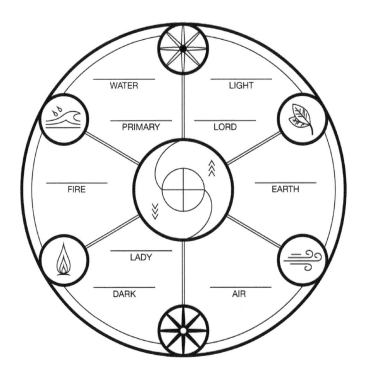

Fig. 2A: Totem Wheel

Affirmation One:

Hang your Totem Wheel near to where you meditate, pray, or otherwise communicate with the spiritual side of yourself. Sit or stand before your Totem Wheel and recite the following:

I Am
And I seek to know myself

*I have come to a place in my life's journey where I would
know who walks with me*
I have come to a time when I would know my totems

*Totem that is my true essential self; Totem of the Mother,
Totem of the Father; Totems of Earth, of Air, of Fire, and of
Water; Totems of Darkness and of Light;*

In the right time, in the right way,
in love and in light,
*I have come to honor the spirits of my animal-self and
declare*
my intent to learn,
to listen,
and to live in harmony with what
I Am.

Continue with your day, remain open to any impressions
you may receive. Make note of any strong mental images,
dreams, or experiences you have.

Affirmation Two:

For each totem you come to know, decide what its five
most dominant characteristics or qualities are and list them
here:

Characteristics of Earth Totem Animal

_____
_____
_____
_____
_____

Characteristics of Air Totem Animal

_____
_____
_____
_____
_____

Characteristics of Fire Totem Animal

_____
_____
_____
_____
_____

Characteristics of Water Totem Animal

_____
_____
_____
_____
_____

Characteristics of Light Totem Animal

_____
_____
_____
_____
_____

Characteristics of Dark Totem Animal

_____
_____
_____
_____
_____

Characteristics of Lord Totem Animal

_____
_____
_____
_____
_____

Characteristics of Lady Totem Animal

_____
_____
_____
_____
_____

Characteristics of Primary Totem Animal

_____

_____

_____

_____

_____

For each totem you discover, utilize its corresponding affirmation below, filling in the blanks with the type of animal and its five characteristic from above.

<u>Earth Totem Affirmation</u>

I am
Through my flesh, I am the Earth within me. I am the soil, the stone, and the trees.
I am myself
I am the _____ (totem) within me.   And I honor myself.
I am _____
I am _____
I am _____
I am _____
I am _____
I am the _____ (totem)
I have come to know my true self
And I give gratitude, acknowledgement, love
to myself, my essential self, my sacred-self,
and I _accept_ myself as
I am

Air Totem Affirmation

I am
Though my breath, I am the Air within me. I am the wind and the sky's bright horizon.
I am myself
I am the _____ (totem) within me. And I honor myself.
I am _____
I am _____
I am _____
I am _____
I am _____
I am the _____ (totem)
I have come to know my true self
And I give gratitude, acknowledgement, love
to myself, my essential self, my sacred-self,
and I *accept* myself as
I am

Fire Totem Affirmation

I am
Through my life-energy, I am the Fire within me. I am the
heat, the flame, and the sun   b l a z i n g
strong.
I am myself
I am the _____ (totem) within me.   And I honor
myself.
I am _____
I am _____
I am _____
I am _____
I am _____
I am the _____ (totem)
I have come to know my true self
And I give gratitude, acknowledgement, love
to myself, my essential self, my sacred-self,
and I *accept* myself as
I am

Water Totem Affirmation

I am
Through my blood, I am the Water within me.   I am the rivers, the rain, the infinite rolling   sea.
I am myself
I am the _____ (totem) within me.   And I honor myself.
I am _____
I am _____
I am _____
I am _____
I am _____
I am the _____ (totem)
I have come to know my true self
And I give gratitude, acknowledgement, love
to myself, my essential self, my sacred-self,
and I *accept* myself as
I am

Light Totem Affirmation

I am
Through my heart, I am the Light within me.   I am the glorious day shining my light on all   things.
I am myself
I am the _____ (totem) within me.   And I honor myself.
I am _____
I am _____
I am _____
I am _____
I am _____
I am the _____ (totem)
I have come to know my true self
And I give gratitude, acknowledgement, love
to myself, my essential self, my sacred-self,
and I *accept* myself as
I am

Dark Totem Affirmation

I am
Through my heart, I am the Darkness within me. I am the
glorious night casting my   shadow on all
things.
I am myself
I am the _____ (totem) within me.   And I honor
myself.
I am _____
I am _____
I am _____
I am _____
I am _____
I am the _____ (totem)
I have come to know my true self
And I give gratitude, acknowledgement, love
to myself, my essential self, my sacred-self,
and I *accept* myself as
I am

Lord Totem Affirmation

I am
I am the great Lord within me. I am the Father of all things, the spark that energizes.
I am myself
I am the _____ (totem) within me.   And I honor myself.
I am _____
I am _____
I am _____
I am _____
I am _____
I am the _____ (totem)
I have come to know my true self
And I give gratitude, acknowledgement, love
to myself, my essential self, my sacred-self,
and I *accept* myself as
I am

Lady Totem Affirmation

I am
I am the great Lady within me. I am the Mother of all things that nourishes and grows.
I am myself
I am the _____ (totem) within me.   And I honor myself.
I am _____
I am _____
I am _____
I am _____
I am _____
I am the _____ (totem)
I have come to know my true self
And I give gratitude, acknowledgement, love
to myself, my essential self, my sacred-self,
and I *accept* myself as
I am

Primary Totem Affirmation

I am
I am the Divine Soul within me. I am a being of spirit and a being flesh.
I am myself
I am the _____ (totem) within me. And I honor myself.
I am _____
I am _____
I am _____
I am _____
I am _____
I am the _____ (totem)
I have come to know my true self
And I give gratitude, acknowledgement, love
to myself, my essential self, my sacred-self,
and I *accept* myself as
I am

Shamanic Journeys

I strongly recommend you read the section on shamanic journeying in the main body of the book before you attempt these exercises.

Shamanic journeying is a discipline of the mind and a form of self-hypnosis used to cultivate heightened awareness. It seeks a sense of travel or movement throughout the inner reaches of the mind and spirit known as the Non-Ordinary Reality or NOR.

Journeying is a matter of beginning with a visualization, embracing it, and becoming a part of it to the point that you are no longer aware of the waking world. It is similar to dreaming, except that you are not fully asleep. The imagery will begin to take on a life of its own, will find its own story, and your journey is following that story. If you find yourself pulling away from the journey and waking up, don't become discouraged; just follow the drumbeat back in.

You will need a quiet and comfortable place to conduct your journey where you will not be interrupted and a recording of shamanic drumming to play. Plan to spend a minimum of ten to fifteen minutes on each journey, if not more. Before you begin, it is important that you ground yourself, either using the method provided above or another method that suits you. If your mind and spirit are not grounded, you will not be able to journey properly.

Any of the shamanic journeys provided here may be used as-is or altered to suit your own preference. You will need to familiarize yourself with the narrative beforehand.

Please note that I have put the narrative itself in plain type and put *additional instructions for heightening your awareness* of the experience in italics. I have described this first journey in greater detail than I have the others to help you get a feel for the process; subsequent journeys have only a basic narrative, leaving the details up to you.

Finding A Totem Guide

A good introductory-level task for you to accomplish during a shamanic journey in the NOR is searching for a Spirit Guide to help you find your totems. It should not require that you stay in the trance for very long or get into it very deeply.

Because you are now ready to know your totems, the Spirit Guide will all but certainly manifest as an aspect of the here-and-now, and so is to be found in the Middle World by shamanic reasoning.

After you have made yourself comfortable in your sacred place and grounded yourself, begin your drumming, close your eyes, and envision the following:

— — — —

Feel the environment around you; feel your own breathing, in and out, and hear nothing but the drumming. Feel the softness of the mat or the pillows below you, feel comfortable and content and cozy as you lie there. Feel nothing else but this moment, feel the drumming as though it were a river and the movement is carrying you away. Feel your mat or your pillow or your carpet as though they are bedding, and feel that you have been sleeping there and it is time to wake up.

Within your mind, feel yourself stretch and shift. See yourself opening your eyes to the diffused light of morning sun through a tent, and smell the cool fresh air of the outdoors flowing in. You are getting up from the floor of a large tent, a tan canvas caravan with sturdy wooden stakes and ropes pulled across the ceiling. Look to your side and find your bag, where you were laying your head, and fold your blanket away. You have slept in the old linen robes you always wear. The warm light of morning is coming in through the canvas above you and you are already late.

Shoulder your bag and head outside. Fall into line as the community packs-up and begins to travel across the landscape, slowly at the speed of work horses loaded with everyone's belongings.

Notice the details around you: the insects buzzing in the air as you trod the grasses, the foot-prints of the person walking in front of you and the footwear they're wearing, the rising sunlight in your eyes. Do you know where you are going? Or where you've just been? Look to the side of the path; you notice things the others overlook. If something invites you, pick it up. What is it? And why is it significant to you alone? If you begin to be lead astray, follow and explore as you are inclined. Allow yourself to follow what leads you, by whatever beckons to you or calls to you, freely and innocently as a child would. If the landscape changes, embrace it and explore it. Notice the changes, take-in the details of where you are.

You notice that the Wise One, the Medicine Maker, the Holy One, the Spirit Walker of your people, is missing. The Wise One likes to sleep separately sometimes, in their own tent, and won't know that the others are moving on. Begin to look more purposefully for signs of their passage.

What do you see? What signs can you find that they have passed this way? Search with purpose for what might lead you to the Wise One of your people— call-out to them if you feel they will answer. Be open to whatever wants to lead you toward the Holy One who has been left behind.

Allow yourself to find the shelter made in the night by the Medicine Maker of your people. Approach the shelter, and enter it as you are bid. It's dim inside, lit by fire, but you can see the tools of their path and smell the incense of their magic.

What do you see? How do you feel it's appropriate to approach them? Are things so familiar, you could walk up and say hello? Or are they more formal?

Tell the Holy One you have been searching for them. Tell them why you have really come. You are on a quest to know yourself. Ask them for their help, for guidance, for the benefit of their animal wisdom. Tell them if you were given such guidance, you would follow it; ask for a Spirit Guide to show you the way. A Spirit guide in the form of an animal to teach you about your animal self.

Be patient with their response. What does the Holy One tell you? What do they show you? What animal signs are you aware of in the place of the Holy One? What are you shown?

Allow yourself to be open and led in new directions. If something calls to you, follow. Allow the experience to become its own end. Ask questions. Follow instructions. Explore. Feel. Learn what is to be found within this place.

When you are satisfied that you have completed your work for this journey, envision yourself traveling back to the landscape where you started. Become aware of the drumming again, hear it as the foreign sound it has always been, coming into your ears from headphones rooted in the ordinary waking world. Go back to the camp of your people, which has been set up again just as you left it. Go back to your spot on the ground, get back into your bedding, wrap your arms around your pillow or blanket, and feel yourself open your eyes in the waking world.

— — — —-

If at any point you are introduced to your Totem Guide— or to a Totem!— it is important to acknowledge and thank it for revealing itself and offering its help. Remember: you have declared your intentions to know your totems, so you are now open to meeting them at any time, regardless of your intended goal in the NOR.

If you desire to journey to visit with your Totem Guide again, you may begin in the caravan tent and look for them in the place where you found the Wise One or where they directed you to go. You may also journey to any place in the NOR that you were shown. Pay attention, as such places can become sacred places to your spirit guides, to your totems, and to you. The place this journey began, the canvas caravan full of a community of kindred travelers, is itself inspired by a significant power dream I had many years ago that I was compelled to share with all of you.

Additional Journeys

Begin the visualizations of any journey with a neutral, but peaceful and comfortable, natural landscape. From there, you may decide to journey upwards, downward, or laterally across the landscape to access the Upper World, the Lower World, or the Middle World, depending on your goal in the NOR. If you are traveling upwards or down, look for some natural means of getting there: climb a tree, scale a cliff, or ride in a hearty wind up into the Upper World; climb down through a hole under a log or dive to the bottom of a pond to go to the Lower World. To help you access the Middle World, go around a large tree or through its hanging branches, walk into a cave, through a doorway, cross a river or bridge, jump across a bonfire, etc.

At any given time, any of your totems could be found in any of the Three Worlds. I have designed the journeys here to give you a good chance of finding them, but you are welcome to alter the details of them as you see fit, as your Totem Guide sees fit, or to let your journey itself go where it may and change direction.

For Totems of Earth, of Air, of Fire, of Water, of Light, and of Dark

Envision yourself sitting quietly at the base of a great tree. Its trunk is enormous and its branches are so wide that you are cast in deep shadow. The grass beneath you is scarce and damp, and exposed roots are green with moss.

Get up and begin to walk around the base of the tree, touching it with your hand as you go. It is knotted and ancient, yet it grows tall and strong and its branches rise so high above you, you cannot see the sky between them.

Ask that your Totem Guide show itself, and see it appearing in front of you, just around the edge of the tree trunk. Tell your Totem Guide that you would like to find whichever totem you are journeying to find this time.

Be patient; allow it to lead you or even carry you if it wants. If you are shown something you do not understand, ask questions. Don't force it, or get frustrated, if it seems like your Guide doesn't comply with your requests. Follow what your Guide tells you; its instructions are more important than mine now. But if your Totem Guide indicates that you should lead, proceed on:

Decide which World you want to journey to, and remember any of them can be accessed through the basic tree visualization. If you wish to visit the Middle World again, pass through a hole or hollow in the trunk like a doorway, or walk around the tree like you just did and find something new on the other side. If you want to find the Upper world, climb up into the branches and beyond until you feel yourself burst through the top of the sky; to find the Underworld, look for a hole at the base of the roots and climb down, down until you fall through the bottom of the world.

Explore, touch, feel, listen, smell. Walk slowly, be mindful of what there is to find. Be open to being lead by the experience itself, and let a narrative develop of its own accord. Follow and listen to your Totem Guide, it is there to help you.

For Earth

Go with your Guide across the landscape of the Middle World searching for a cliff or hillside and find the entrance to a cave. The cave may take you down, turning into an Underworld journey, or it may remain in the Middle World.

Proceed into the cave with caution and respect. Declare aloud your desire to find your Earth totem. Examine the entrance for signs of human or animal occupation, and perhaps see a bear's scratches, a lion's scrapes, or a rodent's nest.

Notice a human's fire pit. Light a torch and carry it with you.

As you proceed inside, look for signs: tracks or foot prints, bones or wallows, or cave paintings on the walls. Be mindful of water, if you find any, as diving into it can be a path to lead you elsewhere.

Expect the unexpected; the cave may shift, change, or take you to places that logically should not exist inside a cave, and that is all right. The NOR follows its own rules.

If you find your Earth totem (or any other at any time) be sure to acknowledge and thank it.

When you feel your journey has finished, travel back up through the cave as quickly as you like; find the mouth of the cave again, set your torch down in the fire-ring, and walk out into the daylight of an open, peaceful, safe natural setting. Follow the drumming back to the waking world from here.

For Air

Go with your Guide up the great tree, up the trunk and into the branches. They are large and strong enough for you to climb across. See that your tree was only one of many within a healthy forest. The branches cross each other, and you can jump from one tree to another. Declare aloud your desire to find your Air totem.

Climb as high as you dare, and be open to finding whatever is at the top. Go from one tree to another, from one kind of tree to another, from a forest to a jungle. Don't be surprised if you find flat areas that feel like land that hold structures or something else entirely; the NOR follows its own rules

Look for animal signs, for nests and discarded feathers, for claw-marks and insect nests. Poke your head inside hollow trunks— go inside if you are bid. If you find yourself at the end of a branch and feel inclined to jump— do it, and fly. Or, find yourself returning to the earth and follow the land where you are led.

If you find your Air totem (or any other at any time) be sure to acknowledge and thank it.

When you feel your journey has finished, travel back to the first tree, the one you started in; you may travel as quickly as you like, flying if you can. Climb back down through the branches and down the trunk until you're standing on the earth again in the peaceful and safe wood.   Follow the drumming back to the waking world from here.

For Fire

Go with your Guide across the landscape until you see a clearing ahead.   It's strange: there is a campfire within a ring of stones, blazing, but no one is there.

Approach and declare aloud your desire to find your Fire totem. There is a small pile of wood by the fire and, hidden behind it, a musical instrument.   What is it?   A flute?   A rattle? A small hand drum? Pick it up and play something. You are all alone here.   Sing, chant, dance! Play to the wilderness around you, play to your own joy.

Others, people or animals or other spirits, may hear your music and join you at the fire. If you feel inclined, feed the fire until it gets as large as you like— or let it grow small into embers. You may be led by someone or something to follow a path elsewhere. Jumping into fire itself can be a passageway in the NOR to lead somewhere else.   Stay with the fire or go off as you feel inclined. Sing or dance or play your instrument as you feel appropriate.

If you find your Fire totem (or any other at any time) be sure to acknowledge and thank it.

When you feel your journey has finished, return to the fire, if you were led away. Inspect it to be sure it is contained within its stones; feed it a few pieces of wood in gratitude. Walk back the way you came through a natural, peaceful setting. Follow the drumming back to the waking world from there.

For Water

Go with your Guide across the landscape until you come to a stream or a river, to flowing water. Examine the shore for signs of animal life; look for the bubbles of a clam's wallow, for a nest with duck's eggs, for the scrapes of an alligator coming ashore, or for the tracks of land animals coming to drink. Declare aloud your desire to find your Water totem.

Find an overhanging tree or other hidden place and find a canoe. Pull it into the water and get in, along with your Totem Guide. There is an oar inside the canoe, so you have some control to steer, but the current has final say over where you go.

Allow the water to carry you away, to go where it will. It may grow larger, or empty into a lake or sea— or it may dry up all together. It may flow through any sort of landscape, from meadows to forests to deserts.

Watch the water, and what lives in her. But also watch the landscape as it drifts past, and around bends, and look for what is hidden between the trees or stones. Mind what you are able to steer toward with your oar— and what slips past as the current takes control.

If you find your Water totem (or any other at any time) be sure to acknowledge and thank it.

When you feel your journey has finished, see a good flat place to land your canoe along the shore and head there. Once you are securely on land, walk back into a natural landscape that is a peaceful, safe natural setting. Follow the drumming back to the waking world from here.

For Light

Go with your Guide across the landscape until you come to the base of a steep and tall cliff. Climb it, with your Guide following. Come to the top and find yourself standing on a great windswept mesa, on a flat-topped desert mountain. Declare aloud your desire to find your Light totem.

You are standing below a vast, seemingly endless blue sky — standing high above everything in the known world below you. The breeze is light. The sun is shining down on you and you face it and greet it like a respected elder. Your face is turned to it and the light is nearly blinding, but you welcome the warmth on your face.

The mesa around you is alive in its short desert grasses, herbs, and sands. Look for animal signs, for human signs. Allow yourself to stay, to climb down and off, or to be carried away— or to fly away— as you are bid.

If you find your Light totem (or any other at any time) be sure to acknowledge and thank it.

When you feel your journey has finished, return to the base of the cliff where you started and walk back into the peaceful, safe natural setting. Follow the drumming back to the waking world from here.

For Dark

Go with your Guide across the landscape until you come to the base of a steep and tall cliff— the same cliff from your Light Guide journey. Climb it, with your Guide following. Come to the top and find yourself standing on the same great mesa, on the flat-topped desert mountain.

Greet the sun. But find a place to sit, and wait and watch as the sun sets.

Allow this to happen organically. The shift may be quick, acting according to the upside-down nature of the NOR; or it may happen more realistically, to test your patience and commitment.

Find yourself standing on the mesa at night. Watch it, feel it, as the same place becomes something new. Declare aloud your desire to find your Dark totem.

The character of the land changes. You can hear, but not see, animals and unknown night hunters moving around in the darkness. The cries of birds and insects, the growls of cougars or hyenas punctuate the silence. The mesa around you is alive— oh, it is alive alright— but you are alone and vulnerable now.

Invite the moon to rise. What phase is it in? Full or new, waning or waxing? Greet the moon as a respected elder. Can you see stars, or is it cloudy?

Allow yourself to stay, to climb down and off, or to be carried away or to fly away as you are bid, into cracks in the cliffs deep underground, or into a dark sea— but be forewarned that if you move off out of fear, you will likely never find your Dark totem.

If you find your Dark totem (or any other at any time) be sure to acknowledge and thank it.

When you feel your journey has finished, return to the base of the cliff where you started and walk back into the peaceful, safe natural setting. Follow the drumming back to the waking world from here.

For Totems of the Lady, the Lord, and the Primary Totem

As these totems represent a more complete, and therefore personal, aspect of yourself, the "right" shamanic journey to find them is open to the most interpretation. If you feel compelled to journey to a certain landscape — a desert or wood, a tundra or jungle— or if you feel it appropriate in some unspoken way to look for them in the Middle, Upper, or Lower World— then do that.

But if you have no inspiration, or if your own journey proved fruitless, or if you do not yet trust yourself to make such decisions, then attempt this journey I have created. You may do it all at once, as it's written, or divide it up into several journeys.

————————-

Find yourself at the base of the great tree, the one we have used before, and find your Totem Guide there with you. Stand, and begin walking slowly around the great trunk. Turn a corner and find a small pool of water trickling out from the ground between some stones among the roots.

Sit at the edge of the pool and, taking your Guide with you, drop backward into the water. There is no bottom. You fall down, down into endless warm waters.

XXIX

Swim easily, and breathe the water as the creature of the seas you have become.

You see light from another direction.   When you find it, surface. You are in a clear still pool in the middle of a vast, endless grassy landscape.   The sky is nondescript and grey, the air moving gently.

Climb out of the water and explore.   The place is familiar, yet foreign; still yet expectant. It is a place between places, archetypal and primal, a template for creation, like a dream and yet real.   It is a place that is both the past and the future, a world removed and set aside from the world we know.

Begin to walk through the grass. What do you see? There is more to the land than what I have described. The grass hides many secrets, clues, signs to be found in the soil between the blades. Stones? Shells? Pieces of glass and ceramic shard from a culture long gone?   The bones of animals or their tracks?

You see a strange formation ahead and go to it.   It's one thing here that's clearly man-made: a wooden pole stuck upright in a pyramid of stones.

This is a marker.   It is a cairn, a traveler's alter, set-up by those who have come before, and added-to by every person who has traveled by it.   You must add to it to proceed. The traditional way is to add a stone to the pile.

What does the altar look like? Is it simple, or ornate? Is the pole carved or decorated? Are there any other objects there?

Add your stone.   But also, stand before it and offer a prayer. Declare aloud that you are on a journey to find your most sacred inner self: you are here to find your Lady totem, your Lord totem, and/or your Primary totem.

The alter hears you. Paths clear their way through the grasses and radiate outward from the cairn in many directions, leading off to many different places. The altar with its upright pole has become a crossroads, a marker between destinations.

For the Lady

Hold in your mind the desire to find your Lady totem and pick whichever path feels appropriate to that calling. Follow it where it leads.

Take as long as you need to get there; learn and observe as you go.

Find yourself, eventually, coming to a dwelling of some kind, a home that is part of the natural landscape and that you may not have seen or found without the path. Approach the entrance.

What sort of dwelling is it? A house or lodge of wood and stone, or a tipi or yurt made of hide? A hole in the side of a hill, or tucked beside a river? Is it humble? Is it tidy? Or is it natural, more like the den of an animal, or a wild witch? Does the place feel familiar, as though you could enter certain you are welcome and expected? Or should you knock, or call out? Is the door locked?

Find yourself entering. Explore the dwelling as much as you are inclined, but find yourself heading for the kitchen and the hearth. There will be a woman there. Greet her, and show her your respect.

Who is this woman? Is she familiar? Take in everything about her, what she looks like, how she dresses, how she behaves. Is she older and motherly? Is she younger, standing with authority? Is she ancient and unnerving, a canny old crone? Does she display any animal signs, in her bearing, dress, or decorations? Is there anyone else with her in the kitchen, or in the house?

Tell the woman why you are there, to find your Lady totem, and that you hope she will help you. Listen to her, patiently. Do as she asks, even if what she says makes no sense, or seems unrelated to your journey. Have patience, show respect, do as she says. Call her "Mother."

If you find your Lady totem (or any other at any time) be sure to acknowledge and thank it.

When you are certain you are finished there, and you are certain you have the woman's blessing to go, then leave her house and take the path back the way you came, back to the traveler's altar. From there, you may return to the pool of water or take another route back to the waking world. Or, you may proceed along another path.

For the Lord

Begin at the Travel's Altar. Hold in your mind the desire to find your Lord totem and pick whichever path feels appropriate to that calling. Follow it where it leads.

Take as long as you need to get there; learn and observe as you go.

Find yourself, eventually, coming to a place deep, deep down in the wild trees and brush. There is a clearing beside a river that you may not have seen or found without the path. There is a healthy fire burning within a circle of stones, with many logs pulled around it as seats. You can see the ground is trampled flat and bare from generations of feet. Take a seat, be patient, and wait.

What do you see? What kind of wilderness surrounds the clearing? Is it a forest? Or a jungle, a desert, or prairie land? What is the season? Are spring flowers blooming, or are winter snows falling?— or both at once? Look to the trampled earth. Can you make out footprints? From people? Or from animals? What else is there? Tools, supplies, or instruments? Does anyone else join you?

A man emerges from behind the brush at the river's edge. He is dressed in the costuming of a Holy Man. He is wearing a mask, but he takes it off when he sees you.

How do you see him? Does he wear the robes of a priest, and of what tradition? Or the feathers and furs of a shaman or medicine man? Or the colorful hodgepodge rags of a wild man of the wood? Is he old and wise? Strong and handsome? Or young and full of life? What kind of mask was he wearing? And what expression does he now wear? Is he welcoming and happy you have come? Or is he stern? Is there any animal sign in this clothing?

Greet him respectfully. Call him "Father." Tell him you are on a journey to find your Lord totem, and that you hope he will help you find it. Tell him you are pleased to be there to hear him teach and that you look forward to learning from him.

Sit patiently, and wait for him to approach the fire and begin his lesson.

What does he do? Does he deliver a sermon, or share a legend? Does he sing, or dance, or pantomime? And what does he say? What wisdom is he sharing? Know that he may well decide to take you somewhere else in the NOR to communicate his lesson.

If you find your Lord totem (or any other at any time) be sure to acknowledge and thank it.

When you are certain you are finished there, and you are certain you have the man's blessing to go, then leave the clearing and take the path back the way you came, back to the traveler's altar. From there, you may return to the pool of water or to another route back to the waking world. Or, you may proceed along another path.

For the Primary

Begin at the Travel's Altar. Hold in your mind the desire to find your Primary totem and pick whichever path feels appropriate to that calling. Follow it where it leads.

Take as long as you need to get there; learn and observe as you go.

Find yourself, eventually, meeting a child along the way. The child is alone, but not really lost. Tell the child what you are doing — that you are in search of your totem, of the face of your own soul— and ask if they would come with you on that journey.

What does the child look like? What race and culture are they? What color are their hair, skin, and eyes, and how are they dressed? How old is the child? Are they male or female, or can you tell? Are they friendly and curious, or shy? When you talk, do they understand you? Does the child speak at all?

The child agrees to go with you. Now the child leads you as though they have a fun secret to share. You travel deeper and deeper into the wilderness. The path grows faint and thin. The going is not easy. Do not lose the child.

What sort of wilderness are you in? Thick forest or jungle, or a hot desert, or heavy snows? Or many, or none? Or is the wilderness composed of scenes and places unique to the NOR?

Eventually, you find that the child has lead you to a Holy Place, lost to time and culture, nearly ruins and all but reclaimed by the wilds of nature. The child doesn't speak, but simply points to it and smiles. The place is your Sacred House.

What do you see? Is it an ancient stone temple or sanctuary? A humble lodge? Or a natural space? A cave or canyon? The space could take any form, but it will strike you as special, as sacred. What is there? Look at details, for marks left by people or animals, for signs left by one who has come before— by You.

Look for a door, for an entrance. You will see water in some form near that entrance. Dip your fingers into it as a sign of respect to the place; do this any time you visit your Sacred House in the NOR. Declare aloud your desire to find *yourself*, and enter. Take your Guide in with you, if it wants to go; leave the child behind, unless they insist.

The inside of your Sacred House may well defy logic. It may be full of many rooms and hallways, or whole landscapes, larger and more complex than should be able to fit inside the dwelling space. It may change each time you visit it. Take your time, look into everything, explore: you are not snooping, this is your house. Open drawers and take the lids off pots, look into the branches of trees and behind tapestries if you are inclined. Things like fires, mirrors, caverns, vessels of water, stairs, and doorways can be portals to take you elsewhere in the NOR. Always, be aware of traces, of signs, both human and animal: read anything that has text, observe anything that bears images. Call-out to your totem, to your sacred self, at any time, and many times.

If you find your Primary totem (or any other at any time) be sure to acknowledge and thank it.

When you are certain you are finished there, leave your Sacred House and take the path back the way you came, back to the traveler's altar. From there, you may return to the pool of water or to another route back to the waking world.

Or, you may proceed along another path. The lessons to be learned in the NOR are endless— and timeless. The shaman returns as often as she is called to.

A Totem Circle

Please be aware that a magick circle has the potential to be the most powerful and direct method of uncovering your totems. There will be space in the ritual to back away if you change your mind, but you should still not engage in this ritual exercise unless you are certain you are ready to know your entire essential self!

Begin by selecting an appropriate place; a place that feels sacred or special to you, where you will be uninterrupted in your work, and that is large enough to physically accommodate your rite. If you keep an altar or special place where you go to meditate or pray, you may use it if it feels suitable and appropriate to you, and if the area around it is large enough. Otherwise, it may be wise to find another location and sanctify it anew. Most natural spaces are already spiritually clean and do not require extra work.

Circles are often drawn using a magick blade called an *athame*, a magic wand, or a staff, etc., and you may use any of these. Or, you may also use your own bare hands, as we do.

For this ritual, you will build a simple altar to be used in the center of the circle. Place these items on a small table or other surface, or you may place them on the ground in the center of the space if you are outdoors (be mindful of lit candles!). You will need:

a symbol for earth; a stone or crystal, a pentagram, a special leaf, or piece of wood

a symbol for air; incense in a stick or censor, a feather or feather fan

a symbol for fire; a candle or tea light

a symbol for water; a dish, cup, or shell filled with water

a symbol for day; an image of the sun, a white feather, or other white object

a symbol for night; an image of the moon or stars, a black feather, or other black object

a symbol of the Lord; a male figurine, a gold candle, or a blade or wand

a symbol of the Lady; a female figurine, a silver candle, or a cup or chalice

a bell (or rattle, or other ritual noise-maker)

a lighter

some sort of nice bread or cake, plated

some sort of alcoholic beverage, juice, or plain water, in a nice cup or chalice

other items you feel are appropriate to the spiritual path you walk

other items you feel are appropriate to the occasion or other decorations, such as a tablecloth, flowers, other seasonal items, etc.

I have written this circle as a means to uncover totems that are yet unknown. However, at any time, you are welcome to cast a circle by using these invocations and include your totems from the beginning. Simply include their name/animal type in the invocation for the corresponding element after the line: "through the power of my _____ totem." Then you may use the circle ceremony to accomplish any task you wish.

For clarity's sake, *actions* to take are written in italics, while words to be spoken aloud are indented.

Don't forget to ground just before you begin.

To sanctify the space before you start:

Place you alter in the center of the space. Place the symbols for the Lord and Lady in the center, and the six elemental symbols in a circle around them, mirroring the six-spoked wheel design of the Totem Wheel. Place the bell and the athame/wand if you have one within reach; put any other decorations and the cakes and ale wherever they fit best.

Stand at the center, close your eyes, and address whatever form of Divinity you understand (altering my language as necessary).

Great Earth Mother, Great Green Father of the Wood, I ask that you give your love   and your blessing to this space and the work that will be done here. Set it aside,   as a sacred space; may it be cleansed, empowered, and protected. So mote it be!

See, with your mind's eye and your heart, the space becoming peaceful, clean, and protected. You may also smudge it with sage or incense if you like.

To cast your circle:

Light all candles and incense on the alter.

Stand at the Northern end of your space. Feel yourself rooted to the earth and grounded. Use your magical tool or point with your dominant hand. Envision and invoke good colorful energy flowing through your body and out through your fingers. Starting at the North, use that line of energy to draw a big circle around the space, walking clockwise, and encircling the East, South, and West corners.

> As the moon
> Goes 'round the earth
> I mark the space
> And claim its worth

Make a second pass completely around the circle you just drew. This time as you pass your hand over the line, envision the energy rising up from the ground and joining at the top, like a large bubble around the circle. The wall of that bubble is glowing with life-energy.

> As the sun
> Goes 'round the sky
> I build the space
> And amplify

Make a third pass completely around the circle. Now, envision the bubble growing strong as you run your hand around the line. It keeps out anything that is not invited; it lets in everything you call by your Will. The space inside the bubble is special, sacred, clean, vibrant, happy, and safe.

> As the earth
> Goes 'round the sun
> I fill the space
> My will be done

Return to the center. Put down your wand (if you used one) and take up the bell.

> The circle lives
> And now is sealed
> What I would *Know*

XL

Will stand revealed

Face the North and address it with both hands held open.

Spirit of the Earth, Powers of the North
keeper of the stones and caverns
I call you to my circle
though the power of my Earth totem
to bless it with stability
Hail and be welcome!

Ring the bell

Face East with both hands held open

Spirit of the Air, Powers of the East
keeper of the winds of change
I call you to my circle
through the power of my Air totem
to bless it with inspiration
Hail and be welcome!

Ring the bell

Face South with both hands held open

Spirit of the Fire, Powers of the South
keeper of the flames and lightning
I call you to my circle
through the power of my Fire totem
to bless it with passion
Hail and be welcome!

Ring the bell

Face West with both hands held open

Spirit of the Water, Powers of the West

keeper of the waves and tides
I call you to my circle
through the power of my Water totem
to bless it with joy
Hail and be welcome!

Ring the bell

Raise both hands above your head

Spirit of the Day, Powers of Above
walker of a straight path
I call you to my circle
through the power of my Light totem
to bless it with truth and light
Hail and be welcome!

Ring the bell

Lower your hands toward the ground

Spirit of the Night, Powers of Below
walker of the crooked path
I call you to my circle
through the power of my Dark totem
to bless it with shadows
Hail and be welcome!

Ring the bell

Hold both of your arms out as though to embrace everything at once. Then make two fists and cross your arms over your chest.

Great Spirit of the Almighty Lord
Father of us all
I invite you to my circle
through the power of my Lord totem

to bless it and to oversee it
Hail and be welcome!

Ring the bell

Hold both of your arms out with your palms up and your elbows at your hips

Great Spirit of the Almighty Lady
Mother of us all
I invite you to my circle
through the power of my Lady totem
to bless it and oversee it
Hail and be welcome!

Ring the bell

May the work I do here be blessed
toward my greatest good
by my Will, so mote it be!

Vigorously ring the bell nine times, one for each totem. Feel the energy raising in you and filling the circle

Take a step back, stand up straight. Address all the spiritual powers you have just called

I am a being of flesh and bone, of light and of shadows, of instinct and of Will. And I   have come to stand here now unadorned, unashamed, naked before the truth of   who I really am.

As I approach the sacred elemental powers I have called to the corners of this circle,   I stand ready to see the true faces of my own soul— new to me, yet never forgotten.

XLIII

I call out to my totems, and welcome them!

This is your last chance to change your mind. When you called each quarter, you got a little taste of what the energy of each corresponding totem will taste like. If you decide now you are not ready to face any of your totems, skip their direction and go on to the next. **Do not acknowledge their direction at this time, as even indirect acknowledgement may be enough to call the totem to you.

Face the North or walk to the Northern edge of the circle, holding your arms open.

> Power of Earth, come to me!
> I stand ready for my totem of Earth to come forward
> that I may know myself
> and honor myself
> and that the magic of the Earth may flow through my soul
> through that in me which is the Earth
> Totem of Earth, I welcome you!

Allow yourself a few moments, or as long as you need, to stand open to spiritually receive from that direction.

Face the East or walk to the Eastern edge of the circle, holding your arms open.

> Power of Air, come to me!
> I stand ready for my totem of Air to come forward
> that I may know myself
> and honor myself
> and that the magic of the Air may flow through my soul
> through that in me which is the Air
> Totem of Air, I welcome you!

Allow yourself a few moments, or as long as you need, to stand open to spiritually receive from that direction.

Face the South or walk to the Southern edge of the circle, holding your arms open.

> Power of Fire, come to me!
> I stand ready for my totem of Fire to come forward
> that I may know myself
> and honor myself
> and that the magic of the Fire may flow through my soul
> through that in me which is the Fire
> Totem of Fire, I welcome you!

Allow yourself a few moments, or as long as you need, to stand open to spiritually receive from that direction.

Face the West or walk to the Western edge of the circle, holding your arms open.

> Power of Water, come to me!
> I stand ready for my totem of Water to come forward
> that I may know myself
> and honor myself
> and that the magic of the Water may flow through my soul
> through that in me which is the Water
> Totem of Water, I welcome you!

Allow yourself a few moments, or as long as you need, to stand open to spiritually receive from that direction.

From the center of the circle, face above, holding your arms open.

> Power of Day, come to me!

I stand ready for my totem of Light to come forward
that I may know myself
and honor myself
and that the magic of the Light from Above may flow
through my soul
through that in me which is the Light
Totem of Light, I welcome you!

*Allow yourself a few moments, or as long as you need, to
stand open to spiritually receive from that direction.*

Now face below, holding your arms open.

Power of Night, come to me!
I stand ready for my totem of Darkness to come
forward
that I may know myself
and honor myself
and that the magic of the Dark from Below may flow
through my soul
through that in me which is the Darkness
Totem of Dark, I welcome you!

*Allow yourself a few moments, or as long as you need, to
stand open to spiritually receive from that direction.*

Make two fists and cross your arms over your chest

Divine spirit of the Lord, the Father, come to me!
I stand ready for my totem of the Lord to come
forward
that I may know myself
and honor myself
and that the magic of the Father may flow through
my soul
through that in me which is the Lord
Totem of the Lord, I welcome you!

Allow yourself a few moments, or as long as you need, to stand open to spiritually receive from that direction.

Now hold your arms open, palms up, elbows at your waist

Divine spirit of the Lady, the Mother, come to me!
I stand ready for my totem of the Lady to come forward
that I may know myself
and honor myself
and that the magic of the Mother may flow through my soul
through that in me which is the Lady
Totem of the Lady, I welcome you!

Allow yourself a few moments, or as long as you need, to stand open to spiritually receive from that direction.

Wrap your arms around yourself. Lift your head to a level gaze. If there are others with you in the circle, face them and make eye contact with them.

Great Spirit of my own Sacred-Self
I stand ready for my totem of my own immortal soul to come forward
that I may know myself
and honor myself
that the magic of my true essential being may flow through me
through my animal self
Totem of this Man/Woman, I welcome you!

Allow yourself a few moments, or as long as you need, to stand open to spiritually receive

**There are no time restraints placed on this ritual. You may stand open to receive for as long as you feel appropriate. Be patient, it may not come right away. If nothing does, accept for now that this totem may not wish to show itself at this time. Do not try to force it, or use words like *call* or *summon*. Accept that the timing is not right, and that the totem knows better than you.

For any totem that does reveal itself, you may say:

> Thank you, (animal), totem of (element)!
> You are part of me, and I honor you, for all to hear!
> May we walk together now in friendship,
> and in full knowledge of each other

For any totem that choses not to reveal itself at this time, you may say:

> Thank you, totem of (element), for hearing my request
> I respect you, and I respect your wisdom
> Know that I remain open to meeting you
> when you feel the time is right

When you have finished interacting with your totems, return to the alter.

Take-up the plate containing the bread/cake

> From the seed to the stalk
> And the stalk to the grain
> We accept this bread
> And its strength we attain

Eat the bread. If you are outdoors, drop a bit on the ground as nature's share; if you are indoors, set a piece aside to take outside later.

Take-up the chalice

> From the seed to the vine

And the vine to the flower
We accept this wine
To renew us of power

Drink the beverage. If you are outdoors, pour a bit on the ground as nature's share; if you are indoors, leave a bit in the cup to take outside later.

**You may do or say anything additional here that feels appropriate to the moment

When you are ready to take-down and close the circle:

Stand at the center. Take-up the bell. Stand with your arms crossed over your chest while making two fists. Then, open your arms and hold them up, open above your head.

> Great Spirit of the Almighty Lord
> Father of us all
> I thank you for coming to my circle
> through the power of my Lord totem
> Go if you must, stay if you will
> So mote it be!

Ring the Bell

Stand with your elbows at your waist and your arms out. Then, raise your arms and hold them up, open above your head

> Great Spirit of the Almighty Lady
> Mother of us all
> I thank you for coming to my circle
> through the power of my Lady totem
> Go if you must, stay if you will
> So mote it be!

Ring the bell

Face Below with your arms held open

> Spirit of the Darkness, Powers of the Night
> I thank you for coming to my circle
> I release you though the power of my Dark totem
> So mote it be!

Ring the bell

Face Above with your arms held open

> Spirit of the Light, Powers of the Day
> I thank you for coming to my circle
> I release you though the power of my Light totem
> So mote it be!

Ring the bell

Face the West with your arms held open

> Spirit of the Water, Powers of the West
> I thank you for coming to my circle
> I release you though the power of my Water totem
> So mote it be!

Ring the bell

Face the South with your arms held open

> Spirit of the Fire, Powers of the South
> I thank you for coming to my circle
> I release you though the power of my Fire totem
> So mote it be!

Ring the bell

L

Face the East with your arms held open

> Spirit of the Air, Powers of the East
> I thank you for coming to my circle
> I release you though the power of my Air totem
> So mote it be!

Ring the bell

Face the North with your arms held open

> Spirit of the Earth, Powers of the North
> I thank you for coming to my circle
> I release you though the power of my Earth totem
> So mote it be!

Ring the bell and set it down. Take-up the wand/athame, if you used one.

Go to the Northern corner. Begin to walk counter-clockwise around the circle. Envision that your hand is directing the energy of the circle to flow back into the earth

> As the day
> Fades into night
> I end this circle
> And this rite

Walk around a second time. Continue to direct the energy into the earth.

> As the night
> Fades into day
> The magick rests
> Is put away

Walk around a third time.

> As the winter
> Turns to spring
> I pull the line
> Release the ring

Stop when you are at North again and face any others present.

> And as the summer
> Fades to fall
> Merry met, merry part
> So say we all!

As stated, this basic outline for casting a circle may be used at any time, and altered to suit your own needs. You may always create your own circle. Just remember they are methodic; you must undo, release, or put away everything you raise, and thank and dismiss every spiritual entity you call.

Appendix Two:
Glossary

air totem: part of the **essential self** that stands for the mind; the part in charge of thoughts, ideas, intellect, and creativity

and/and (or **and/and logic**): neo-pagan philosophy of understanding the physical world and the metaphysical/spirit worlds to operate by different rules and by different logic; where things of the spirit that appear to be contradictions or opposites to each other can also be equal to each other or the same.

animal speak: an animal's methods of communication with others of its kind including body language, posture, facial expression, actions, and vocalizations; the method by which a totem animal may likely be perceived to communicate with its bearer; not to be confused with the book by Ted Andrew of the same name

animus/anima: the **archetype** of psychologist Carl Jung that most closely relates to our concept of animal totems; the totality of an individual's unconscious self, or that which is the inner, hidden, or unexpressed self, taking a variety of forms either animal or human

anthropological totem: a spirit being, sacred object, or symbol that serves as an emblem of a group of people, family, clan, lineage, or tribe; used in the past by the discipline, but discouraged in modern times due to the inaccuracy of using a single term for a concept used by many cultures

archetypes: unconscious, universally understood symbols that supersede all learned, cultural symbology; idea proposed by psychologist Carl Jung to define the symbols found in the **collective unconscious**

astral projection: the metaphysical or spiritual practice of projecting one's soul out from the body to travel the astral planes

balance: a state in which you are able to function well in your own life, comfortable with the influences of all of your totems and corresponding aspects of yourself, where no one totem has an unfair or unhealthy influence over another

circle (or **ritual circle**, **magick circle**): a ritual in the traditional Wiccan style, or one inspired by that style; an area of space marked-out or otherwise set aside with intent to raise spiritual energy, to create sacred space, and/or to provide spiritually protected space within it, to perform sacred rites therein, where spiritual powers are called upon to bless, empower, and/or protect the sacred space within the circle and assist with carrying-out the work and the rite performed, varying by tradition, but usually including the four elemental powers of Earth, Air, Fire, and Water, and some face of dualistic divinity expressed as the Lord and Lady.

collective unconscious; the idea that all human minds have the same unconscious structures, influencing how we understand and contextualize our experiences; idea proposed by psychologist Carl Jung to explain similarities in symbols and metaphor used across cultures

crisis-shift: when a person has experienced abuse, trauma, or profound stressor to cause a **defensive shift** in response and that totem never shifts back to its original location; when a totem other than the **primary totem** assumes the role of primary due to profound stress

cognitive dissonance: the uncomfortable feeling that comes from holding two conflicting ideas at once

cultural bias: when interpretations or judgements are clouded by the specific cultural experiences of the person making them

cultural relativism: the idea that the actions of an individual should only be judged moral or immoral by the standards of their own culture, and not by the standards of the observer.

dark totem (alternately, **below totem** or **night totem**): part of the essential self that stands for the hidden or shadow self; the part in charge of all that we wish we weren't, that we would discard if possible, what we are ashamed of or afraid of in ourselves, what we try to hide from others, and how we see ourselves in the past

defensive shift: a shift from the influence of one totem to another that happens unconsciously and instinctually in reaction to any situation; represents an unconscious shift between the dominance of one aspect of your character to another

domesticated animal: an animal whose physiological form as well as temperament has been altered by humans, often through selective breeding to favor desired traits

earth totem: part of the **essential self** that stands for the physical body and physical needs; the part in charge of holding steady in times of crisis, the part that defines what an individual finds comforting and secure, and the part that decides what is most essential to life when taken against all else

either/or (or **either/or logic**): in neo-pagan philosophy, the name given to the idea that the spirit world follows the the same rules of logic that exist in the physical world; where things that are contradictions cannot be the same, and things that are opposites cannot be equal; following patterns of Euclidian logic, mathematics, in the style of Greek philosophy as applied both to the physical and metaphysical worlds

essential self: your higher self, divine self, primal self, animal self, and/or natural self; what you are when you are able to clearly know yourself; your soul; your **totems** are the face of your essential self

fakelore: a play on the word "folklore," an inauthentic and usually manufactured story, myth, song, or other idea presented as the authentic or traditional folklore of a culture

familiar: an individual living animal with whom a person shares a metaphysical or spiritual relationship

family totem: a **totem** that is inherited directly through a family line or cultural heritage; a type of totem possibly common to our ancestors but usually absent in modern people due to modern individualistic, rather than tribal and communal, thinking patterns

ferrel animal: a **domesticated animal** that has returned to the wild, while retaining their altered form.

fire totem: part of the **essential self** that stands for passions, reactions, and impulses; the part in charge of your feelings that are fleeting in nature

geomancy: a method of divination that interprets markings found on the earth or otherwise the configurations of nature; in regards to totemic geomancy, a method by which one interprets omens, messages, or other metaphysical meaning from wild animal sightings

Gray (or "the Gray" or "being Gray"): within contemporary neo-pagan philosophy, a belief that no rule, especially of ethics, behavior, or human culture, can remain good and just without allowance for exceptions; a philosophy of wisdom rooted in balance and logical exceptions, especially on moral and ethical issues

group totem: an animal spirit representing a family line, an extended clan, or other family group rather than only an individual; our tradition's term for what is usually meant by **anthropological totem**

guided meditation: when one **meditates** according to directions provided by another, usually an experienced guide or teacher, often following a narrative or story; any meditation in which a person follows directions laid-out by another person; quite similar to a **shamanic journey**, except it is always lead by another person's guidelines

humors (or *humours*): from antiquated European folklore, the four essential fluids of yellow bile, black bile, blood, and phlegm within the body, each of which corresponded to an element and qualities of hot/cold and wet/dry; believed to be the source of most human aliments when imbalanced; believed to be the source of the **four temperaments**

Identifying Questions: the questions used in this path of totemism to define an animal totem's precise role in its natural environment, to be used to understand its influences on its bearer's character; they cover environment, social grouping, sexual differences, size, and diet, with the later addition of how it fares in the human world

imbalance: when one totem dominates a situation habitually, for a prolonged period, or otherwise inappropriately, in a way that negatively affects its bearer's life; when a person shifts toward the influence of a totem too often, too strongly, or otherwise inappropriately, against their **Will**

kind: animals that common perception and common-sense reasoning would group together by shared characteristics, behaviors, and/or ecological role that may or may not include a close genetic relationship

Lady totem: the totality of one's ideal femaleness and the face of one's passive (or alternately, active) side or energy; one of the three **center totems**

lesser crisis shift: when a person learns to make an inappropriate **defensive shift** in response to abuse, trauma, or profound stressor; when someone has learned to respond to certain situations with an inappropriate behavior and corresponding inappropriate totem; unhealthy, potentially toxic learned behaviors and responses

light totem (alternately, **above totem** or **day totem**): part of the essential self that stands for the ideal self; the part in charge of what we wish to be, hope to be, what we think we ought to be, how we'd want others to see us, and how we see ourselves projected into the future

Lord totem: the totality of one's concept of ideal maleness and the face of one's active (or alternately, passive) side or energy; one of the three **center totems**

lucid dreaming: exercising control of one's dreams while fully asleep

magick: the process of focusing spiritual or metaphysical energy on a specific task by willpower to affect change

meditation: a discipline of the mind used to cultivate internal peace, calm, heightened and focused awareness, and a state of mental stillness

neo-shamanism: a modern tradition of direct interaction with the **three layered world** of the **non-ordinary reality** or spirit world, usually through **shamanic journeying**, often for the purpose of healing; created by anthropologist M. Harner and inspired by his work with several native cultures of the Amazon, but also built on his personal experiences and knowledge

non-ordinary reality (or **NOR**): the realm that is at once of the spirit and of the mind that one seeks to enter during a **shamanic journey**; alternate term for the spirit world as well as the realm of dreams and the imagination; understood by neo-shamans to be **three-layered** and containing the Lower, Middle, and Upper Worlds.

non-physical creatures (or **metaphysical, non-corporeal, spirit, or energy creatures):** entities or beings that have no physical bodies and are comprised of spiritual or metaphysical energy only, but that have independent identities and lives similar to animals or people; overlapping with what the general population would think of as "mythical" creatures from folklore such as dragons, fairies, unicorns, giants, sprites, dryads, etc.

offensive shift: a conscious shift from the influence of one totem to another in reaction to any situation; represents a conscious shift between the dominance of one aspect of your character to another; a conscious choice to shift into the energy of a totem to take advantage of the power it lends you

primary totem: the animal that is directly reflective of our entire **essential selves**; a person's "main" totem or otherwise most prominent totem; what is usually meant when a person simply says "totem"; one of the three **center totems**

shaman: any person who interacts with and receives information from the spirit world directly, as opposed to through the interpretation of a religious authority, sacred text or ritual, or other outside media, often for the purpose of healing; a person who creates their own rituals, practices, and general spiritual methodology through their own inspiration rather than accepting one of an existing tradition; usually in neo-pagan context, meaning a practitioner of **neo-shamanism**

shamanic journey: a mental discipline similar to **meditation** but with the intent of active interaction with the **non-ordinary reality** or spiritual realm; the mental and spiritual discipline of active meditation; a means of self-hypnosis; a practice within **neo-shamanism**

shapeshifting: an advanced exercise of totemic communication in which a person seeks to unify their spirit and their totem's into a single entity; often accomplished by imitating the **animal speak** of a **totem** while in a **trance** state

spirit guide: a temporary **tutelar spirit** in animal form; an animal spirit that communicates with or works with a person for a limited time or for a single issue

tamed animal: an animal that has been taught to accept the authority of humans, often by being raised by them or imprinting on them, but has not been physically altered from their natural form

temperaments (four): from antiquated European folklore, four basic personality types, each a result of a **humor** being more prolific in an individual; melancholic (quiet and analytical), choleric (moody), sanguine (optimistic and sociable), and phlegmatic (peaceful and content)

three-layered world: a cross-cultural concept of a spirit world that comes in three layers or multiples of three, typically occurring along a central axis that creates realms higher and lower than the one we currently occupy; in **neo-shamanism**, the three levels of the **non-ordinary reality** constituting the Upper World (light/future/ideal), Middle World (reality of the present), and Lower World (dark/past/primal)

totem: a manifestation of the essential self or spiritual self; a permanent, personal tutelary spirit taking an animal form often relatable to an aspect of its bearer's character or personality; your spiritual essence, your soul, shown to you in its more pure animal form

totem circle: to call and evoke each of a person's own **totems** to sit at each Quarter and position when casting a magick **circle**.

totem guide: a **spirit guide** specifically tasked with leading you to your totems

tutelar spirit: a personal, protective or guiding spiritual entity; a "spirit helper" or "guardian spirit" without predefined form

totem wheel: a map of your nine totems that visually represents the elements and your totems and their relationship to you; a **meditational** aid consisting of a wheel shape with a central axle and six spokes echoing many existing metaphysical constructs

trained animal: an animal that may still be thought of as a wild animal but that has been taught to obey some commands by humans or to respond to certain humans

trance (or **trance state**): an altered state of consciousness, usually purposefully induced to interact with the spirit world or non-ordinary reality; being in a state of self-hypnosis, a state of wakeful dreaming, or allowing your unconscious mind to dream while you are relaxed but still awake enough to interact with the dream with purpose.

underdeveloped animals: animals that are too physiologically and/or intellectually simple to be seated as totems, as they would not provide a bearer with adequate survival instincts to live a successful human life; animals such as amoebas and other single-celled organisms, corals, most mollusks, insects, etc.

water totem: part of the **essential self** that stands for emotions; the part in charge of your "feelings" that have depth, connection to past experiences, and longevity

Will (or The Will): within contemporary neo-pagan philosophy, meaning the combination of and/or exercise of sentience, self-awareness, and/or free-will; the uniquely human ability to understand our lives objectively, to know that we exist in an abstract sense, to make complex decisions factoring-in a variety of ideals, options, ethics, concepts of cause-and-effect, and a sense of time that differentiates past, present, and future; our choice in how we act and our awareness of this choice; by neo-pagan philosophy, a sacred defining factor of our humanity

Appendix Three:
References

Andrews, Ted. *Animal-speak: The Spiritual & Magical Powers of Creatures Great & Small.* Woodbury, MN: Llewellyn Publications, 2000.

Auel, Jean M. *The Clan of the Cave Bear: A Novel (Earths Children Series #1).* New York, NY: Crown Publishers, 1980.

Harner, Michael. *The Way of the Shaman: A Guide to Power and Healing.* San Francisco: Harper & Row, 1990.

Pullman, Philip. *His Dark Materials.* Surrey, UK: Ted Smart, 2000.

Sentier, Elen. *Elen of the Ways: Following the Deer Trods, the Ancient Shamanism of Britain.* 1st ed. Winchester, UK: Moon Books, 2013.

Appendix Four:
Authors' Totems

Stephanie's Totems

Primary: Jaguar
Lady: Asian Elephant
Lord: Lion
Earth: Snake (unknown variety)
Air: Eurasian Magpie
Fire: Bengal Tiger
Water: Ermine/Stoat
Light: Cougar/Mountain Lion
Dark: Shark (unknown variety)

Scott's Totems

Primary: Gray Wolf
Lady: River Otter
Lord: Peregrene Falcon
Earth: Orca
Air: Mockingbird
Fire: Bobcat
Water: Beaver
Light: ?
Dark: Snowy Owl

Appendix Five:
Five Identifying Questions for Totemic Knowledge:

1) **What environment does the animal live in?** (The desert? Jungle? Or widely spread?) And does that environment carry a strong elemental connection? (The sea, the sky, or the earth? The frozen ice or dry sands? Strictly nocturnal or diurnal?) And does the animal have to make any adaptations to any seasonal variations or cycles? (Change in physical appearance like coloration or coat thickness? Hibernation, migration, or change in diet?) What is the nature of that seasonal change? (Cycles of cold/warm? Or wet/dry?)

2) **Is it a solitary animal, or does it live in a group?** If a group, how is that group organized, and are there different ranks or roles for individuals? How permanent is the group? Most importantly, what rank does your individual totem hold within that group? What about pair-bonding between mates; does it pair within a larger group or in place of it? How much of what the animal needs to know is learned from others of their species, compared to relying only on instinct?

3) **How different are the males from the females?** Are there strong differences in appearance? Do they behave differently, have different roles, or do they live basically identical lives? Is there much competition between males for status and access to females, or do the males concentrate their efforts on impressing the females directly? Do they form some kind of bond with their mates,

and is that bond just for the season or for longer? Who raises the young— directly, or indirectly?

4) **Is this a large animal, a medium-sized animal, or a small animal?** How likely is it that it could physically over-power another animal? That it could be over-powered? How does its size translate to its food and shelter needs?

5) **Is the animal a predator, a prey animal, or both?** Keep in mind that most all small animals, regardless of what they eat, can be prey to larger predators on occasion. What about scavenging? Keep in mind that most all predatory animals will scavenge if the situation warrants it.

*6) **How well does it fare in the human world?** Can it be tamed? Can it be trained? Can it be domesticated? Can it go ferrel again?